CISTERCIAN FATHERS SERIES NUMBER FIFTY-TWO

Bernard of Clairvaux

SERMONS FOR LENT
AND THE
EASTER SEASON

D1562522

CISTERCIAN FATHERS SERIES NUMBER FIFTY-TWO

Bernard of Clairvaux

Sermons for Lent and the Easter Season

Translated by
Irene Edmonds

Reviewed by
John Leinenweber

Edited and Revised by
Mark A. Scott, OCSO

Introduction by
Wim Verbaal

Cistercian Publications
www.cistercianpublications.org

LITURGICAL PRESS
Collegeville, Minnesota
www.litpress.org

A Cistercian Publications title published by Liturgical Press

Cistercian Publications
Editorial Offices
Abbey of Gethsemani
3642 Monks Road
Trappist, Kentucky 40051
www.cistercianpublications.org

Based on the critical Latin edition of Jean Leclercq and H. M. Rochais, Sancti Bernardi opera, 8 vols. (Rome: Editiones Cistercienses, 1957–77), 4:334–80, 5:1–121.

1   2   3   4   5   6   7   8   9

Library of Congress Cataloging-in-Publication Data

Bernard, of Clairvaux, Saint, 1090 or 91–1153.
   [Sermons. English. Selections]
   Sermons for Lent and the Easter season / Bernard of Clairvaux ;
Translated by Irene Edmonds ; Edited by John Leinenweber and Mark Scott,
OCSO ; Foreword by Wim Verbaal.
     pages cm. — (CISTERCIAN FATHERS SERIES ; NUMBER
FIFTY-TWO)
   ISBN 978-0-87907-452-4 — ISBN 978-0-87907-744-0 (ebook)
   1. Lenten sermons.   2. Easter—Sermons.   3. Sermons, Latin—Translations into
English.   I. Leinenweber, John.   II. Title.
BV4277.B47   2013
252'.02—dc23   2012049284

Contents

An Introduction to Saint Bernard's
Sermons for Lent and Easter

Wim Verbaal

IN THE INTRODUCTION to the Cistercian Publications'
translation of Bernard's *Sermons for Advent and the Christmas Season*, the growth of the entire liturgical collection was treated.[1]
First of all, the question had to be answered for what reason Bernard
took up the charge of writing a completely new homily collection
that could never be used by the Cistercian order because the homi-
lies took too much liberty with respect to the Cistercian customs
as expressed in the *Ecclesiastica officia*. The conclusion had to be that
Bernard did not aim at a liturgical use of his collection but rather
considered it to offer a continuous *lectio divina*, accompanying the
reader through the liturgical year and deepening the reader's insight
into the liturgical sacralization of the year by each renewed reading.

Another problem posed itself regarding the development of the
entire collection, which proved to be more complex than suggested
by the editorial work of Dom Jean Leclercq. The succeeding versions
corresponded to different organizing principles, and although the
basic line did not change fundamentally over the years, each version
demonstrated a shift of emphasis within the project. The final version
(Pf) managed to bring all these former elements together, harmoniz-
ing them into a sublime unifying equilibrium and showing a clear
division in four subgroups. Each of these starts with a sermon or a

---

[1] Wim Verbaal, "The Sermon Collection: Its Creation and Edition," in *Bernard of
Clairvaux: Sermons for Advent and the Christmas Season*, trans. Irene Edmonds, Wendy
Mary Beckett, and Conrad Greenia, CF 51 (Kalamazoo, MI: Cistercian Publications,
2007), vii–lix.

cluster of sermons dedicated to the Virgin (Advent, Purification, Annunciation, Nativity, and Assumption) and ends on the human level (Paul's Conversion, Benedict, Summer Toil, and Humbert).

As far as Bernard's compositional directives are concerned, different underlying strands come to the surface, which can be reduced to three organizing principles that give a clear idea of Bernard's purpose for the collection. Fundamental to them all is his concept of time. In the first place, the collection conforms to the linear time concept, both of human life from conception or expectancy (Advent) to death or commemoration (Humbert), and of the history of salvation from the desire for liberation to the victory over death, as well as to the linearity of the reading process, which expects progress during reading.

Besides, the collection gives expression to the temporal circularity of the natural and liturgical year, both in its entirety and in its details. In its totality, the collection wants to be read year after year, aiming at a continuous rumination of the liturgical year, thus obliging the reader to lift his experience onto the level that conforms to the liturgical signification of the year, thanks to the repetitive reading of the sermons. In its details, the collection demonstrates how each smaller subgroup or subunit seems to offer a circular reading, bringing the reader back to his point of departure only to realize that this starting point is no longer the same as the one he departed from.

Finally, Bernard introduced a pointed time concept, giving the reader the impression that, actually, there is no time at all. The liturgical allusions in his sermons are not limited to the occasion to which the sermon itself is dedicated, thus implying that each liturgical event includes every other one. Furthermore, as a writer Bernard feels free to handle time according to his own writing purposes, thus creating anti- or even a-chronological events.

In reading the first subgroup, composed of the sermons from Advent until the conversion of Paul, these different compositional strands all appeared and were even reinforced by the themes that seemed to be specific for this unit: desire and recognition. The vocabulary of desire abounds in the sermons for Advent, while from Christmas onward the vocabulary of acknowledgment is privileged, reaching its peak in the sermons for Epiphany and the voluntary submission of the reader to a spiritual leader.

Bernard's most important aim in writing, however, is not to offer the reader some intellectual entertainment. He wants to educate the reader. He wants the reader to conform to the evolution as presented inside the sermons. For this reason, Bernard attacks him, he assails him, trying to get a hold on his inner capacities. Within the reading process, thus, Bernard tries to train each of the three capacities of the soul: *ratio* (reason), *voluntas* (will), and *memoria* (memory). Each of them has to be converted, and in the sequence of the sermons Bernard first elaborates the conversion of memory (Advent with a peak in Adv 3), then will (from Nativity to Circumcision), and finally reason (from Epiphany on).

This threefold conversion, however, can be recognized in many of the singular sermons, too, and most clearly in the Conversion of Paul. In this sermon, will is the last to be converted, after memory and reason. This sequential shift was linked to the fact that Bernard, at the end of the sermon, leaves the reader with the image of the blinded Paul, waiting for the man who will release him from his darkness and give him back the light. In fact, the conversion of reason in the sermon did not lead to the acknowledgment of insight but rather to the consciousness of its lack. The "conversion sermons," as the entire unit from Advent to Paul was called, did not aim at true knowledge of God's mysteries but rather at the recognition of the deficiency of man's unconverted reason to understand God's glorious truth. For this reason only, some glimpses of God's glory had been allowed to his eyes, notably in the sermons for Epiphany. Inevitably, man thus became aware of his own blindness and remained stuck in his desire for liberation out of the captivity of his own defects. It can be expected that the unit of sermons following will first of all try to heal this mental blindness of the reader by giving him the recognition of insight.

THE SERMONS FOR LENT

Developing Ideas in a Growing Concept

As has been demonstrated by the sermons for Advent and the Christmas season, it is illuminating to have a closer look at the growth and development of each group of sermons throughout the succeeding versions. Both the earliest version (B) from 1138–40 in its rather moralistic tenor and the later, purely liturgical, version (M) from around 1140 give an insight into Bernard's search for the best composition to fit his basic intentions. The miscellaneous collection L in its two halves, exegetical (L^A) and liturgical (L^B), on the contrary, illustrates both Bernard's hesitations and his organizational capacities.[2]

The sermons for Lent differ in their evolution from the preceding group in their more complex and varying constitution. The conversion sermons from Advent to Paul had formed, from the beginning, a rather coherent unit, changing only in the number of sermons dedicated to each of the liturgical events. In the sermons for Lent, however, one gets to know a more hesitant and searching Bernard. The greatest differences between the succeeding versions are caused by the separation or fusion of the Temporal and the Sanctoral on the one hand and by an apparent uncertainty about what to do with the exegetic sermons on Psalm 90, *Qui habitat* (QH), on the other hand.

The Monastic Prayer: The First Version (B)[3]

In his earliest transmitted draft for a liturgical homiliary, which he probably never meant to publish,[4] Bernard gave a place of prominence to the exegesis of Psalm 90, although he had only written the first six of his sermons.[5] Actually, they constitute the entire Lenten cycle in this compilation, preceded only by the sermon *On the Divine Will* and fol-

---

[2] See, for a characterization of the different versions, their dating, and their basic tenors, the introduction to CF 51 with bibliography.

[3] The collection B contains the following texts, indicated by the sigla they received in the final edition: *1.* Div 14; *2.* Adv 4; *3.* Adv 5; *4.* VNat 2; *5.* Div 85; *6.* Sent 3.15; *7.* Sent: *Laqueus* (edited as an appendix to QH 3); *8.* Div 75; *9.* Sent 1.5; *10.* Sent 1.6; *11.* Sent 1.7; *12.* Circ 3; *13.* Sent 3.16; *14.* Sent 3.17; *15.* Div 73; *16.* Epi 1; *17.* Epi 2; *18.* Div 29; *19.* OEpi; *20.* Div 86; *21.* pEpi 1; *22.* *De voluntate* (Sermones varii VI). Most of these texts are written in a first editing. For the entire collection B, see SBOp 4 (1966) 130 and 133-135. Also Jean Leclercq 'La tradition,' *Recueil* 2 (1966) 214–217.

[4] See CF 51: xxxiii–xxxiv.

[5] Of these, QH I and II still constituted a unity. The group thus counted only five sermons with the future QH IV in its center. See *Sancti Bernardi Opera* [hereafter

lowed by the first version of his sermon on Saint Benedict. The Lenten cycle thus counted only seven sermons of a largely exegetic nature.

The opening sermon *On the Divine Will* was eliminated entirely from the final collection, although it appears in some intermediary versions where it forms part of the Lent sermons proper (Quad). In these cases it occupies the sixth position. The modern editors published the text as part of the Various Sermons (*Sermones varii*), together with some other texts that did not fit into any series.[6]

The body of the sermon treats the obstacles that hinder human will from adhering to the divine will in the way the angels do. Four of these obstacles are described: our wicked affection that makes us enjoy the wrong things, the weakness of our body, our greed that makes us long for things we cannot fulfill, and our ignorance. Each of these is countered by one of the four cardinal virtues: our wrong affection by justice, our weakness by fortitude, our greed by temperance, and our ignorance by prudence. Each couple of opponents is simply mentioned, without one of Bernard's other inventive elaborations like the *psychomachia* or the liberation of the king's son from captivity.

The last paragraph suddenly introduces a new theme in its double exegesis of two verses of the Pater Noster: *adveniat regnum tuum* and *sanctificetur nomen tuum*. As the preceding paragraph ends with a short *peroratio* and *conclusio*, this last exegetic paragraph might have been added afterward. The reason could have been to transform the sermon into a transitional text from the preceding block of sermons around Epiphany to the exegetic sermons on Psalm 90. This can find a confirmation in the introduction of several verses of the Pater Noster in the sermons on Psalm 90. In QH 1.4 the words *Pater noster qui es in caelis* were only introduced in the final version, just as *Adveniat regnum tuum* was then added to QH 4.3. In QH 5.1, *Et ne nos inducas in tentationem* was added, while QH 15.6 retook the entire opening: *Pater noster qui es in caelis, sanctificetur nomen tuum.*[7]

SBOp], ed. Jean Leclercq and Henri-Marie Rochais, vol. 4, Apparatus (Rome: Editiones Cistercienses, 1966), 389.

[6] SV 6; SBOp 6/1:37–39.

[7] SBOp 4:388 and 399, both in the Apparatus series.

These changes demonstrate the importance Bernard attached to the allusions to the Pater Noster. Apparently, he considered them essential for the sermons on Psalm 90 as a reading for Lent. As soon as he had eliminated the sermon *On the Divine Will* from his liturgical project and reintroduced the exegesis on Psalm 90, he counterbalanced its loss by the insertion of several parts of the Lord's Prayer into the exegesis.

An important difference occurs, however. Originally, in the sermon *On the Divine Will* the verses of the Lord's Prayer had received a proper exegetic treatment, even when it was very short and as a kind of appendix. Incorporated in the exegetic sequence on Psalm 90, they appear as an illustration, as an argument in the actual explanation. They lose their focused position and become more of a founding principle, which makes it possible to realize the content of the exegesis. As will be shown, this points indeed to one of the fundamental lines according to which the entire unit of Lent was organized.

The five sermons on Psalm 90, of course, have first of all an exegetic motivation.[8] One might wonder why Bernard inserted them into B before finishing them. It could strengthen the assumption that B is nothing more than a preliminary collection, never destined for publication. But there might be more behind it. These early sermons form a nice, coherent, and formal unit, opening and closing with two sermons of almost identical length, surrounding three rather small sermons such as could have been pronounced in the chapterhouse.[9] Starting from QH 7, the length of the new sermons increases considerably. Now, QH 7–10 make their appearance in L[A], the exegetic part, while QH 11–17 are introduced only in the final collection Pf. This might imply that, originally, Bernard perhaps did not intend to treat the entire Psalm 90 but wanted to restrict his explanation to the opening verses. Only after deciding to lift it out of his liturgical

---

[8] The sermons on Psalm 90 have been translated separately in CF 25. They are treated here only for the understanding they offer of the liturgical collection.

[9] As mentioned, B contains the future sermons QH 1–6 together with the prologue, of which QH 1 and 2 still form one unity of seven paragraphs—of similar length as QH 6.

project and making it into a separate exegetical unit, he started to elaborate on its interpretative opportunities.[10]

For this reason it can be important for understanding the significance of the Lenten sermons to consider the original concept of including in an early version only the first six sermons on Psalm 90 with the prologue. This early reading differs in some places significantly from the later ones, notably in the prologue and in the last sermon, besides, of course, the split of the original first sermon into two, QH 1 and 2. The opening of the prologue was almost entirely rewritten from the first to the second version. With one exception, the two versions do not differ so much as to the content, but the style was strongly heightened, putting more emphasis upon the central concern of the *consolatio* (the comfort) the abbot-writer owed to his monks in their suffering. The only true change is the first source of comfort. In the original version, the monks had to remember God in order to find relief. In the final version, Bernard changed this rather abstract allusion into the concrete reference to "him who died for you." Instead of the distant God, Christ appears, sharing the suffering of the monks, even surpassing them in his voluntary death on their behalf.[11]

Unlike this still rather formal adaptation, the last sermon in B later underwent a complete rewriting, making it into an entirely new sermon—QH 6. Again, the content did not change radically. Originally the four temptations were enumerated and treated with their counterparts but in a less satisfying way. The third temptation—hypocrisy—clearly is not finished. It does not get any countervirtue and its description somehow breaks off in the middle of the argument. In the final sermon (QH 6), hypocrisy is replaced by the temptation of cupidity that receives a more convincing treatment and is opposed to the knowledge of the temporality of the world. Actually, it is opposed to the truth of worldly temporality.

---

[10] Bernard never felt compelled to consider biblical texts as undividable units. This is most clearly illustrated by his exegesis of only the first part of the Song of Songs. See Wim Verbaal, "Les *Sermons sur le Cantique* de Saint Bernard: un chef-d'oeuvre achevé?," *Collectanea* 61 (1999): 167–85.

[11] *Mortificamini, sed propter eum qui mortuus est pro vobis. Quod si abundat tribulatio vestra pro eo, abundabit consolatio vestra per eum* [QH Praef.1; SBOp 4:383].

And indeed, in his rewriting Bernard did increase the importance of truth. In QH 6, each of the four temptations is countered by a different truth. The first temptation is the novice's fear of the flesh. It can be disarmed by pondering on the truth about our sins, the infernal pains, the heavenly promises, and Christ's suffering for us. The second temptation, desire for vainglory, can be disarmed by the acknowledgment of our corruptibility. The third temptation, cupidity, is countered by the truth of the world's ephemeral nature. The fourth temptation, ignorance, to which Christ was not subjected in the desert, is disarmed by truth itself.

Truth becomes an essential element in the rewritten sermons as they are inserted in the final liturgical collection Pf, a fact that gives us a hint of the underlying thought that came to organize this section. In the original sequence, Bernard elaborated primarily the confrontation of two opposing forces: the devil with his temptations and the protection God offered to his followers. Later, this element did not disappear but it got a completely new interpretation. The weapon of God was truth in its different aspects, thereby changing the more warlike confrontation into something more like an intellectual confrontation.

Just like the final collection Pf, the block of sermons for Lent closes in B with the sermon for the Feast of Saint Benedict (Ben). Once again, however, the text has undergone important adaptations from the first to the final version; these do not touch the content but seem mostly limited to a literary refining of the language. Yet one remarkable change must be mentioned: when compared to the final version in Pf, the initial text has a much stronger monastic flavor. In rewriting the sermon, Bernard eliminated almost consequentially all references to the monastic situation, including his personal involvement and that of his monks. Because of its treating a very monastic subject—Benedict being the father of monasticism—this "demonasticizing" of the sermon cannot be disposed of in a few words. It demonstrates Bernard's desire to break out of the purely monastic circles and to reach a broader audience.

The sermon as a whole offers a nice example of Bernard's capacity to meld texts from different origins into a new and coherent entity. Different themes succeed each other but seem loosely connected. After a short introduction that only alludes to Benedict's name by the wordplay on *benediction* (Ben 1), a second equally short introduction follows comparing the writer as an abbot with the father of monasticism (Ben 2). Then suddenly the reader finds himself or herself[12] in a sermon treating the Palm Sunday procession. Benedict disappears, only to return as the tree from which the monks may pluck twigs to lay on the road before Christ (Ben 3). Immediately, the sermon changes perspective once more, becoming an exegesis of Psalm 1:3—*tamquam lignum quod plantatum est secus decursus aquarum*—and developing the theme of fertile and infertile trees (Ben 4–6a). Only then is the original theme picked up once again, examining Benedict's fruits (Ben 6b–8). Suddenly, however, the writer leaves the fruits and focuses on the seeds, treating the sowing of the different orders in heaven and earth with a small digression on Lucifer (Ben 9–12). In this last part, nothing more is said about Benedict.

Thus, the sermon on Saint Benedict falls roughly into two halves, one treating the third verse of Psalm 1, the other treating Christ's sowing after Luke 8:5. Benedict himself appears only in the opening, in a transitional sentence to introduce the exegesis of the psalm, and in the conclusion to the exegetical part. This reinforces the impression that we have to deal with an assemblage of different texts, written for different occasions and put together to fit into the first collection as the climax of a still largely monastic sequence of sermons.

In this sense, it is comprehensible that the line of thought for the Lenten cycle in this early collection B is mostly moralistic from a monastic perspective. The structuring principle, however, seems to have been dominated by a wish for exegesis with focus upon the psalms: the block opens with a sermon treating the Pater Noster, consists largely of an exegesis on Psalm 90:1-6, and closes with a sermon concentrating on Psalm 1:3. Also this emphasis on the reading of Psalms seems to point to a purely monastic context.

---

[12] [Editor's note: Verbaal explains, "Bernard was never thinking of an audience of women while writing these sermons. I do not know if he would have agreed with opening his audience to women. I think he would have written differently for them. Anyway, nowadays of course, both men and women do read Bernard and the use of both masculine and feminine pronouns is a normal way of acknowledging that fact."]

Striving for Unity: The Second Version (M)[13]

When compared to B, the second version—M—displays a much less complicated structure. The liturgical perspective is clear from the beginning. The block of sermons for Lent, made up of the sermons between those for Epiphany and those for Palm Sunday, contains five of the six sermons *In Quadragesima* (Quad), thus leaving no doubt about the purpose and objective of these five Quad sermons. All of them would be inserted into the final collection Pf. Only their order changed: in M they appear successively as Quad 1, 2, 6, 3, and 4. Of course, this different sequence will imply also another interpretation of the entire block.

In both collections the series opens with the same ideas on Lent as a period of anointment (Quad 1) and of conversion (Quad 2). Both are also exegetical sermons: Quad 1 starts from Matthew 6:17, *Unge caput tuum et faciem tuam lava*; Quad 2 takes its lead from Joel 2:12-13, *Convertimini ad me in toto corde vestro, in ieiunio et fletu, et planctu, et scindite corda vestra et non vestimenta vestra, ait Dominus omnipotens*, which was used as a reading during Tierce at Lent.[14] Then follows in M the future Quad 6, which deals with three ways to mortify oneself vis-à-vis the world—as the passing stranger, as the dead, and as the crucified. The sermon is not a true exegesis but is built along the lines offered by different biblical quotations. The last two sermons in M take up again explicitly the theme of Lent, treating the search for Christ in its sacramental value (Quad 3) and as the fruit of mortification (Quad 4).

Thus a circular movement is visible with, at its center, the three ways of mortification. The movement starts with the ingression into Lent as a period for Christian military service.[15] The central idea is offered by the unity with Christ as it is guaranteed by the anointment of his self-sacrificial love and has to be restored or strengthened by our communication in his suffering. The movement then seems to continue upon this idea of restoration of the bond between Christ's suffering and

---

[13] M consists of the following texts: *1*. Adv I; *2*. Adv II; *3*. Adv III; *4*. VNat II; *5*. VNat I; *6*. Nat II; *7*. Nat III; *8*. Nat IV; *9*. Circ I; *10*. Circ III; *11*. Epi I; *12*. Epi II; *13*. OEpi; *14*. pEpi I.

[14] SBOp 4:359, Apparatus.

[15] *Hodie, dilectissimi, sacrum Quadragesimae tempus ingredimur, tempus militiae christianae* [Quad 1.1; SBOp 4:353].

human mortification, first concentrating on a person's conversion: in humility (Quad 2.1), in the heart by way of the four affections (Quad 2.2–3), in the body by mortification and tears (Quad 2.4) and, finally, once again in the heart by its inner laceration (Quad 2.5–6).

This final form of mortification is elaborated in a more visible way in the middle sermon (future Quad 6), in which the three images of stranger, dead, and crucified one express an increasing degree of detachment. Only this growing detachment makes the next step possible, in which mortification receives its sacramental value because of its passionate search for the Lord (Quad 3.4). Hereafter the fruit of mortification will be the strengthened unity of the community, mirroring the unity of the body with the head (Quad 4.2) as it finds its clearest expression in the liberated prayer (Quad 4.3–4).

So the line connecting the different sermons seems to be the restoration or strengthening of unity, both inside the community and between the body of the faithful and Christ as its head. Apparently, the way to build this unity can only be by way of mortification, taking its start in the desire to share the sufferings of Christ for humankind but, finally, leading to a desire of detachment in order to be freer in praying and rising up to God. The circular movement thus implies a strong linear impulse. The end remains open in a certain sense, thus leading to the following sermons for Palm Sunday and its procession.

The sermons for Purification (Pur 1–3) that will open the sequence of Lent in the final collection Pf can already be found in M, but there they do not belong to the Temporal. They form part of the Sanctoral, in which they follow the first sermon on Annunciation (Ann 1), constituting the opening sequence for a block of sermons dedicated to the Virgin. In M the Pur sermons thus remain separated from the guiding principles in the Lent sermons.

The Liturgical Shortcut: The Third Collection (L^B)[16]

In the liturgical part of the third collection, L^B, only two sermons for Lent appear: the future first sermon for Septuagesima (Sept 1)

---

[16] L^B contains the following texts concerning the period before Lent: *1.* VNat III; *2.* VNat V, *3.* VNat VI; *4.* Adv VI; *5.* Adv VII; *6.* VNat IV; *7.* Nat I; *8.* Nat V; *9.* Innoc;

and a sermon on the Ten Commandments and the seven obstacles to following them. This last text disappeared from the liturgical collection and ended in the separate series of sermons on various subjects as Div 22.

Sept 1 opens the Lent block in L^B and is preceded by three sermons on the water jars of the wedding feast at Cana. Sept 1 indicates a clear liturgical break within the sequence, as the theme of Lent is particularly emphasized after the introduction of the opening paragraphs, when the actual sermon starts.[17] The body of the sermon treats the desire for fulfillment, which is resented by man while living (Sept 1.3). Yet, true realization of this desire will only be possible after the earthly Septuagesima in the heavenly Jerusalem (Sept 1.4). Seven obstacles hinder us from reaching this fulfillment available to humankind by the Ten Commandments, each of which has to be overcome by a specific spiritual exercise (Sept 1.5). The time of Septuagesima is dedicated to this training.

In its numerical elaboration at the end, the sermon parallels preceding texts in which the numerical element of the six water jars offers Bernard all kinds of exegetic opportunities. Yet, in Sept 1 this numerical accent is no longer the most obvious element of the sermon. It has submitted to the theme of desire, thus bringing in an impulse of forward movement. These dynamics are even reinforced by the obstacles that are introduced in the last paragraph, causing the forward rush to be hampered and even to halt.

The outset in Sept 1 is both intensified and elaborated in the following sermon (Div 22), which deals with the shortcut offered by Lent. Although the road is steep, it is short for those who have relieved themselves of all excess so that they may take the shortest road upward (Div 22.1–2). The greatest danger is formed by the wish to take up the burdens of life and thus to impede oneself on the way up (Div 22.4). On the contrary, the way becomes only more passable when one feels indebtedness toward the sufferings of Christ for humankind (Div 22.5–9).

---

10. Div 51.2; *11.* Div 53; *12.* Div 51.1; *13.* Sent I.11; *14.* Circ II; *15.* Sent I.14; *16.* Sent I.15; *17.* Epi III; *18.* Div 55; *19.* Div 56; *20.* pEpi II.

[17] *Initium Septuagesimae, fratres, hodie celebratur* [Sept 1.3; SBOp 4:346].

The desire awakened in Sept 1 thus spurs us on the steep road that leads immediately to the victory of the Word as it is expressed in the following sermon on the passion of Christ, the future 4 HM. The order is neat and clear, showing in M how Lent for Bernard has to be a spiritual progression, leading to the recognition of Christ's liberating passion.

The third collection, L, contains still other texts that were inserted into the final version. Here, though, they do not yet belong to the liturgical part but can be found in the exegetic half (L^A), which in origin constituted a separate volume.[18] To start with, this exegetic part opens with the enlarged exegesis of Psalm 90, in which is contained the future sermons QH 1 to 10. This coherent block begins a series of exegetic texts on Psalms and separate verses that seems to be organized roughly according to the order of the psalms themselves.[19] The appearance of QH as the opening sequence in L^A proves that Bernard by this time had left the idea of incorporating this exegesis in his liturgical collection. The reason might have been that he wanted to develop it into a separate treatise or that it just did not fit anymore into his new concept, dividing the liturgical collection into a Temporal and a Sanctoral.

The future second sermon for Septuagesima (Sept 2) also occurs in the exegetic part of L, where it takes the fortieth place. It follows a block of texts treating different fragments from the books of Wisdom. As it deals itself with the sleep of Adam (Gen 2:21-26), it seems to constitute a rupture with what precedes. Yet, the text just before (the future Div 82) offers a reading of Proverbs 4:23 dealing with vigilance of the heart, while the text following Sept 2—which will end up in the edition of the *Sententiae*, first series (Sent 1.13)—also deals with a verse of Genesis (Gen 48:22) and explains it in the sense of the unity of man with God as one of his members. This last line is elaborated also in the two succeeding texts of L^A. Thus, the place of Sept 2 within the exegetic half is explained both by the biblical text

[18] See Verbaal, CF 51: xxxviii.
[19] L^A contains 94 texts, starting with QH 1 with prologue. Texts 1 (QH 1) to 22 treat the Psalms.

central to its discourse and by a more interpretative subunit around man's unity with God.

Finally, the future Quad 5 appears in L[A] at the seventy-first place. It is preceded by a large block of texts, in which the central theme is not so much formed by a biblical verse as by numerical exegesis. Texts 60 to 70 in L[A] deal with a symbolic application of the number "three" on all kinds of subjects, including the three regions with their inhabitants; three testimonies in heaven, on earth, and in hell; three kinds of peaceful men; a threefold fall and resurrection; and so on.[20] The future Quad 5 is followed by nine texts giving other numerical exegesis, in which the number "four" is emphasized, such as in the four degrees of love, four steps in our progression, and four obstacles for our confession.

The numerical structure of Quad 5 is less obvious. Careful reading, however, shows that the text can be divided into two parts, of which the first half (Quad 5.1–4) treats four different ways of experience in the battle between the body and the soul. The second half (Quad 5.5–9) deals with prayer and closes on two triple experiences in prayer (Quad 5. 8 and 9).

More important than the numerical element, however, is the theme of praying which dominates the second half and which connects Quad 5 to the text immediately following it, the future Div 107. This text also deals with praying, applying to it a numerical exegesis. It distinguishes four correct praying attitudes and three intentions, starting from the two obstacles for a fruitful prayer. Thus, Quad 5 was born as a numerical meditation on praying.

Summary

The development of the sermons for Lent shows a much less linear evolution than was the case with the sermons for the first unit, those for Advent and the Christmas season. Bernard seems to have been wavering over the best approach for this part of the liturgical

---

[20] The one exception is text 61 (the future Sent 3.17), treating the four obligations in imitating Christ.

year. Initially taking his start from the opening verses of Psalm 90, it seems that he wanted to concentrate on the confrontation between vices and virtues, based upon an exegetic treatment of some psalms (B). Apparently, he then decided to leave this plan and to insert other texts, mostly explicitly written for Lent and giving a stronger expression to a forward and upward movement (M). The meditation on Psalm 90 was continued as an independent exegetic treatise and inserted into his exegetic "archive" (L^A). In the parallel liturgical "archive" (L^B), the movement as found in M was even reinforced because of the small unit dedicated to Lent. In the final collection (Pf), all these texts were brought together and completed by texts that originally did not have any link to liturgy at all but rather belonged to his exegetic archive. Also, entirely new sermons, which only occur in Pf, were introduced.

In spite of this seeming amalgam of texts, Bernard managed to create a coherent unit around Lent in which he developed the ideas already present in the former collections. Some of them may be shortly rehearsed. One of the basic lines in Bernard's meditation on Lent is the necessity of exegesis. Both B and M show a strong exegetic emphasis. They differ in the sense that B is almost entirely exegetic, while in M only half of the sermons have an exegetic tenor. This importance of exegesis will remain one of the fundamental elements in composing the final sequence.

A second component that seems to reappear frequently is the confrontation of opposing elements: vices and virtues, progressions and impediments, mortifications and their fruits, etc. This component lends itself perfectly to a numerical treatment, thus helping to compose the more complex sermons into coherent unities.

Closely linked to this idea of oppositions is the basic line of progression, of movement, which can be recognized in almost every preceding collection. Much stronger than in the sermons for Advent and the Christmas season, the sermons for Lent are based upon a linear, progressive movement from a starting point of dissatisfaction and desire toward a feeling of unity and hope of fulfillment.

Finally, linking this forward movement to the idea of struggle, inherent to the multiple oppositions inside the different series, all of them lay much emphasis on the importance of praying. In B, the Lord's

Prayer itself constitutes one of the fundamental guidelines in the succession of sermons, while in M the entire block of Lent results in the prayer ascending to heaven.

All of these different strains were taken up by Bernard and woven into the inextricable net, formed by his last collection, proving him to be once more a writer of uttermost talent and, above all, a spiritual teacher of the highest degree.

The School of Lent

In Pf Bernard tried to merge all the different strains he had developed over the years in his meditation on the purpose of a liturgical homiliary. It brought him to an entirely new interpretation of what Lent ought to be for a spiritual reader. All the former readings remained but were cast into a new frame. This composition gave a new and stronger emphasis to elements that had been present from the beginning and so gave a different sense to the texts without Bernard's actually rewriting them.

Reading Progressions: Linear Movements

When comparing the final liturgical block of Lent with the preceding versions, it is hard to realize that its composition had not been figured out at the beginning. With few exceptions, no text has undergone a drastic rewriting. The exceptions are mostly situated in the exegesis on Psalm 90 (QH), while the others were taken out of the previous collections, almost without any internal change. They were put in a new arrangement. That was all; yet the entire concept changed radically. The old ideas were not abandoned but they were treated from a new perspective, thus opening up toward new interpretations.

What exactly did change and how did Bernard obtain the realization of his new conceptual idea? The first element, which should alert a scholar studying the growth and sense of Bernard's liturgical collection, is the new start his sequence on Lent got in the final version. In all the preceding versions, the sermons for Lent were closely linked to the final sermons on Epiphany. In each of them, B, M and L[B], the first sermon for Lent followed immediately after one or more sermons on the change of water into wine at the wedding of Cana. Both in the earliest one, B, and in the archival collection, L[B], the sense of the Epiphany sermons lies clearly in the search for the Truth. In the sermons for Lent, this quest was continued in a deepened meditation on the biblical Word, thus giving a prominent place to the exegesis of biblical texts in the readings of Lent.

In Pf, this recognition of the Truth still remained central to a good understanding of the sermons on Epiphany and those that follow. Yet the link to Lent was made less intimate and direct. Actually, the recognition of Christ's divinity as demonstrated by his threefold manifestation at Epiphany was suddenly broken by Paul's blindness. In our reading we demonstrated this to be the blindness of a man who came to realize that he misses true insight.[21] The sermons for Lent, then, have to offer an answer to this desire of man, born out of his incapacity to grasp the Truth. From this point of view, not so much changed when compared to the previous collections.

However, after Paul's blindness, it is not the sermons on Lent that follow. Bernard has instead inserted the sermons for the Purification of the Virgin (Pur). As shown in the introduction to the sermons for Advent and the Christmas Season, each of the four subunits within the final liturgical collection opens with a sermon or a group of sermons on the Virgin. They give a first hint at one of the central ideas that will run through the new subunit, just as the last sermon on the human level will show one of its possible concrete actualizations.

At first sight it does not seem a strange choice to let the period of Lent start with the solemnity of Purification. Mortification seems to strive for a purification of the flesh and the body. Yet when reading these three sermons it becomes almost immediately clear that Bernard is not at all occupied with Mary's purification. Only in Pur 3.2 does he touch slightly upon the question of whether the Virgin needed at all to submit herself to Jewish custom. As a whole, however, the three sermons concentrate more on other subjects.

---

[21] See CF 51: xlviii–li.

The most important elements introduced by these sermons are the ideas of the procession and the presentation of Christ. As far as the procession is concerned, Bernard stresses the importance to progress and not to halt, because "in the path of life, not to make progress is to regress."[22] This emphasis on forward movement breaks through the passivity to which the reader was brought at the conclusion of the Christmas season, sitting with Paul in order to wait for deliverance out of his blindness, preferring to be drawn by the hand than to presume leadership over those who have their eyes open but do not see anything.[23]

The Purification sermons, however, immediately set us in motion: "Today the Virgin Mother brought the Lord of the Temple into the Temple of the Lord."[24] There is movement, both in a passive and in an active way. The child, the Lord of the Temple, is carried toward the temple. The Virgin Mother leads him (*inducit*) as if she was taking him by the hand just as Ananias will have to do with the blinded Paul. Yet huge differences are introduced, for it is not the blinded man in his incapacity to understand who asks for guidance here. It is the Lord of the Temple himself who is brought into his own temple. Human misery is replaced by divinity itself, but not in its divine, inaccessible form. God is carried as a small weeping child, having taken upon himself man's weakness.

Actually, the entire sentence is constructed around conflicting senses. The Lord of the Temple is carried as a small vulnerable child into the temple, which is both his property to govern and the visible sign of his all-embracing power. A virgin, who is also mother, is carrying the child, and the man who assists is considered father, although the child is not his son. And this happens today, not in some far away biblical time, but now, before our eyes, and in our midst.[25]

---

[22] Pur 2.3: *in via vitae non progredi regredi est.* SBOp 4:340.

[23] Pl 8: *semper, quod in nobis est, abiecti eligamus esse et ad manus trahi.* SBOp 4:334. ("Let us beware of this vice, brothers. Always, as far as we can, let us choose to be abject and to be led by the hand," CF 51: 202.)

[24] Pur 1.1: *Hodie templi Dominum in templum Domini Virgo Mater inducit.* SBOp 4:334.

[25] The word *hodie* has a clear function in Bernard's writing. Mostly, it signals the opening of a new sequence, while stressing the topicality of the subject treated. Its repetition in the opening sermons of Lent shows this double importance: what is being told is possible every current day *and* Lent wants to get started in order to find

In this one sentence, readers are once again confronted with their own incapacity to understand the congruency of incongruent truths. This sentence throws them back upon the situation they were confronted with in the second sermon for Epiphany (Epi 2), where they had to see God truly there, where there was no reason to see him this way.[26] Yet in the sermon for Epiphany, God was recognized by the Magi, by the thief at the cross, and by the centurion under the cross. So, now, God is recognized in the shape of the small baby by the just man who expects him and by the widow who confesses him.[27]

All elements of the Advent and Christmas sermons return: God taking on a human body in its most vulnerable shape, thus combining the incompatible, like his Virgin Mother; Joseph, loving and assisting the Son that is not his own; the desire for insight and recognition in Simeon the Just; and the confession of the Truth by Anna, who has lost all. From these four persons, "today's procession" takes its start—i.e., from fertile chastity, selfless love, recognition in desire, and confession in detachment. By the insertion of the three sermons on the Purification, the sermons for Lent, though being a new start, constitute perhaps an even tighter connection to the results of the Christmas Season.

Bernard's rearrangement of the sermons for Lent did not limit itself to the insertion of sermons from the original Sanctoral. He also brought together sermons which before had never belonged to each other. First of all, he combined two texts to comment upon Septuagesima, taking them both from his archive, one from the exegetic and one from the liturgical part. Sept 1 belonged from the beginning to Bernard's liturgical projects. It opens with an introduction on the consolation man can find when he opens himself to the words of the Lord (Sept 1.1–2). The actual sermon then[28] treats of the desire

---

its conclusion in the resurrection. *Hodie* appears in Pur 1.1 and 2, Pur 2.1 (five times!), Pur 3.1, Sept 1.3, Quad 1.1 and 3, while it does not appear in QH. Similarly, it is used to open (and close) the sermons of Advent and the Christmas Season (Adv 1.1) after which it disappears until Pl 1.

[26] See CF 51: lvi–lvii.

[27] Pur 1.1: *Agnoscit iustus quem exspectabat, Anna quoque vidua confitetur.* SBOp 4:334.

[28] Note Bernard's formulation of the sentence, characteristic of so many of his opening sequences: *Initium Septuagesimae, fratres, hodie celebratur.* SBOp 4:346.

for fulfillment (Sept 1.3, based on an exegesis of Wisdom 11:21), as it will only be attained after the earthly Septuagesima in the heavenly Jerusalem (Sept 1.4). On earth, seven obstacles lie in the way of this fulfillment (Sept 1.5). Sept 1 thus takes up two of the central themes from the preceding sermons: the forward movement, which is no longer seen as a procession but rather as a progression, and its impulse in the desire for fulfillment.

The content of this fulfillment is the subject of Sept 2, which originally belonged to the exegetic half of Bernard's "archives." In comparing Adam's sleep (Gen 2:21-26) to Christ's, Bernard opposes man's bodily weakness both to Adam's contemplative freedom and to Christ's redeeming sleep in death. Several lines are taken from the preceding sermon. First of all, the story of Adam brings into practice what was announced at the conclusion of Sept 1: "It is because of [this] that . . . the lamentable story of human transgression is recounted from the beginning."[29] Indeed, the new sermon deals with an episode from the beginnings of humankind, comparing man's situation before the Fall with his present condition. Pondering over the freedom Adam enjoyed, man cannot but realize the bitterness of his actual state. This realization ought to kindle his desire for release and his gratitude for the sleep of death, by which Christ has redeemed him. Sept 2 thus becomes a sermon of desire, putting before the reader's eyes both the initial and the actual state of humankind as well as the opportunity for restoration that Christ offered him by his death.

Sept 2 does not, however, limit itself to a description of man's vocation to transcend his present condition. In its subject itself, the sermon focuses upon one of the basic elements of human condition: his need of sleep out of the infirmity of his existence. Man has to sleep because life is toilsome, because even the use of the senses is tiresome. Sleep is the condition of corporeal man after the Fall. Thus, Sept 2 actually deals with the first of the seven obstacles, enumerated in the last paragraph of Sept 1: the needs of this miserable body.[30]

---

[29] Sept 1.5: *Unde . . . humanae transgressionis historia miserabilis ab exordio recensetur.* SBOp 4:349.

[30] Sept 1.5: "Our first hindrance—a heavy burden—is the compulsions of this miserable body! With its constant demands for sleep, food, clothes, and other such

That Sept 1.5 is offering the underlying idea for the entire cycle of Lent is confirmed by the sermons for Quadragesima, which follow. Quad 1 deals indeed with the second impediment, purifying the vices of the heart. Quad 2 takes the third and the fourth obstacles, prosperity and adversity in the world, together. Quad 3 fights the fifth impediment, ignorance; Quad 4 the sixth, the suggestions of the adversary; and Quad 5 the seventh, deceitful brothers.

Bernard never dedicates a sermon explicitly to one of the seven obstacles. They are only touched upon slightly or can be deduced by their opposite. Quad 5, for example, does not have deceitful brothers as its actual subject. It rather gives the writer the profile of a leader who is concerned about his monks and wants to support them by his advice and words. Quad 5 thus rather attacks the idea of deceitful brothers by offering the image of a trustworthy leader and brother. Bernard's occupation with the spiritual health of his monks and readers is shown to originate from the knowledge of his own weaknesses. Fraternal love thus becomes effective thanks to self-knowledge, giving finally in Quad 5.8 strength to prayer in order to conquer the different obstacles (purification of the heart, weakness of the flesh, strengthening of the soul, safeguarding from the enemy), whereas knowledge and fraternal love express themselves in the prayer itself.

Now, prayer had become the central theme of Quad 4 as the most effective way to endure the mortifications of Lent, thus giving an impulse to the forward movement as it was initiated by the procession of Pur and concretized in the enumeration of the obstacles in Sept 1.5. Progressing "in the path of life" becomes synonymous with the effectiveness of one's praying. The enemy tries to hinder this effectiveness in three ways. He either brings the mind to despair, putting the enormity of a person's crimes before his eyes, or he seduces him into too much confidence in divine clemency, or he deprives him of his fervor, thus leaving his prayer tepid. The first two obstacles are conquered by memory, bringing to mind either divine clemency,

---

things our body is frequently a hindrance to us in our spiritual activities." *Primum enim impedimentum nostrum et occupatio gravis, ipsa est necessitas huius miseri corporis, quod, dum modo somnum, modo cibum, modo vestem ceteraque similia quaerit, haud dubium quin frequenter impediat nos ab exercitio spiritualis.* SBOp 4:348.

which soothes despair, or the proper sins committed, which strengthens humility (Quad 4.3–4).

The importance of prayer within the cycle of Lenten sermons was stressed by the insertion of Quad 5, brought into close connection with Quad 4. Besides, the insertion of Quad 5 strengthened the fundamental significance of Sept 1.5, offering something of a framework for the entire cycle from Sept 2 to Quad 5. This also explains the change within the sequence of Quad. As Quad 6 treats of three kinds of mortification (being a stranger to the world, being dead, and being crucified), it does not fit into the new scheme and has had to abandon its place as the center in the cycle. Instead, it was moved toward the last place.

Apparently Bernard thought the sermon too important to leave out. By its shift, however, the impression of the sequence of Quad changed considerably. In origin, Quad constituted something of a cyclical composition, opening with the unity between Christ and man—thanks to the ointments of Christ's love and our participation in his suffering (Quad 1)—passing over conversion into true compunction of the heart (Quad 2) and over detachment from the world (Quad 4), and ending in a new unity with the church and God (Quad 3)—thanks to mortification and praying (Quad 4).

Now, in Pf a more linear movement replaces this circular composition: unity with the church and God (Quad 3) becomes the immediate result of the conversion of the heart (Quad 2), not leading to detachment from the world but to stronger mortification and prayer (Quad 4 and 5). This strengthened prayer pushes us into the world as stranger, dead, or crucified (Quad 6), thus giving more fervor to our prayer and the actual sense to our mortification. Quad 6 becomes the conclusion of the preceding movement, offering itself an open ending because it concludes with the exhortation to "press on with their usual battle, more than usual, so that a great victory may result, for the glory of our King, and for our salvation."[31] Quad 6 thus gives the antidote against the third obstacle to fervent prayer, which had not been treated in Quad 5, but also opens up to the succeeding exegesis of Psalm 90, in which the battle with the enemy is fought and explained.

[31] Quad 6.4: *amplius solitae est insistere pugnae, ut magna quaedam victoria Regi nostro ad gloriam, nobis proveniat ad salutem.* SBOp 4:380.

The open conclusion of Quad 6 and its exegetic continuation in QH singles out another of the new themes that have been introduced into the cycle of Lent. Indeed, the peaceful procession of Pur has changed into an advancing army. Military language and images get an increasing importance from Quad 1 and onward. The readers are exhorted to adhere closely to their Head, to follow him closely, to imitate him and not to betray him (Quad 1). They have to be watchful and to win ground upon their enemy, to attack him on his proper territory by abstaining from his means of seduction (Quad 3). The old theme of opposing virtues and vices, as it can be read in the earlier versions, did not disappear. Now it functions as preparation for the actual battle that has to be fought in the exegesis of Psalm 90.

In the final cycle it is the theme of learning that receives the emphasis. In addition to military imagery, the language of school and learning is important in the Lent cycle. Conversion in humility is opposed to the danger of overestimation of one's self, to the danger of the inflated ego, which Bernard always associates with the teachers in the schools (Quad 2). Language of teaching reaches a peak in Quad 2 and Quad 4, thus alternating with the more military language in Quad 4 and Quad 3. Lent may thus be considered a battle. It is an intellectual battle, a war to be fought by insight and endurance. Blinded Paul has to suffer until his labor has won him the insight he desires. He will only learn this, however, from the teacher who explains the psalm of spiritual war to him. The peaceful procession offering Christ's human weakness to the temple has become, in its military advance, an intellectual progression in order to regain the light of insight in the living Word.

Training and Retraining: Circular Movements

The shift of Quad 6 from a central to a concluding position shows an important compositional change in Bernard's project. Instead of a circular composition, he introduced a strong, linear movement, breaking open the closed structures of the earlier collections. This intervention is remarkable in view of Bernard's clear preference for cyclic compositions in both single texts and larger collections. As mentioned in the general introduction to CF 51, Bernard likes to give the reader vertigo by turning him around, leading him by a long road to the idea of having arrived at the point of departure, which is no longer the same.[32] Thus, Bernard's replacing this favorite tactic by a more straightforward linear composition makes one wonder if Bernard did not retain the circular movement but in another less visible way.

On a smaller scale, indeed, circular movements can be recognized. Already the disposition within the sequence of Quad and the alternation of military and educational inspiration shows a tendency toward a spiraling composition. Inside the single sermons, however, another repetitive scheme closely linked to the theme of schooling becomes visible. Because schooling ought never limit itself to a training of the mind, as far as Bernard is concerned the monastic school as a school of love or charity has to take man in his entirety into account. Monastic schooling thus has to be oriented toward the totality of man's spirit. Education demands the participation of all of man's spiritual capacities: memory, will, and reason.

As has been demonstrated before, already in the subunit of the Advent and Christmas sermons these three capacities of the soul were involved. In the Advent sermons, Bernard concentrated upon the conversion of memory, in the Christmas sermons upon the conversion of will, and in the Epiphany sermons upon the conversion of reason. Conversion, however, did not lead to insight but rather to the recognition of failing insight, leaving the human being blinded by our own impotence. We had to wait for the Man sent by God who would open our eyes and lead the human being by the hand toward the light. The Lenten sermons will accomplish this task. They continue where the cycle of Christmas sermons stops. Their aim is not to convert but to open the eyes—i.e., to teach by training the human spirit.

Many of the educational sermons within the sequence of Lent indeed seem to take up the training of each of the three capacities of the soul. Quad 2, for example, starts at the position where the Christmas season had left the human creature: starting from Joel 2:12-13 in its liturgical form, it treats of the human's need for conversion. Yet it does not do this in the way the Christmas sermons do.

---

[32] CF 51: xlix–l.

Rather, it treats conversion as a movement from exterior to interior mortification, as a procession of intention—i.e., giving direction to the affectivity of the heart. In order to achieve this purpose, Quad 2 treats successively the conversion of reason (Quad 2.2–3), of memory (Quad 2.4), and of will (Quad 2.5). Reason has to be trained in order to distinguish between true and false motives for joy, sadness, fear, and love. Memory must be trained in order to make us weep in penitence over the sins in our past as well as to make us weep in longing for their future fulfillment. The will must be trained in order to submit self-will to the will of God.

This threefold scheme repeats itself in almost every succeeding sermon. In Quad 3, vigilance is demanded from memory in order to avoid falling prey to despair (Quad 3.1), from will in order to follow more devotionally the leaders Moses, Elijah, and Christ (Quad 3.2), and from reason in order to get knowledge of and insight into the true meaning of Lent (Quad 3.3). This last subject is picked up in Quad 4.1, where Bernard explains "how you should fast and what its result should be."[33] That Bernard first appears as a rational teacher is clear from his scholastic opening (*quo fructu et quemadmodum*). He continues in teaching the right way of love by maintaining unity, cherishing peace, and loving the brotherhood (Quad 4.2). After having thus given direction to reason, he continues in directing the will. As seen before, the end of the sermon gives direction to memory, showing which tactics of the enemy can be countered by way of memory (Quad 4.3–4).

In Quad 5, reason, memory, and will are trained in a more simultaneous way, each implying the others. Out of self-knowledge (reason) is born the fraternal love (will), which pushes Bernard to console his audience (Quad 5.1–2). He exhorts them not to consent to the suggestions of the enemy, linking closely will and consent (Quad 5.3–4). Passing on to prayer, he opposes faith in the truth of the Bible to the futility of our own experience—i.e., scriptural memory as opposed to personal (Quad 5.5). Finally, in Quad 6, memory is the driving

---

[33] Quad 4.1: *dignum reor aliquatenus exponere, quo fructu et quemadmodum oporteat ieiunari.* SBOp 4:368.

force in the stranger, spurning him on in desire; reason dominates in the dead, replacing worldly desire with the desire for Christ; and will triumphs in the crucified, inverting worldly desires into their opposite out of love for Christ.

Thus, the readers find themselves time and again confronted with their underdeveloped capacities. Reason, will, and memory never seem to have finished their training, but rather continuously need to be retaken, retrained, and reoriented in order not to lose track and not to change into regressive forces, causing man to fall back instead of to progress.

This spiraling movement, however, can be recognized also in the overall composition of the sermons for Lent. From the linear movement, traced by the seven obstacles of Sept 1.5, a shift of emphasis can be distilled. The beginning of the learning movement concentrates more specifically on the rational aspects, stressing the understanding of the body and its needs (Sept 2) and of the heart and its vices (Quad 1). Then follow two sermons that give more attention to memory, stressing the need for conversion to the humility of the Christmas infant (Quad 2) and to fighting ignorance by being vigilant (Quad 3). Finally, the will is trained in giving direction to prayer (Quad 4) and in fraternal love and consolation (Quad 5). Thus, each of the three capacities gets its own learning, which, however, always implies both the other ones. Man remains one and indivisible.

The Beginning Is the End: Pointed Movement

Being pushed forward, the reader is at the same time turned around in circles, continuously returning to his point of departure. Even while realizing that no return leads him to the same place, but that somehow a distance has grown between where he was and where he is now, the simultaneity of this progressing in a linear way, and this finding himself always back at the same point, cannot but provoke a disorientation. The reader feels overwhelmed and gets lost in the complicated interplay of forward and circling movements, giving him a kind of floating feeling as if he escaped the laws of gravity. An increasing uneasiness as regards his submission to time strengthens this experience of emptiness. Indeed, Bernard manages to give the reader the impression that his progression is not chronologically bound—i.e., that progressing in Bernard's school of Lent does not imply a movement in time. The reader does not have an impression either of proceeding or receding. Although being put continuously into motion, he feels as if the movement is not directed along visible lines, be they linear or circular. He rather experiences an imploding movement, a kind of inward expansion, leaving him in the center of a dynamics that never transgresses his own borders.

This bizarre experience is, first of all, the result of Bernard's joining both ends of the liturgical sequence, Christmas and Easter, Birth and Passion. This joining already constituted one of the main structural elements in the sermons for the Advent and the Christmas season. In Lent it is repeated but in a different way. There is the impression of varied repetition, of a nonidentical rehearsal. In the opening sequence for the liturgical year, the longing desire of Advent was followed by the devotional souvenirs of Christmas, which for its part led to the acknowledgement of Epiphany—i.e., that the human being's vision still was blinded. A similar line of thought appears in the Lent series, as is very clearly illustrated by the opening sentence of Quad 4: "Because the season of the forty-day fast is near [*advenit*], I exhort you of your charity to undertake it with complete devotion [*tota devotione suscipere moneo*]. I think I should explain [*dignum reor exponere*] how you should fast and what its result should be."[34]

In the earlier sermon cycle, Advent is followed by devotion and concluded by the teaching of its results. Simultaneously, however, everything receives new significance. It is not the Nativity that is near, but "the season of the forty-day fast" (*ieiunii quadragesimalis tempus*). It is not the Child who has to be considered "with complete devotion," but once again Lent itself. Neither is it necessary to get insight into the divine nature of the Child, but rather into the reasons behind Lent. Christ is replaced by Lent, by the season of fasting.

Indeed, the Christmas season reappears in the period of Lent. The Purification of the Virgin takes place forty days after the Nativity, as

---

[34] Quad 4.1: *Quia ieiunii quadragesimalis tempus advenit, quod tota devotione suscipere moneo caritatem vestram, dignum reor aliquatenus exponere, quo fructu et quemadmodum oporteat ieiunari.* SBOp 4:368.

Bernard explains in Pur 3.1, equating this first period of forty days with the period of fasting, which is near. The sacrifice brought after these forty days leading to Purification is thus the same as the one brought after the forty days of fasting. Yet, at the same time, it is not the same: "That [sc., the Easter sacrifice] will be the evening sacrifice; this [sc., the sacrifice of purification] is the morning sacrifice. The one is more joyful, but the other more complete; this one takes place at the time of his birth, the other at the fullness of his years."[35]

So, there is a clearly marked temporal interval between the sacrifice of purification and that of Easter, the one taking place in the morning (of both day and life), the other in the evening. Yet, as the sermon continues, the sacrifice of purification becomes ever more like the Easter sacrifice. For the reason behind this ceremony to which the Virgin Mother actually did not need to submit herself is the voluntary sacrifice of Christ. Just as Christ underwent circumcision voluntarily and will sacrifice himself voluntarily at Easter, so now he undergoes the oblation of purification voluntarily (Pur 3.2). Circumcision, Purification, Easter: they come forth from one will and actually imply one another. Fundamentally, they do not differ from each other.

Likewise, they imply the final voluntary sacrifice that has to be offered by us: "He offered himself; who are you who hesitate to offer yourself? Who will accord to me that such great Majesty condescend to accept my offering?"[36] Christ will have to accept my offering in the same way that Simeon accepted his. The crucial term for both is *suscipere*, because the importance of the oblation lies not only in the one who offers but also in the one who accepts. The human person has to accept the gift of the Word who has become human. Only then will the Word accept man's gift of himself. The oblation of Christ is the oblation of the human, both in the morning and in the evening. Christ's self-sacrifice in humankind is humankind's self-sacrifice in Christ, in both the past and the present, and also in

[35] Pur 3.2: *Illud erit sacrificium vespertinum, istud est matutinum; istud quidem iocundius, sed illud plenius; istud enim tempore nativitatis, illud iam in plenitudine aetatis.* SBOp 4:343.

[36] Pur 3.3: *Ille seipsum obtuli; tu quis es qui te offerre cuncteris? Quis mihi tribuat, ut oblationem meam dignetur maiestas tanta suscipere?* SBOp 4:343.

eternity. Only by accepting Christ in this sense will the human being realize that the procession of Purification, the journey of Lent, and the procession of Palm Sunday take place simultaneously and continuously inside himself.

THE EASTER SERMONS

In Easter, the reconciliation of God and humankind is celebrated. The human creature has accepted the oblation of Christ, and his proper oblation is in its own turn accepted by the Divinity. As a consequence, all blinding ought to disappear. Man's eyes should open to the mysteries of life and the secrets of his pains and sufferings. God has come down to meet the human being in his sufferings. The human now can see the glory of God in the suffering humanity of Christ. The blindness of Epiphany is broken by the divine splendor that radiates from a human being in his broken state. Easter is the solemnity of concordance in discord, of harmony in opposition, of life in death. Easter will be the turning point in the liturgical year—after Easter the year cannot be the same. This will be the challenge to the success of Bernard's liturgical project.

An Idea Taking Size

With the block of three sermons for the Annunciation, the new subunit begins. As demonstrated in the general introduction of CF 51, this unit comprises the sermons for Holy Week and Easter, for the period from Easter to Pentecost, and for the entire summertime until the block on the Assumption of the Virgin.[37] This series counts thirty-six sermons, which is 28 percent of the liturgical sermon collection.[38] When compared to the earliest collection, this is a remarkable increase.

[37] CF 51: xxx–xxxi.

[38] Just to recollect the distribution over the four subunits: the Christmas and the Lent season each total 29, the Easter-summer season 36, and the fall season 34 sermons—i.e., 23 (twice), 28, and 26 percent, respectively.

The oldest liturgical collection B contained only fourteen sermons for the equivalent period. But it is clear that Bernard considered this too small. M already counts sixteen sermons for the Temporal and fifteen sermons for the Sanctoral, thus coming closer to the final sum. L^B totals twenty sermons, but this number does not tell that much in view of the particular character of the collection.

The increase, however, is not a result of Bernard's insertion of sermons for extra celebrations, thus inserting into the calendar festivities on which it was not allowed to preach according to the general chapter. As noticed, Bernard's liturgical collection did not limit itself to the preaching festivities that were recognized by the *Ecclesiastica officia*.[39] Certainly, in this Easter and summer unit he added sermons for nine additional celebrations: Wednesday and Thursday in Holy Week (4 HM and 5 HM), the Easter Octave (OPasc), the Rogation Days (Rog), the vigil of the feast of Peter and Paul, and the fourth and sixth Sundays after Pentecost. In addition, four sermons were added that were not linked to any celebration: *On the Altitude and Depth of the Heart* (Alt) and *On the Work of the Harvest* (Lab 1–3).

But compared to the ten additional preaching opportunities in the last subunit of the end of the year and to the six additions in the much shorter Christmas season, Bernard still seems not to have felt a strong need to enlarge his liturgical space for his literary preaching. Most of his additions fall in the liturgically empty period of the summer season. This proves Bernard's desire to cover the entire year and to offer a continuous meditative reading, thus not limiting his collection to the purely liturgical events.

A more important means to increase the Easter and summer subunit seems to have been the rearrangement of sermons inside the official solemnities. In order to have a good understanding of Bernard's reasons to develop this subunit, it can thus be clarifying to have a closer look at the successive versions of his collection.[40]

---

[39] See CF 51: xv–xvi.

[40] As the summer sermons have been published separately in CF 53, we will limit ourselves here to the sermons for Holy Week and Easter. These count exactly seven sermons each because Holy Week is concentrated around Palm Sunday and includes 4 HM, whereas 5 HM will be shown as intrinsically closer to the Easter themes. The

Ups and Downs: The First Collection (B)

In the oldest collection, B, the Easter group is not clearly demarcated. The group of Lenten sermons consists mainly of the exegesis of the opening verses of Psalm 90, the future QH 1–4. They are introduced by the sermon *On the Divine Will* and followed by the sermon on Saint Benedict (Ben), the future first sermon on the Annunciation (Ann 1) and the future second sermon for Palm Sunday. This last text being clearly related to the liturgical celebration, the Easter group can be considered to have started. Yet, for the two sermons in-between, it is less clear to which part of the liturgical year they belong.

The sermon on Saint Benedict—which, for this reason, we have neglected in our analysis of the Lenten group—indeed causes a problem in the interpretation of the entire collection. Actually, it causes a problem as a sermon too. First, it belongs to the longer texts within the collection.[41] Apparently, this length is the result of one of Bernard's more often used techniques of compiling older texts into one new sermon. Ben indeed seems to comprise several lines of thought, originally constituting distinct texts, which have been fused in order to give the actual sermon.

It opens with a first introduction, containing a word play on *benedictio*, which already refers to the central subject of the sermon (Ben 1). This is followed by what seems to be a second introduction as a meditation on the nature of the abbacy and Benedict's exemplarity (Ben 2–3ª).[42] After having mentioned the three loaves that Bernard wants to receive from Benedict in order to offer them to his readers, Bernard abruptly breaks off this line of thought. The text continues with a picture of all those spreading either their own garments or

---

rupture between 4 HM and 5 HM is the more remarkable when taking into account that the reader finds himself exactly halfway through the entire collection.

[41] With its twelve paragraphs it belongs to the group of relatively larger sermons. The length of a liturgical sermon averages around seven paragraphs, which is already longer than the normal length of a chapter sermon—normally restricted to three to five paragraphs—as can be deduced from the sermons on various subjects (Div).

[42] That the second paragraph originally constituted a proper beginning can also be deduced from the typical opening formula: *Celebramus hodie.*

branches in the procession of the Lord. Suddenly, the reader sees himself transported to Palm Sunday, near but not yet celebrated.[43]

The text develops briefly the idea of those looking for branches and turns in the end to Benedict as "a tree, tall and fruitful, *like a tree planted near running waters*" (Ben 3ᵇ–4ᵃ). Now, the sermon continues for some time as an exegesis on this third verse of Psalm 1, treating first the water, then distinguishing three kinds of trees according to their fruitfulness (Ben 4ᵇ–6ᵃ). Benedict disappears, only to return much later. First, Benedict serves as an illustration of how to live true fruitfulness; then, Benedict's three fruits are developed—i.e., the three virtues that had been presented earlier in the sermon as three loaves Benedict had to offer (Ben 6ᵇ–8ᵇ).[44] Having developed the fruits of Benedict, the sermon then turns toward Christ as a tree himself, but also as he who sows. Now the act of sowing becomes the central concern of the sermon, treating respectively how man has become the sowing ground for the Trinity, the angels, the apostles, martyrs, confessors, and virgins (Ben 8ᶜ–12). In this last part of the sermon, nothing more is said about Benedict.

Already from this short summary it becomes clear that the sermon on Saint Benedict shows us a kind of patchwork of different texts and ideas masterfully woven together by one continuous development of the plights and fruitfulness of an abbot. Two apparently distinct introductions on Benedict (on his name and on his abbacy), an exegesis of Psalm 1:3, and a separate meditation on the act of heavenly sowing are linked and spanned by the central idea of vegetative growth and fruitfulness: the tree, its fruits, and the seeds.

This heterogeneous character of the sermon is even reinforced by the liturgical references. In its primary version, Ben contained half-

---

[43] Ben 3: "Since this charge has been entrusted to me, even though I have nothing of my own to set before you I shall ask Saint Benedict for three loaves to feed you with. May his sanctity, his righteousness, and his piety restore you. Remember, my beloved, that not all those in the Lord's procession spread out their garments."

[44] Ben 7: "As I was saying, blessed Benedict did not think when he was still tossed about by such temptations that it was the time to bear fruit; the time did come, however, and he produced fruit *in its season*. Three of these I touched on before, his sanctity, his righteousness, and his piety."

way, at the opening of the section on Benedict's fruits, a clear liturgical reminiscence of the Vigil of Christmas. At the end of paragraph
6, instead of the actual closure—"No matter how sharply temptation
may rage, believe that you are not therefore abandoned by God. Remember that Scripture says, *Call on me in the day of trouble; I will deliver
you, and you shall honor me*" with the quotation of Psalm 49:15 (50:15
Heb)—Bernard wrote: "No matter how sharply temptation may
rage, believe that you are not therefore abandoned by God. Be firm
and soon you will see God's help above you."[45] The final words stem
from the responsory *Constantes* for the Vigil of Christmas.[46] Bernard
may have introduced them into the sermon on Benedict with the
intention of causing a liturgical disorientation in the reader, or he
may have forgotten them while rewriting this text into a sermon on
Benedict. However this may be, before inserting the final version of
this sermon into his liturgical series, he cancelled this liturgical link
and replaced it by a psalm text.

Toward the end of the sermon another liturgical incongruity appears. While talking about the act of heavenly sowing, Bernard suddenly refers to the gospel of the day: "You heard today in the gospel
the Lord promising his disciples, saying, *You will also sit on twelve thrones,
judging the twelve tribes of Israel.*"[47] The quotation comes from Matthew 19:28 and belongs to the reading at a celebration for the apostles.[48] Yet, Benedict was honored by a proper liturgy with its adapted
readings. Once again, thus, this textual fragment might have belonged
to another preaching from another occasion. Bernard did not feel
the urge, though, to eliminate it when adapting the text for its final

[45] Ben 6 (final version): *et disce, quantumcumque acerba tentatio saeviat, non credere
propterea derelictum esse a Domino, sed memineris scriptum esse: Invoca me in die tribulationis:
eruam te, et honorificabis me.* Ben 6 (primary version): *et disce iam, quantumcumque acerba
tentatio saeviat, non credere propterea derelictum esse a Domino, sed constans esto, et cito videbis
auxilium Domini super te.* SBOp 5:6 + Apparatus.

[46] SBOp 5:6, Apparatus.

[47] Ben 11: *Hodie audistis in Evangelio promittentem Dominum et dicentem discipulis:
Sedebitis super sedes, iudicantes duodecim tribus Israel.* SBOp 5:10–11.

[48] SBOp 5:11, Apparatus and *Bernhard von Clairvaux. Sämtliche Werke,* vol. 8, ed.
Gerhard Winkler (Innsbruck: Tyrolia Verlaganstalt, 1997), Anmerkung 24, p. 969.

position.[49] Apparently he did not feel any tension between Benedict the abbot and master, and the apostles. This is not surprising when his own frequent assimilation to Paul is taken into consideration.[50]

These two originally liturgical references to the Vigil of Christmas and to the feast of an apostle—together with the repeated allusions to Palm Sunday—make the sermon on Saint Benedict, liturgically speaking, unstable. Its liturgical framework is fluid and causes the reader to lose ground. Yet the liturgical references add a common feature to the text: they strengthen a sensation of expectancy toward the future. Both the Vigil of Christmas and Palm Sunday lead to the great events of the liturgical year, of which the apostles are the testimonies. Benedict thus becomes somewhat of a messenger of the great things to come.

Apparently, this idea did not suit Bernard for his final project and he softened it without eliminating it entirely by cancelling the Christmas allusion. Hereby another basic idea was reinforced, the idea of movement that governs the entire sermon. By the reiterated images of Palm Sunday, the impression of progressive movement, as it was installed and elaborated in the sermons for Lent, is strengthened. It only slowly takes a different form, changing in aspect from a linear and external progression toward an outward development, from the steady trotting of the donkey to the flourishing and fructification of the trees. Simultaneously, the horizontal and linear movement of the animal has become a vertical and cyclical dynamic. The growing of the tree takes its origin at the waters, stretching its branches loaded with fruit toward heaven, from which the seeds are sown "upon all waters." The Palm Sunday procession, passing over the branches, has become a growth toward heaven in order to fertilize the earth. Mov-

---

[49] An additional argument for the heterogeneous origins of the sermon can be found in the different intensity of rewriting as applied to the text. When reworking the text for the final collection, Bernard apparently concentrated on the first half (the exegetical part). The second half, on the contrary, was only slightly adapted.

[50] To Bernard, Saint Paul simply is the Apostle. For one of his clearest self-identifications with Paul, see the first sermon on the Song of Songs (SC 1.1): *Vobis, fratres, alia quam aliis de saeculo, aut certe aliter dicenda sunt. Illis siquidem lac potum dat, et non escam, qui Apostoli formam tenet in docendo.* SBOp 1:3.

ing forward means growing upward and turning back down. Linearity becomes circularity, with the one movement implying the other.

These dynamics are strengthened in the sermon that follows in B, the future first sermon on the Annunciation (Ann 1). Once again, it seems as if Bernard compiled one text out of two different ones, but the lines of fracture between the distinct texts are much harder to detect. With its fourteen paragraphs, Ann 1 is even longer than Ben. While opening with a psalm verse (Ps 84:10-11; 85:9-10 Heb), the first part develops an exegesis of a sentence by Paul (2 Cor 1:12) treating the three testimonies of human and divine glory by the Spirit (Ann 1.1–4). In the original version, this treatment was immediately followed by a first exegesis of the psalm verse, without any transition. Apparently, Bernard thought this too abrupt and inserted paragraph 5 in order to link the two explications.[51] He continued with a biblical exegesis of the psalm verse, paralleling it with Adam's situation in Paradise, his being vested in the four virtues of the psalm, and his being robbed like the man going down from Jerusalem to Jericho (Ann 1.6–8). Then, Bernard takes his reader to heaven, where he develops an allegorical dispute between the four virtues for the sake of humankind (Ann 1.9–14).

The sermon thus seems to consist of three distinct exegetical treatises, one on Second Corinthians 1:12 and two on Psalm 84:10-11. In a new setting, each gets its place, and together they give a new movement to the sermon. The treatment of Paul lays the foundation for the psalm treatment. First the human creature loses the glory that was his original honor as he descends from Jerusalem to Jericho. Then, in order to restore him the Divinity agrees to come down to the state of humankind. Unlike the somewhat unsuccessful procedure in Ben, Ann 1 shows a perfect unity with scarcely detectable junctures.

At the same time, the vertical movement in Ben is repeated in Ann 1, but in the opposite way. While in Ben the dynamics went upward to come down, now all movements go down: the human descending from Jerusalem, God coming down to take up the human state, and even bending down to write with his finger on the ground (Ann 1.12). In these dynamics, however, no mention is made of Palm Sunday,

[51] SBOp 5:16, Apparatus.

or even of the Annunciation, to which it would be linked in the final versions. Apparently, Bernard thought it simply apt to constitute the transition between the solemnities for Saint Benedict and Palm Sunday, thus continuing the dynamics that characterize the sermons for Lent and that come to a rest in the Easter sermons.

This linking of Ben and Ann 1 to the Lent cycle in B seems to be confirmed by the change in exegetical nature with the following sermon, the future second sermon for Palm Sunday (Palm 2). Ben and Ann 1 both still have a strong biblical exegetical strand, based notably on psalm texts, thus continuing in a certain sense the line of the Lent sermons QH 1–4. With Palm 2, the psalm exegesis is interrupted. Instead, a block of sermons of numerical exegesis starts. Palm 2 treats of the four groups in the Palm Sunday procession. The following sermon, *On the Supper of the Lord* (5 HM), treats the three sacraments. This is followed by the future first sermon for Easter (Res 1), treating the three days and the seven seals of the Apocalypse (Rev 5:5), and the future third sermon for Easter (Res 3) on the sevenfold healing of Naaman (2 K 5:10). Then the numerical exegesis is momentarily abandoned when the next two sermons—the future fourth sermon for Easter (Res 4) and a sermon ending up in the series on various subjects (Div 12)—concentrate on the way of man, thus retaking the idea of movement. The Easter cycle closes in B with two numerical sermons again: Div 13 on the threefold mercy of God and the future Res 2 on the three ointments and aromatics of the women at the grave.

The oldest liturgical version thus seems to concentrate upon the restoration of man after his fall. Bernard parallels this theological item with the way the human being has gone and the way he has to go. The movement of Lent continues in Ben and Ann 1 but takes up a more vertical direction, bringing together man's fall and descent with divine mercy, humbling itself to human state. They meet in the sacraments, such as they are exposed in the sermons that in B seem to prepare the actual Easter solemnity (5 HM, Res 1, Res 3 and Res 5) and that open up the true meaning of the human being's destination (Div 12). He can only rise to this destination when undergoing God's mercy in the threefold application of the balsams (Div 13 and Res 2). Important in this reading is the attention paid to the human in his fallen state. Divinity and Christ's passion almost become secondary themes, completely submitted to man's destiny.

Faith's Death and Resurrection: The Second Version (M)

In the second collection, almost the entire Easter cycle of B is reproduced and contains few differences from the final version. Only a few changes occur, mostly of a predictable character. By the separation of the Sanctoral from the Temporal, Ben and Ann 1 disappeared from the Easter series. Ben disappeared entirely from the collection, while Ann 1 now opens the Sanctoral, immediately preceding the three sermons for Purification. As Ann 1 does not have any intrinsic link to the Annunciation, it is clear that the Sanctoral in Bernard's project is not in the first place concerned with the Virgin but rather in a human form with the incarnation.

In M, the Easter sermons are introduced by a new text, a first sermon for Palm Sunday (Palm 1). Then follows exactly the same series as in B: Palm 2, 5 HM, Res 1, Res 3 and Res 4. Only in the transition to Ascension did Bernard go in a completely new direction. He replaced all the sermons by new ones: Div 111, two sermons for the Octave of Easter (OPasc 1 and 2) and the Sermon for Rogation Day (Rog). Div 12 on man's way, Div 13 on the threefold mercy of God, and the future Res 2 on the three ointments and aromatics all disappeared.

Res 4 treats the way the life of Christ actualizes itself in human existence. Bernard distinguishes all those groups in society for whom the life of Christ has not yet come into being: those for whom he is not yet born, for whom he has not yet suffered, for whom he did not already rise, for whom he did not ascend to heaven, and to whom he did not yet send the Spirit. This rather negative approach of humankind is continued in M by Div 111, which treats notably the negative forms of faith: faith that is numb to worldly misery and thus has to be considered dead (Div 111.1), the human creature's unbelief as regards the promises of future beatitude (Div 111.2), his lack of faith in an experienced teacher (Div 111.3), faith without good works (Div 111.4). Man has to convert from these false forms of faith and to return in a six day's journey to the way of salvation (Div 111.5). The six days are then treated, one by one, leading finally to the glorious vision of God (Div 111.6–7).[52]

---

[52] Div 111 in SBOp 6.1:385–89.

These six days form an easy transition to the central theme of the two sermons for the octave of Easter that follow. Bernard presents the six days indeed as six testimonies of the reviving faith. The importance of giving testimony returns both in OPasc 1, treating in its second part the sacraments as testimonies on earth, and in OPasc 2 about the testimonies in heaven and on earth. Thus the sacramental nature of the Easter cycle as developed in Palm 2, 5 HM, Res 1, and Res 3 is even reinforced by the new transition to Ascension. The moral aspect, on the contrary, seems to have lost importance.

In its eschatological sense, however, this moral aspect reappears in the Sanctoral, which has been separated from the Temporal in this collection. The series of solemnities for saints limits itself almost exclusively to sermons that will become part of the festivities for the Virgin. Within the project of M, however, they do not seem to refer primarily to Mary, as the development within the sermons seems to suggest. The future Ann 1 became the opening sermon of the Sanctoral, which might imply that the central idea of this part deals with the restoration of humankind by God's descent from heaven, manifesting itself in fertile faith—i.e., in the good works that constitute the life of faith. The focus of these sermons is not so much Mary herself as what happened in and through her, what originated in heaven and came into being thanks to her, finding in her its culmination.

Ann 1 opens by asking for the significance of Easter (Ann 1.1–5), giving immediately both the answer (the Fall and its results on earth: Ann 1.6–8) and the solution (the incarnation as a divine decision: Ann 1.9–14). In order to make God's descent possible, a response is awaited from the human, who must set out to prepare to host the Spirit in his own life. Thus, the prophets put the human being into movement for an inward procession into his heart (Pur 1.1–4), followed by the Light procession of unity (Pur 2.1–3) and leading to the sacrifice of his humility (Pur 3.1–3). Mary appears as the perfect embodiment of human plenitude in her virginity, her humility, and her fertility (the future sixth sermon for the Assumption, Asspt 6.1).[53] Only thanks to

---

[53] Asspt 6 was formerly edited as Div 46, for which reason Jean Leclercq often refers to the sermon under this title.

Mary's humble plenitude does the incarnation mediate between God and humanity (the future second sermon for the Annunciation, Ann 2.1–2) and the Spirit descend from heaven to earth (Ann 2.3–5). The descent of the Spirit is answered by the ascent of Mary in her assumption, heralding humanity's ultimate destiny. Almost the entire cycle of sermons for the Assumption now follows, stressing the coincidence of Mary's ascent and the descent of Christ as the living Word—i.e., as the Word that operates (the future Asspt 1–4).

The Sanctoral cycle logically follows Easter and Pentecost, concluding the liturgical unity of the Temporal cycle. While the Temporal celebrates the completion of the unique mystery of Easter on earth, the Sanctoral focuses on its perpetual meaning for humanity, for whom Mary is the mediator. In her, the descending movement of Word and Spirit meets the ascending movement of the human as it is evoked by the word of God in the prophets and the Bible.

The divine resolution to become incarnate (Ann 1) needs, as its counterpart, human plenitude as embodied by Mary (Asspt 6). Only then can the descent of the Spirit be realized (Ann 2), meaning the immediate ascent of Mary, for her ascent corresponds to the descent of the Word (Asspt 1) into a human body (Asspt 2–3), and even into Lazarus's grave, where the descending movement once again changes into an ascent: Christ in front of Lazarus is like Mary in front of us (Asspt 4).

The Easter sermons of the Temporal cycle concentrate on the death and resurrection of faith that takes place in the human being and have a rather theological significance. The Sanctoral in M is not to be read as an independent cycle paralleling the Temporal; rather, it forms a true sequel and continuation of what precedes it. In the Sanctoral in M, the activity of the eternal, divine truth described in the Temporal cycle is reenacted on the human level; the descending movement of the Spirit and the Word is brought together with the ascending impulse of the human. This overlap of the two movements will prove essential to the interpretation of the final collection.

A Liturgical Summary: The Third Collection (L)

Bernard's numerical and liturgical archive does not offer much that is new as regards the Easter cycle. None of the sermons that would become part of the final Easter collection can be retrieved from the exegetical half L^A. The liturgical part L^B contains two sermons that will be reused in the final collection: Res 2, which had disappeared after B, and a new sermon, *Of the Lord's Passion,* for Wednesday in Holy Week (4 HM). Both form part of a larger unit that somehow summarizes the entire Lent and Easter cycles.

As mentioned in the paragraphs on Lent, the line of thought in L^B is very clear and neat. Sept 1 opens Lent in the desire of fulfillment, giving special attention to listening to the word of God and to the battle against the obstacles on the way to fulfillment. Div 22 that follows shows a shortcut in the way of Lent, when man is ready and willing to take the steepest road and the heavier weight upon his shoulders.

Continuing in this line, 4 HM analyzes vice in its different triads or trinities—i.e., according to its several threefold appearances (4 HM 5–7)—but it leads in the end to the victory of divine clemency (4 HM 8–9) as it was lived and illustrated in Christ's passion (4 HM 10–14). Res 2 then builds upon the threefold exegesis in 4 HM, treating the threefold character of the ointments but interpreting them in the sense of the human's resurrection to renewed life.

Next follows a sermon on the seven seals (Div 57) that resumes the apocalyptic imagery that B linked to the Easter mystery. However, here it has also a moralistic meaning, referring to man's resurrection from vice. This is illustrated by the three women at the tomb, treated in the following sermon (Div 58), which precedes a sermon on Ascension (Div 60).

L^B thus proves how closely related are the themes of Christ's death and resurrection and man's rebirth from the death of vice, in which he was held captive after the Fall. The parallelism between the divine descent in the incarnation and man's descent from Jerusalem to Jericho as it is elaborated in Ann 1 returns in L^B as the structuring theme for the entire Lent and Easter cycle. L^B, however, gives a rather straightforward view of this idea. It is far from the complicated playing with ascending and descending movements that was fundamental to the arrangement of the Sanctoral in M. In the final collection, it will be exactly this complex simultaneity that gives M its decisive significance.

Summary

The older collections prove that Bernard had a very clear view of what he wanted to express in the sermons for Easter. The entire cycle does not change that much from B to M. Neither will it change very much when reworked into the final project. Bernard's only doubts seem to have been about the place of sermons for the Sanctoral: did he have to treat them independently as a human continuation of the disclosure of the sacramental value of the Easter mystery? Or did he rather prefer to include them inside the development of the Temporal, not separating the sacraments from their eschatological actualizations?

In the end, he took the second road, but with significant consequences. The increase of the summer period can be considered a result of his merging the Sanctoral and the Temporal of M. By this fusion, Mary's importance was again linked to the sacrament of the divine descent. She remains the human counterpart of the divine resolution, but as the indispensable condition for its actualization, Bernard must have thought her inseparable from the story of the incarnation. Thus, the sermons for the solemnities linked to her feasts now open each phase in the actualization of man's restoration. This means that the illustration of man's return to his original glory had to be done in other ways. Bernard brought it down to a more human level, closing each phase with an example of humanity in its purer forms: Saint Paul, the converted sinner; Saint Benedict, the experienced master; Saint Paul and Saint Peter, the harvesters of the Spirit like the farmers in the fields; and finally Humbert, no saint but an all-too-human monk.

The development of the Easter sermons demonstrates how Bernard was trying to bring his different lines of thought into harmony. He wanted to stress the sacramental meaning of the Easter events, but not without concretizing them in the human life. While the sermons of Lent were treated as a linear progression of learning and training of the soul in its three qualities, in Easter all movement had to come to a rest but without losing its dynamics. The horizontal procession turned into vertical movements as already elaborated in the sermon for Saint Benedict. Faith in man had died but was called again to new life. The man had gone down from Jerusalem, but only to bring God

xlviii   *Sermons for Lent and the Easter Season*

down, who, however, could only descend if humanity would meet him by ascending.

Indeed, Bernard did not eschew a difficult task. The final version had to prove him to be not only the spiritual master that he aspired to be but also the master writer who knew how to create and to revive by way of his words. He proved to be both, and even more.

Breaking the Seals

In the final collection the number of sermons for Easter and the summer season increased considerably, making it much more difficult for the reader to have an overview. The entire block of thirty-six sermons can, however, be distinguished in several subunits, of which only the first two will be treated here. Each of them, like the third subunit, counts seven sermons, thus stressing in a numerical way the importance of the central subjects treated.[54]

In addition, the pattern and construction of the subunits show that a change takes place inside the development of the liturgical series. The sermons of the first block treat the Annunciation, Palm Sunday, and Wednesday of Holy Week. Those of the second block consist of the sermon for Maundy Thursday, the actual Easter sermons, and the sermons for the Octave of Easter. The third block, finally, opens with the sermon for Rogation Day, followed by the Ascension sermons.[55] The Palm Sunday unit, thus, opens with two series of three and closes with one final sermon, while each of the other blocks opens with a kind of introductive sermon that is followed by the core of the treatment, respectively, four Easter sermons

---

[54] It is unnecessary by now to stress the importance of numerical exegesis in helping to understand the construction of Bernard's thought. Three blocks of seven sermons, each around the central solemnities of the liturgical year, will have to remind us to keep in mind the several triads or trinities that reappear over and again in Bernard's thinking, of which the most important are Father, Son, Spirit, and memory, reason, will.

[55] The Pentecost sermons fall out of this numerical series. They only count three texts, thus somehow summarizing and concluding the entire movement.

plus two sermons for the octave, and six Ascension sermons. This structural inversion corresponds to a change in approach as will be clear from the reading.[56]

Telling Stories: A Linear Experience?

The sermon for the Birth Day of Saint Benedict ends with an enumeration of those who sowed their virtues upon humanity: "The whole Trinity has sown on our land; the angels and apostles have sown, the martyrs, confessors, and virgins, all have sown."[57] Each of these categories passes before the reader's eyes, each with the virtues its members bestowed upon humankind: the Trinity sowed the heavenly bread, truth, and love; the angels, seeds of steadfast wisdom; the apostles, wisdom of the eternal life; the martyrs, endurance; the confessors, justice; and the virgins, self-restraint. Comparatively much attention is paid to the angels in their opposition to Lucifer[58] and to the apostles in their devotion to the Lord because of his "words of eternal life."[59] Martyrs and confessors are taken together in one short reflection, leading up to the equation of the martyrs with Peter and of the confessors with Abraham, the first having "left everything at once," the other putting "his worldly goods to good use."[60] The enumeration as well as the sermon closes with the virgins, mentioned in one short phrase only: "As for the holy virgins, it is clear that they sowed temperance, for they trampled lust under foot."

It is likely that the reader will feel a bit confused by this abrupt ending. We already mentioned the probability that Bernard had been compiling different texts to make the sermon for Saint Benedict and that the last part on sowing did not fit in so easily with the preceding

---

[56] Is it necessary to repeat that 4 HM is located halfway in the liturgical collection? The division in two halves of the entire collection reminds one of the two strains of thought elaborated in the sermons on the Song of Songs: the time of engagement and of marriage (the *Sponsa*) and the time of fertility and motherhood (the *Mater*).

[57] Ben 10: *Seminavit in terra nostra tota Trinitas, seminaverunt angeli pariter et Apostoli, seminaverunt et Martyres, et Confessores, et Virgines.* SBOp 5:9.

[58] Ben 11, SBOp 5:10–11.

[59] Ben 12, SBOp 5:11–12.

[60] Ben 12, SBOp 5:12.

parts. This impression is reinforced by the sudden and rough ending. One could assume that Bernard wished to end with the sowing by the confessors, thus still linking the end of his sermon to Saint Benedict. Of course, Saint Benedict may be reckoned among the virgins too, but the very concise way of treating them, actually only mentioning them, may suggest that Bernard did not want the reader to leave the sermon with the image of Saint Benedict as a virgin. There is another reason for this abrupt and unanticipated ending.

As we saw, already in the earliest version the sermon for Saint Benedict was followed by the first sermon for the Annunciation. Thus it seems as if Bernard, by his particular ending of the Benedict sermon, wanted to bridge the gap between the two sermons, announcing in a certain way the next text on the Annunciation and its principal figure—the Holy Virgin. This hypothesis, however, implies that both texts have to be understood in a continuous line, just as the sermons on Psalm 90 do. Whereas the continuity of a psalm exegesis within a series of sermons seems rather evident, the assumption of a similar continuity over a series of sermons for different occasions has far-reaching consequences. It obliges the reader to see the sermons (and thus the festivities they celebrate) joined in a linear sequence, all obedient to the same progressive development, to the same "story line."

The sermon for Saint Benedict, while concluding the sermons for Lent, at the same time opens the story of the Annunciation. This fact seems to imply, however, that in the story Bernard wants to tell the reader the event narrated by the Annunciation sermons can only take place after the part of the story told in the sermon for Saint Benedict. This kind of sequence differs from the one imposed by the liturgical year for it implies a much stronger causality. Whereas the succession of the solemnities during the year obeys mainly the chronology of the liturgical calendar, Bernard imposes upon them an internal development in which one solemnity must, by a kind of internal law, automatically lead to the following episode in his story. In the story Bernard tells, consequently, the Annunciation can only take place *after* the reader has gone through the preceding episodes—i.e., after the events told in the sermons for Advent, Christmas, Epiphany, Lent, and Saint Benedict. The chronological succession of events, by which the Annunciation looks ahead to the return of the liturgical cycle of the next year, is thus completely ignored, even annihilated. In Bernard's story, the Annunciation results from the preceding liturgical episodes, thus turning the chronology upside down.

The cancelling of temporal linearity by the story line of his sermons is one of the central issues in the following block of the Annunciation and the Palm Sunday sermons. The three sermons for Annunciation actually tell one continuous story, starting in Ann 1 with the original and eternal glory of the human being, continuing with his loss by his descent from Jerusalem to Jericho, and ending with the allegorical lawsuit in heaven between the four divine virtues (Mercy and Truth, Righteousness and Peace). Each of the virtues pleads her case in front of "the Father of lights." But as God the Father can never judge in a way inconsistent with himself, the case is referred to the Wisdom of King Solomon, "because all judgment, Scripture says, was given to the Son" (Ann 1.11).

There follows the renewed pleading of Mercy and Truth, arguing against each other, Mercy in favor of humankind, Truth in favor of divine Justice. They can only be calmed by Peace, after which the divine Judge "bent down and wrote with his finger on the ground," thus passing judgment on humankind: "Let there be a good death, and each possess what she asks,"—i.e., "if a person not deserving of death dies out of love" (Ann 1.12).

Truth and Mercy start their quest in search of the one who is innocent and full of love, but Mercy does not find in heaven a love great enough to die for humankind, nor does Truth find on earth a faultless soul. On their hopeless return they are consoled by Peace, who announces that there is only one who meets the requirements: "May he who gave counsel bring help" (Ann 1.14). The Son understands what she means and decides to descend in order to free man. He summons Gabriel to announce to the daughter of Sion that the King will come.

The second sermon describes the descent of the divinity. First the question has to be answered why the Son, and not the Father or the Spirit, descended. But as the Son is Son of the Father and the plenitude of the Spirit rests on him, the descent of the Son implies the descent of the Spirit and testifies to the presence of God. By this descent of the Son, "the simple story of our restoration" (Ann 2.1) gets its start, leading to "the new man, the true man" (Ann 2.5), who will feed "us with the bread of life and understanding," and give "us the water of saving wisdom to drink" (Ann 2.4).

The descending movement of the second sermon encounters an ascending movement in the third sermon. This one opens with the invitation to the reader to attend the meal "set before us on the table of this wealthy Householder by the testimonies of Holy Scripture" (Ann 3.1) and consisting of mercy and righteousness. Then Bernard starts his story from its beginning. The Pharisees bring in the adulteress and argue against her, expecting Jesus to pronounce his judgment. As in the scene in heaven of Ann 1, Jesus "*bent down*, and having turned toward mercy—he did not think as the Jews did—he *wrote with his finger*, not now on tables of stone, but *on the ground*" (Ann 3.2). Bernard implores the Lord to bend down his heavens and to come down (Ann 3.2), thus rehearsing the event of Ann 2. As in Ann 1, the answer of Jesus leads to a peaceful solution of the insoluble problem.

Yet, the story continues after Jesus has sent the adulteress away. "But let us consider, my brothers, where these Pharisees depart from. Do you see the two old men—for they began to go away, beginning with the elders—hiding in Joachim's orchard?" (Ann 3.4). The eldest Pharisees left Jesus first and Bernard invites the reader to follow them in order to see where they go. The reader is introduced into the garden of Joachim and is allowed to spy upon the two men trying to seduce Susanna and, when failing to do this, accusing her falsely of adultery.

Bernard's story line takes a surprising turn. Not only do we pass from a true adultery to a seduction and false accusation, which throws doubts about the sincerity of the first one, but we also pass from the same men before Jesus to Joachim's orchard in Babylon and thus to the time of Daniel. Time is turned upside down, as in the liturgical story line. Actually, time is submitted to a higher and more abstract linearity, in which mercy precedes righteousness. Jesus first shows mercy upon the adulteress, after which Daniel can do justice toward Susanna (Ann 3.5).

Only then Gabriel arrives in front of Mary and announces the restoration of man's glory thanks to the descent of the Son (Ann 3.7). And once again the reader is thrown into confusion. Ann 3 starts with Jesus showing mercy upon the adulteress and ends with the annunciation of Jesus' birth. Temporal linearity is broken down and completely replaced by the a-temporality of divine acting.

This annihilation of time continues in the following block of sermons for Palm Sunday. Bernard's procedure, however, changes. He does not confuse the reader by putting stories together in a nonchronological succession. He rather returns to a linear progression similar to that used in the sermons for Lent and in the sermon for Saint Benedict. In a self-evident way, the reader is again confronted with movement, thanks to the Palm Sunday procession, which was already announced in the sermon for Saint Benedict. While in the Benedict sermon, however, the movement truly implied *movement*—a linear progression changing from a horizontal to a vertical direction—the Palm Sunday procession leaves the reader with an impression of *immobility*.

The block opens with Bernard's assertion of the sound reasons for the church to join the procession of "today" with the passion, even when this conjunction is "singular and wonderful" (Palm 1.1). Procession and passion, applause and sorrow, glory and humiliation are treated as one, taking place "in the same city, by the same people and at the same time" (Palm 1.1). But just as in the life of Christ procession and passion are taken together, forming an indivisible unity, Bernard now also emphasizes the unity of the earthly and the heavenly processions linked in the person of Christ who enters the heavenly Jerusalem in eternal glory as he enters the earthly Jerusalem in temporary glory. The descending movement of the Son as developed in the Annunciation sermons turns again upward, into the ascending movement of the Son of God, both by his passion on the cross and the still-distant ascension toward heaven.

While heaven and earth in the Annunciation sermons were moving toward each other, in the Palm Sunday sermons the processions form a parallel movement, taking place at the same moment in heaven and on earth, in the spirit and in the church. Indeed, the first sermon opens with the earthly procession and its connotation of ephemeral glory, showing by the example of Christ how worldly joy leads to the grief of the passion (Palm 1.1). However, those who know to continue the procession in the spirit have the ability to pass through the labor of the passion into the glorious procession that opens up heaven (Palm 1.2). The heavenly procession is welcomed by those in heaven (Palm 1.3) just as it is proceeding on earth by the dedication of the participants (Palm 1.4).

This last element is elaborated in the second sermon, in which the patience and humility of Christ are presented as his answer to the pains of the passion and the glory of the entrance. The accent slowly shifts from the simultaneous parallelism between heaven and earth to the simultaneity of the two chronologically subsequent events, procession and passion, glory and pain. The second part of this sermon then concentrates upon the obligation of change, of *commutatio*. As the procession changes into the passion and all worldly glory and joy into pain and suffering, likewise the participants in the procession have to be changed by the procession.

Bernard gives special attention to the beast carrying Christ. He likens it to those "for whom the discipline is heavy and all things burdensome, who must often be prodded and urged forward," and he exhorts them "to change from beasts into human beings, if they can" (Palm 2.6). Only then can they be said to partake in the procession alongside the other groups. And if they cannot change, they are begged to remain where they are and to carry humbly their burden until God moves them on to something better—i.e., until their hard-headed immobility is brought into movement, putting them on the road of the procession, which leads to the immobile parallelism of heaven and earth. The linear movement of procession and time has become an inward movement of change from earth to heaven.

Time, thus, has lost its power over the human being. It has become a key to heaven, to the human's spiritual change. And the only one who had the power to break the seals of time was the living Word. "God made all things by weight, number, and measure, but particularly at the time when *he was seen on earth and lived with humankind*, whatever he did, spoke, or suffered among us was so arranged that not the smallest detail, not one iota was devoid of sacramental content or passed without mystery" (Palm 3.1). Every day gets its power and is developed in its sacramental content. The day of the procession recapitulates the transition of glory into the passion and Christ's answer to both: humility and patience. The day of the Last Supper shows his human gentleness. The days of his passion, rest and resurrection are briefly treated. They are abbreviated and they still have to come, only promising the liberation from our toil.

Time is mystery and sacramental. The last sermon in the block of Palm Sunday, the sermon for Wednesday in Holy Week (4 HM), re-emphasizes the sacramental value of time: "Stay awake, brothers! Do not let the mysteries of this time pass through you fruitlessly" (4 HM 1). Indeed, time is not just passing man by. It passes through him. As such, it has to bring about changes in man to keep him from remaining fruitless. In the sermon for Wednesday in Holy Week, the entire schooling seems to come to an end. It recapitulates the training as it was imposed upon the reader by the sermons of Lent, appealing one by one to the reader's memory, reason, and will. Most important is his memory of the passion, which lends him patience in his deeds, humility in his manner, and love in the cause (4 HM 2). Memory thus becomes the soil on which memory helps to strengthen patience, reason to strengthen humility, and will to strengthen love. Memory, reason, and will now return during the entire sermon, each linked to the specific virtue it nurtures. Memory is linked to patience in deeds in order to meet justice, which is different for every human being and for this reason is called *singularis* (4 HM 2). Reason evokes the wonderful humility in memory of the appearance of Christ at the cross (4 HM 3). Reason leads to the conclusion that at the ground of the entire passion there must have been an immeasurable love, which brought about such voluntary suffering (4 HM 4). The importance of Christ's sacrifice is its voluntariness: "He was offered because he willed it. Not only was he offered and willed it, but he was offered *because* he willed it" (4 HM 4). A change in will is the final aim of the entire schooling, and the way is shortened in the week of the passion where the virtues get joined and linked together. "How can the remembrance [*memoria*] of patience not keep all passion at a distance? How can the consideration [*ratio*] of humility not utterly drive out the pride of life? The worthy love that engages the mind in meditation and claims for itself the whole will [*voluntas*] quenches the vice of curiosity altogether" (4 HM 5).

"Nothing better can happen in the world than what God has done during these days; nothing can benefit the world more than that each year it should celebrate his memorial by a perpetual observance with the soul's desire, and gush forth the memory of his abundant goodness" (4 HM 1). The eternity of the observance (*ritu perpetuo*) observed each year (*singulis annis*) revitalizes memory (*memoriam eructuet*) by the celebration of his memorial (*celebret memoriale*) and to do this is the soul's desire (*in desiderio animae*). Thus time becomes eternity in the short period of Passion Week by the celebration of the separate moments, when done with an ardent spirit as it is done in Bernard's words. His preaching was a *celebrare*, closely joined to the *hodie*, the actual moment of reading, because it is *now* that the sacraments of the liturgical year must proceed to their fulfillment in the reader.

> [H]ere our hands have handled the Word of life, and what was from the beginning we have seen with our own eyes. This Word, because it had united in itself pure flesh and a holy soul, freely controlled the actions of his body, both because he was wisdom and righteousness, and because he had no law in his members at war with the law of his mind. My word is neither wisdom nor righteousness, yet it is capable of both, and they can be either absent from it or present with it, but being absent is easier. (4 HM 13)

Bernard's words merely mediate between the Word and the reader. It depends on the reader if they prove to be capable of wisdom and righteousness, or capable of bringing the divine virtues to life within him, so that he is no longer alone in his labor and toil but, embracing the living Word, is directed toward God's justice and righteousness in the passions of life. Then only can he await divine benediction; because that is what remains—the blessing. And nothing else awaits him after the embrace but the kiss: *Let him kiss me with the kiss of his mouth* (4 HM 14). At this moment, the reader has become equal to the spouse. The time of his engagement comes to a close, he is ready for the marriage.

Perpetual Observance: A Circular Experience.

Celebrating Easter means celebrating Bernard's victory over time as a writer and storyteller of the liturgical story—not at all fictitious but the possible reality of every man. In the story he tells, chronological time is submitted to the narrative requirements of Bernard's story, which has to be every reader's story. By his storytelling, following a narrative line which is perfectly logical, although it opposes the historical chronology as the reader knows it, Bernard brings about in the reader the sentiment of being lifted out of his earthly sense of time and transposed to a new temporal experience, which is no longer obedient to human reality but to the will of the writer. Time has a new meaning, wholly sacramental, because, thanks to the words we read, it evolves both on an earthly, human level and on a heavenly, divine level.

This sense of the dissolution of linear temporality, caused by the simultaneous validity of historical chronology and its narrative inversion, of earthly progressive movement and heavenly motionlessness, is even reinforced by the continuous return of earlier liturgical solemnities. Already it was announced that Bernard loved to play with liturgical allusions that did not fit the actual solemnity he was preaching. In the sermon for Saint Benedict, allusions could be found to the liturgy for the apostles and, originally, also to the Vigil of Christmas.[61]

In the Annunciation and Palm Sunday sermons, these allusions become more visible and important. They allude to the entire liturgical year but notably to the preceding solemnities.[62] In the last block, Bernard even refers openly to some liturgical events. In the first sermon for Palm Sunday, he inserts a small attack against those heretics who denied that baptized children were saved. He takes the Innocents as the counterexample: "The One who was born as a child and chose a

---

[61] See above and SBOp 5:6 and 11, Apparatus.

[62] The liturgical allusions begin at Ann 1.14 with two texts taken from the antiphon *Adorna* for the Purification and from the Response *Bethlehem* for the third Sunday of Advent. In Ann 3, allusions to the third week of Lent (3) and to the liturgy of November (5) follow. In Palm 2.3, an allusion is made to the Response *Ecce quomodo moritur* of Holy Saturday, while in Palm 3.5, a text is taken from the liturgy for the Innocents. The liturgical allusions thus seem to follow a clear scheme: Purification of the Virgin, Advent, Lent, November, Holy Saturday, Innocents—i.e., purification of the soul so that it prepares itself to receive the Word (Advent) by deprivations (Lent) and mortification or even death (November, the month dedicated to the commemoration of the dead) in order to be reborn in innocence. That Bernard used his liturgical allusions in a very conscious way may be clear from his elimination of a liturgical reference to the twenty-third Sunday after Pentecost as in the first version of Ann 1.12.

vanguard of children—I mean the Innocents—does not exclude children from grace even today" (Palm 1.3). In the second sermon, he uses a quote from Psalm 90 (91), the psalm central in his Lenten sermons (Palm 2.2) and in both this same Palm Sunday sermon and the sermon for Wednesday in the Holy Week he alludes by the wordplay on *benedictio* to his sermon for Saint Benedict (Palm 2.6 and 4 HM 14).[63]

A similar play with liturgical allusions can be recognized in the new block of sermons, those for Easter. Once again Bernard refers to different events in the liturgical year, and once again they seem to obey a conscious scheme. Most of them, however, seem more appropriate than in the other series. There are allusions to the liturgy of the day in the sermon for Maundy Thursday and the first sermon for Easter (Res 1.7 and 13). Besides, Bernard refers in Res 1 to the liturgy of Passion Week (Pasc 1.2) and to the liturgy for the week after Easter (Res 1.13 and 18).

As the first part of Res 1 is already known from an older version, it is telling to see how Bernard deliberately changed some allusions from the first to the later sermon. He took over the references to the passion in Res 1.2 and to Easter in Res 7. He changed the allusion to the liturgy for the fourth day after Easter in Res 1.13 into one to the liturgy for the second day. Besides, he added several completely different liturgical references: to Epiphany in Res 1.1; to Christmas in Res 1.2; and another one to Easter in Res 1.13. Together with the allusions made to Lent in Res 3.2, to Christmas in Res 3.4, and to Maundy Thursday in Res 3.5, these liturgical references appear to follow a circular composition: Maundy Thursday—Epiphany—Passion Week—Christmas—Easter (twice)—second and third days after Easter—Lent—Christmas—Maundy Thursday. The allusions start and close with Maundy Thursday. Epiphany and Passion Week correspond to Lent and Christmas. In the center, thus, remains a liturgically closed block of Christmas, Easter, and Easter Week. Already, this points to the close link Bernard wants to make between Christmas and Easter, between the start and the end of the Temporal within the liturgical year.

---

[63] As in his liturgical allusions, these open references thus follow a scheme, this time more in liturgical chronology.

This return to the preceding liturgical events is not limited to Bernard's use of liturgical allusions. His exegesis of the sacramental value of Easter in Res 1 brings him to an implied cyclical evolution. After having treated the Easter victory of perseverance (Res 1.1–9) and the Easter opening of the seals by the Lamb and the Lion (Res 1.10–13), Bernard invites his readers to consider thoroughly the meaning of Easter (Res 1.14). He points out three elements: Easter as resurrection (*resurrectio*), passing over (*transitus*), and entering into another state (*transmigratio*). Christ did not fall back (*recidit*), neither did he go back (*rediit*), nor turn back (*remeavit*). Christ did not return to his former way of life but he went over to a new way of life (*novitas vitae*). So the reader is expected after Easter not to fall back into his ancient life but to enter a new life.

Opposed to this new life is the return to one's former life. After having shared the passion of Christ and having been resurrected in him, it is just impossible to combine the former life in sin with his presence in us. "Light has no partnership with darkness, nor Christ[64] with pride, with greed, with ambition, with hatred of the brothers, with excess, with fornication. Why do you owe him less now when he is present than when he was yet to come" (Res 1.16). This return to one's old habits proves that there has been no *transmigratio* yet (Res 1.15). Because this is not the way Christ is honored, whom "you took up [*quem suscepistis*]" (Res 1.16). In a short sentence, the reader is referred to his "taking up" of Christ during the sermons for the Purification, where he was invited to take up the Word as Simeon took up the child.

The sacramental value of Easter lies in the consciousness of Christ's resurrection as a *transmigratio* into us—the readers—that ought to prevent each falling back. Those who have not yet experienced this *transmigratio*, those who still cling to their ancient habits and way of life, do not share anything with Christ, not even through reading. They did not accept the Word of life: "you have no life in you" (Res 1.17). "*Recall it to mind, transgressors,* seek the Lord with your whole heart" (Res 1.17). Those who did not follow have to return. Whither? They are admonished to convert in the true sense and thus to restart, to return

---

[64] 2 Cor 6:14–15.

to the beginning of the period of Lent and go the ways of purification and mortification once more in the hope that at the end the Word can resurrect in them and the eternal life can pass over into them.

Those for whom the living Word has resurrected in their heart, however, are prompted not to diminish their zeal, not to lose anything from the spiritual exercise now at the coming of the sacred resurrection (*sacrae resurrectionis adventu*). They must strive always to pass over further and to grow out of themselves (*transire magis et excrescere studeamus*) (Res 1.14). For them the time opens in which memory enflames the desire for eternal recompense. They live again in a time of Advent.

Indeed, Easter is the sacrament of victory, both over time and over oneself. For Bernard, this means that the solemnity of Easter includes the entire span of the liturgical year. It constitutes the crystallization point of the liturgical mystery. It divides those who believe in the cross, and for whom Christ resurrected and descended, from those who do not believe and who remain buried in the grave. Yet, for them too there still is the chance to revive, to open themselves unto the living Word, but for this they have to return, they must retake the road of Lent. The others, who shared the cross, who died with Christ, and for whom he resurrected, await a new life. Full of desire, they long for this new life to come. The novelty of their life after Easter is the reality of the new Advent, the hope for the Word to become life once again. Not in them, now, for they passed over; they are married to the Word already. They wait for the Word to pass over into others, to bring to life those who are still buried in the tomb of their ancient life. To Bernard, Easter is the solemnity in which the reader of the Word becomes a preacher, in which the Spouse becomes Mother.

Indeed, Bernard's attitude toward the reader of his sermons has changed. When continuing the reading of the following Easter sermons, the reader becomes aware that many of the old problems are still addressed, but that he is now treated almost as a colleague. Bernard no longer seems to put all the emphasis upon the inner evolution of his reader. He rather points him to the inner evolution of another, and all his attention is given to those who fall back into their ancient habits and life. Thus, it is of the highest importance that the reader becomes acquainted with the remedies by which he can heal the souls who have been committed to his care. The second sermon for Easter treats the spices necessary to anoint the dead. The third sermon treats the sevenfold leprosy, the illness, into which the poor man is always in danger of falling. The fourth sermon treats of the sick people themselves, those who do not yet live the Word of Christ. It distinguishes in a very clear way the different failures of man in his spiritual growth.

All of these sermons offer an approach from the healing side. They no longer consider the reader himself in need of the resurrection or the *transitus* to the new life. They want to train him for his new task, that of accompanying other souls upon the road toward life and in their struggle for *transmigratio* into another new life.[65] This new task takes its origin in Easter and will lead the reader through the part of the liturgical year to come.

God in Us: Experiencing the Point

The Word has become life in us. It passed over into us. It prevents us from falling back into ancient habits and customs. Yet, it leads us upon the road we want. It brings us a new Advent, just as it wants to bring those who did not take it up to a new Lent. The liturgical year is no longer submitted to a linear evolution. It winds itself into itself, revivifying what is passed but will never be over, reactualizing what was conquered but will never be vanquished. Life is no linear movement from birth to death. It is a perpetual being born and dying and resurrecting from death into a newborn life.

Easter is the victory over time. The entire liturgical year is condensed into Easter. Likewise, Easter is stretched to encompass the entire liturgical year. Easter is not Christmas, but only Easter can break the seal that closes the mystery of Christmas. It is only thanks to Easter that the sacramental meaning of Christmas becomes clear. And, it is only thanks to Easter that the true Christmas is possible. Easter leads to Christmas, just as the true Christmas automatically leads to Easter. They imply one another. One cannot be without

---

[65] Res 2 has in many manuscripts the title *Ad abbates,* which implies that it is based on a sermon pronounced by Bernard at the general chapter of Cîteaux. See SBOp 5:95, Apparatus. The abbots are, of course, the first ones to deal with the healing of souls.

the other, although it will never be clear which precedes and which follows. Likewise, the birth of Christ cannot be announced without Christ himself having written in the dust both in heaven and on earth, or Saint Benedict having been praised as the father of monks.

In reading Bernard's liturgical sermons, the reader has been lifted out of the temporal or logical sequence of things. He has entered a new world that obeys new rules imposed by no one else but the writer. But the writer imposes upon himself no other rule than obeying the living Word—i.e., giving expression to words—which may be capable of both wisdom and righteousness. He cannot command their reception, the way they are taken up by the reader, but he knows they are "capable of both": they can transmit the living Word and thus revivify the reader to the new life after Easter.

From now on, the reader is no longer a simple disciple of the writer. He has become his successor, another abbot, another mother, taking care of their common pupils. Therefore, he will have to become like Bernard, overseeing human history, organizing it according to the best way of having impact upon his own readers, in order to enflame their desire and will for the new life. Because nothing in past or future is without meaning; not the smallest detail, not one iota is devoid of sacramental content or passes without mystery. Everything can be a *figura* or even a *praefigura* for the perpetual truth of Christ's sacramental life. "See if Christ seems not clearly prefigured in this event" (O Pasc 1.5).

In the first sermon for the Octave of Easter, Bernard speaks of Moses' salvation by Pharaoh's daughter, demonstrating how Moses functions in the history of the Old Testament as the *figura* of Christ. The past thus becomes actualized in the presence of the Christ's eternal now. And similarly, we are the actualization of what was prefigured in Moses' liberation of the Israelites: "The true liberation from slavery in Egypt was accomplished not by Moses but by the blood of the Lamb; it prefigured us who are to be liberated from our empty commerce with this world by the blood of the spotless Lamb, Jesus Christ" (O Pasc 1.5). Past and future are dissolved in the eternal presence of Christ's truth. Even we, living readers, are no more than the actualization of what is lived before and for us by and in Christ. We live in him, since he, after Easter, has chosen to live in us.

Where time has gone, where no past, future, or present exists, where all has become one, and one has become all, where the reader does not exist anymore outside his reading and his reading has become him, where there is only one Word searching to express itself in the multitude of human words in order to revive and to die in order to be born, where Easter has become the solemnity of the human's rebirth, of his transmigration into the new life, the life outside time—there Easter, the union of the Word and his Spouse, is celebrated.

Editorial Note

TO MAKE CLEAR how steeped Saint Bernard was in Scripture, references to scriptural quotations and allusions are identified in the margins. For the abbreviations, see pages lxvii–lxviii.

Direct scriptural quotations, even those containing a minor variation from the Vulgate text, appear in italics. Phrases and allusions taken from Scripture, but not quoted verbatim, are noted but not italicized. Psalms are cited according to the Vulgate numbering.

Table of Abbreviations

BOOKS OF THE BIBLE

Gen	Genesis	Is	Isaiah
Ex	Exodus	Jer	Jeremiah
Lv	Leviticus	Lam	Lamentations
Nm	Numbers	Bar	Baruch
Dt	Deuteronomy	Ez	Ezekiel
Jos	Joshua	Dn	Daniel
Jgs	Judges	Hos	Hosea
1 Sm	First Samuel	Jl	Joel
2 Sm	Second Samuel	Am	Amos
1 K	First Kings	Jon	Jonah
2 K	Second Kings	Mi	Micah
1 Ch	First Chronicles	Na	Nahum
2 Ch	Second Chronicles	Hab	Habbakuk
Ezr	Ezra	Zep	Zephaniah
Neh	Nehemiah	Hg	Haggai
Tb	Tobit	Zec	Zechariah
Jdt	Judith	Mal	Malachi
1 Mc	First Maccabees	Mt	Matthew
2 Mc	Second Maccabees	Mk	Mark
3 Mc	Third Maccabees	Lk	Luke
4 Mc	Fourth Maccabees	Jn	John
Jb	Job	Ac	Acts of the Apostles
Ps[s]	Psalms	Rm	Romans
Pr	Proverbs	1 Cor	First Corinthians
Qo	Ecclesiastes, Qoheleth	2 Cor	Second Corinthians
Sg	Song of Songs	Gal	Galatians
Ws	Wisdom	Eph	Ephesians
Si	Ecclesiasticus, Sirach	Ph	Philippians

Col	Colossians	2 Pt	Second Peter
1 Thes	First Thessalonians	1 Jn	First John
2 Thes	Second Thessalonians	2 Jn	Second John
1 Tm	First Timothy	3 Jn	Third John
2 Tm	Second Timothy	Jude	Jude
Ti	Titus	Rv	Revelation
Phlm	Philemon		
Heb	Hebrews	LXX	Septuagint
Jm	James	VL	*Vetus Latina*
1 Pt	First Peter	RB	Rule of Saint Benedict

WORKS OF SAINT BERNARD

Adv	*Sermo in adventu domini*
Ann	*Sermo in annuntiatione domini*
Asspt	*Sermo in assumptione B.V.M.*
Ben	*Sermo in natali sancti Benedicti*
Circ	*Sermones in circumcisione domini*
Div	*Sermones de diversis*
Epi	*Sermo in epiphania domini*
4 HM	*Sermo in feria iv hebdomadæ sanctæ*
5 HM	*Sermo in cena domini*
Nat	*Sermones in nativitate domini*
OEpi	*Sermo in octava epiphaniae*
O Pasc	*Sermo in octava paschæ*
Palm	*Sermo in ramis palmarum*
Pasc	*Sermo in die paschæ*
Pur	*Sermo in purificatione B.V.M.*
QH	*Sermo super psalmum Qui habitat*
Quad	*Sermo in quadragesima*
Res	*De resurrectione*
Rog	*Sermo in rogationibus*
Sent	*Sententia*
Sept	*Sermo in septuagesima*
VNat	*Sermones in vigilia nativitatis domini*

Bernard of Clairvaux

SERMONS FOR LENT
AND THE
EASTER SEASON

SERMON ONE

On the Canticle:
We have received.[*]

*See Ps 47:10,
used in the Mass
of the Feast of the
Purification on 2
February.

1. TODAY the Virgin Mother brought the Lord of the Temple into the Temple of the Lord.* Joseph too conveys to the Lord, not his own son, but the beloved Son of him who took good pleasure in him.* A righteous man recognized the One he was awaiting, and the widow Anna professed her faith. These four persons first celebrated today's procession that afterward was to be celebrated with the joy of all the earth in every place and by every people. It is no wonder if it was small at the time: the One who was received there was small. No sinner had a place there. All were righteous, all were holy, all were perfect.

*Lk 2:22-36

*Mt 3:17

But are you going to save only these persons, Lord? May your body grow and your compassion[2] grow, too. *Humans and animals you will save, O Lord, when you multiply your mercy, O God.** Then in a second procession, crowds go ahead of him and crowds follow him;* he

*Ps 35:8

*Mt 21:9

---

[1] The Feast of the Purification was regarded as the end of the Christmas–Epiphany season. Bernard uses the theme of purification as an opportunity to prepare his monks for the approaching Lenten season.

[2] *Miseratio.*

3

is carried not by a virgin but by a donkey. He scorns no one, not even those who have rotted like beasts in their dung.* He scorns no one, I say; rather, if they do not lack the apostles' cloaks, if their doctrine, righteous habits, obedience, and godly love cover a multitude of sins,* he will not now judge them unworthy of the glory of his procession. What is more, we find that he has reserved for us the same glory that seems to have been bestowed on so few. Why should he not reserve for those who come later what he granted in anticipation to those of times past?

*JI 1:17

*Jm 5:20

2. David, king and prophet as he was, rejoiced that he might see this day: *he saw it and was glad.** Had he not seen it, how could he have sung, *We have received your mercy, O God, in the midst of your temple?** David received this mercy of the Lord. Simeon received it. We, too, have received it, and all those predestined for life,* for Christ [is the same] yesterday and today and forever.*

*Jn 8:56

*Ps 47:10

*Ac 13:48
*Heb 13:8

In the midst of his temple is his mercy, not in a corner or an inn, because *with God there is no respect for persons.** It stands there open, it is offered to all, and no one is beyond its reach save those who reject it. Your waters are dispersed abroad, Lord God, yet your spring is your own, and no stranger drinks of it.* Those who are yours will not see death until they see the Lord's Christ, so that, untroubled, they may be dismissed in peace.* Why should those who possess the Lord's Christ in their hearts not be dismissed in peace?

*Col 3:25

*Pr 5:15-17

*Lk 2:26, 29

He is our peace,* he who dwells in our hearts through faith.* You, unhappy soul, ignorant of Jesus, the guide of your journey, how are you going to set out? *Some people have no knowledge of God.** How is this? Surely because *the light came into the world and people loved darkness more than light.** *And the light,* it says, *shines in darkness, and the darkness has not overcome it.** It is as if it said: the waters are coursing through the streets, and no stranger drinks from them; and

*Eph 2:14
*Eph 3:17

*1 Cor 15:34

*Jn 3:19

*Jn 1:5

mercy is in the midst of the temple, yet those whom eternal damnation awaits do not approach it! *In your midst stands One whom you do not know,** you unhappy people, and so when you die before having seen the Lord's Christ you will not be dismissed in peace but will be seized instead by roaring beings prepared to devour you.* **Jn 1:26*

*Si 51:41

3. *We have received your mercy, O God, in the midst of your temple.* This thanksgiving is a long way from the words of the person moaning, *Your mercy is in heaven, and your truth reaches even to the clouds.** What about this? Does it seem to you that mercy was *in the midst,* when only the heaven-born spirits possessed it? But when Christ was made a little lower than the angels,* when he became the mediator between God and humankind,* when, like a cornerstone,° he made peace through his blood both as to things in heaven and things on earth*—surely from then on *we have received your mercy, O God, in the midst of your temple.* **Ps 35:6*

*Ps 8:6; Heb 2:7,9

*1 Tm 2:5
°1 Pt 2:6

*Col 1:20

We were by nature children of wrath, but we have obtained mercy.* Of what wrath were we the children, and what mercy have we obtained? We were children of ignorance, of indolence, and of incarceration, and we have obtained wisdom, virtue, and redemption. The ignorance of the woman led astray had blinded us, the irresolution of the man allured and enticed by his own grasping self-interest* had enfeebled us, and the malice of the devil had held us captive once we were justly left unprotected by God. **Eph 2:3; 2 Cor 4:1*

*Jm 1:14

So each and every one of us was born—first, utterly ignorant of the ways of the inhabited city;* then, weak-witted and indolent so that even had we known the path of life,* we were still shackled and held back by our own inertia; and, finally, imprisoned under the worst and cruelest of all tyrants, so that even if we had been prudent and strong, we would have been crushed by our wretched condition of slavery. **Ps 106:4*

*Ps 15:11

Does such misery not necessitate great mercy and commiseration?* Surely if we have now been saved from this threefold wrath through Christ,* *who became for us wisdom from God the Father, and righteousness, and sanctification, and redemption,** what great vigilance are we not going to need, dearly beloved, if—God forbid—our last state is not to be worse than our first,* because we incur his wrath again and are *children of wrath*, not now *by nature*, but by our own free choice?

*Ps 102:4; *Rm 5:9; *1 Cor 1:30; *Mt 12:45

4. Let us then embrace the mercy we have received in the midst of the temple and let us, with blessed Anna, never leave the temple.* *God's temple is holy, and you are that temple*, says the Apostle.* This mercy is nearby, the word is near, in your mouth and in your heart.* In short, Christ dwells in your hearts through faith.* This is the temple and this is his throne, unless for some reason he slips away from you, for *the soul of the righteous is the throne of wisdom.**[3]

*Lk 2:37; *1 Cor 3:17; *Rm 10:8; Dt 30:14; *Eph 3:17; *Pr 12:3 LXX

This is why I want to admonish my brothers frequently—in fact, always—and I beseech you now: let us not walk according to the flesh* lest we displease God. Let us not be friends of the world lest we become enemies of God.* Let us resist the devil and he will flee away from us,* that we may *walk freely in the spirit** and our way of life be from our heart. *The corruptible body weighs down the soul*, enervating and enfeebling it, *and the earthly habitation presses down on the mind that ponders many things** until it cannot rise up to the things of heaven. But *the wisdom of this world is foolishness with God** for someone who has overcome evil and become his servant.* What is more, in the heart we receive mercy, in the heart Christ dwells,* in the heart *he speaks peace to his people, to his saints, to those who are converted to the heart.**

*Rm 8:1, 4; *Jm 4:4; *Jm 4:7; *Gal 5:16, 25; *Ws 9:15; *1 Cor 3:19; *2 Pt 2:19; *Eph 3:17; *Ps 84:9

[3] See Jean Leclercq, *Recueil d'études sur S. Bernard,* vol.1 (Rome: Edizioni de storia e litteratura, 1962), 298.

On the Manner of the Procession and Its Significance

1. THANKS be to our Redeemer, who has so generously gone before us with blessings of sweetness, multiplying our joys by the mysteries of his infancy. A short time ago we celebrated his birth, his circumcision, and his epiphany.[1] Today the feast of his presentation [in the temple]* has dawned upon us. Today *earth's noblest fruit** is offered to its Creator. Today an atoning sacrifice, acceptable to God, is offered in the temple by the Virgin's hands. He is carried by his parents; he is awaited by the aged. Joseph and Mary offer a morning sacrifice;* Simeon and Anna receive it.

    These four celebrated the procession that we today call to mind with solemn joy throughout the four corners of the earth. And because today we ourselves are about to hold this festal procession—contrary to our custom on other solemnities[2]—I think

Lk 2:22-38
Is 4:2

*Nm 12:1; 28:2;
Rm 12:1*

---

[1] *Apparitione.*
[2] The early Cistercians reduced the number of liturgical processions common in traditional monasteries to three and were criticized by traditionalist monks for doing so. See *Twelfth–century Statutes from*

it not inappropriate to consider carefully the manner and the order [in which we will proceed]. We will process two by two, holding candles in our hands—candles lighted, not by just any fire, but by fire previously consecrated in the church by a priestly blessing. In our procession, the last shall be first and the first last,* and we shall sing in the ways of the Lord, for great is the glory of the Lord.*

2. We fittingly process two by two, for the holy gospels bear witness that thus were the disciples sent out by the Savior* with the purpose of commending brotherly love and community life. If someone takes it into his head to walk alone, he disturbs the procession and not only harms himself but is a nuisance to others as well. These are people who segregate themselves, animals³ devoid of the Spirit.* They make no *effort to maintain the unity of the Spirit in the bond of peace.**

Now as *it is not good for a human being to be alone,** so it is forbidden to appear empty handed before God.* When even those whom no one hired are rebuked for their idleness,* what do those who have already been hired deserve if they are found idle? *Faith without works is dead!** Our works must be done with fervor and with desire of heart, so that we may have burning lamps in our hands.* Otherwise we have to fear that he who says, *I have come to send fire on the earth, and what do I will but that it should burn,** may find us lukewarm and spew us out of his mouth.* Clearly this is the holy and

*Mt 20:16
*Ps 137:5

*Lk 10:1

*Jdt 19
*Eph 4:3

*Gen 2:18
*Ex 23:15

*Mt 20:6-7

*Jm 2:26

*Lk 12:35

*Lk 12:49
*Rv 3:16

---

the Cistercian General Chapter, ed. Chrysogonus Waddell, Studia et Documenta 12 (Brecht: Citeaux, Commentarii Cistercienses, 2002), 621 (48), 637 (29), 683 (41).

³ *Animales*. For Bernard's meaning, see, for example, William of Saint Thierry's division of human beings into animal, rational, and spiritual levels of development. William of Saint-Thierry, *Ep frat*, *The Golden Epistle*, trans. Theodore Berkeley, CF 12 (Spencer, MA: Cistercian, 1971). *Animales* identifies those who rely on their physical senses rather than their reason or spiritual senses.

blessed fire that the Father has sanctified and sent into the world* and that is blessed in the churches—as it is written: *In the churches, bless the Lord God.*   *Jn 10:36
*Ps 67:27

Our adversary,* the perverse emulator of divine works, has his own fire, I tell you. And the fire he has, the fire of fleshly desire, the fire of envy and ambition, the Savior came not to kindle in us but to quench. Those who presume to offer this alien fire at the divine sacrifice, even if they have Aaron as their father,*⁴ shall die in their iniquity,*   *1 Pt 5:8

*Lv 10:1
*Ezr 3:18

3. In addition to what has been mentioned with regard to the common life and brotherly love, to good works and holy fervor, we have the greatest need of the greatest virtue, humility. This is so that we may outdo one another in showing honor,* putting before ourselves not only our seniors but even our juniors,* for that is the perfection of humility and the fullness of righteousness.   *Rm 12:10
*RB 63.10

Since *God loves a cheerful giver** and joy in the Holy Spirit is the fruit of love,* let us sing, as it is said, in the ways of the Lord, for great is the glory of the Lord.* Let us *sing unto the Lord a new song, for he has done marvelous things.** In all these matters, if anyone only pretends he is making progress, even making progress from strength to strength,* let him know that he is standing still and not in the procession—in fact, that he is in regression; for in the path of life,* not to make progress is to regress. Nothing ever continues in the same state.* Indeed, our progress lies in this—as I remember having said quite often—that we should never think, "I have grasped it," but should always strain forward to what lies ahead.* We should strive unceasingly to become better, and we should leave our imperfect being constantly open to the oversight of divine mercy.   *2 Cor 9:7
*Rm 14:17;
Gal 5:22
*Ps 137:5

*Ps 97:1

*Ps 83:8

*Ps 15:11
*Jb 14:2

*Ph 3:13

---

⁴ Aaron's sons "offered unholy fire before the Lord, such as he had not commanded them."

On Moses' Precept and the Offering of the Morning Sacrifice

1. TODAY we celebrate the purification of the Blessed Virgin Mary,* which was performed in accord with the law of Moses forty days after the Lord's birth. In the law it was written that a woman who, having received seed, has borne a son is unclean for seven days;* on the eighth day she should circumcise the boy. Then, while she was intent on cleansing and purification, she was to refrain from entering the temple for thirty-three days. After that time she was to offer her son to the Lord, along with gifts.*

*Lk 2:22

*Lv 12:2

*Lv 12:2-4, 6-8; 5:11; Ex 13:2, 12-13

But does anyone fail to notice that in the very first phrase of this declaration the Lord's mother is set free from this precept? Do you suppose that when Moses was about to say that a woman who has borne a son is unclean, that he was not afraid of incurring the sin of blasphemy against the Lord's mother, and prefaced what he said with, *having received seed*?[1] Unless he had

---

[1] *Suscepto semine.*

10

foreseen that the Virgin was going to give birth without seed, what need had he to say "having received
seed"?

This shows clearly that this law does not apply to
the Lord's mother, who—without having received
seed—gave birth to a son. This is just as Jeremiah had
foretold: the Lord would do a new thing on the earth.
Do you ask what new thing? *A woman*, he says, *will
encompass a man.** She will not receive a man by an-   *Jer 31:22*
other man; she will not conceive a human being in
the human way, but she will enclose a man in a womb
inviolate and intact. This was so that, while the Lord
was coming and going,* the eastern gate—as another   *2 Ch 23:7*
prophet says—might remain permanently shut.*   *Ez 44:2*

2. Do you suppose that her mind could not have
been moved to say, "What need have I of purification? Why should I refrain from entering the temple?
My womb, not knowing man, has become the temple
of the Holy Spirit. Why should I, who have given
birth to the Lord of the temple, not enter the temple?
Nothing in this conception, nothing in this birth has
been impure, nothing unlawful, nothing requiring
purification. Surely not, for this child I have brought
forth is the source of purification and comes to make
purification for transgressions.* What will lawful ob-   *Heb 1:3*
servation purify in me who has been made absolutely
pure by the spotless birth itself?"

Truly, O blessed Virgin, truly you have no reason
for purification, nor any need of it. But had your child
any need of circumcision? Be among women as one
of them, just as your son was among the boys. He
willed to be circumcised; does he not will far more
to be offered? Offer your son, hallowed Virgin, and
hold up to the Lord the blessed fruit of your womb!*   *Lk 1:42*
Offer a sacrifice holy and acceptable to God* for the   *Rm 12:1*
reconciliation of us all! God the Father will accept the
new oblation, the most precious sacrifice, of whom he

Mt 17:5

himself said, *This is my beloved Son in whom I am well pleased.**

Yet this offering, brothers, seems benign enough; he is simply presented to the Lord, redeemed by birds, and taken home again. A time will come when he will be offered, not in the temple or between Simeon's arms, but outside the city between the arms of the cross. A time will come when he will not be redeemed by another's blood, but will redeem others by his own,* because he is the redemption God the Father has sent to his people.* That will be the evening sacrifice; this is the morning sacrifice.* The one is more joyful, but the other more complete; this one takes place at the time of his birth, the other at the fullness of his years. What the prophet predicted you can understand as applying to both sacrifices: He was offered, because he himself willed it.* Now he was offered, not out of necessity, not because he was under an edict of the Law, but because he willed it; on the cross, too, he was offered, not because the Jews had prevailed, not because he deserved it, but because he willed it. *I will freely sacrifice to you,** Lord, because you freely offered yourself for my salvation, not for your necessity.

3. But, brothers, what do we offer or what do we render for all he has rendered to us?* He offered for us the most precious victim that he had—indeed, none more precious could exist. Let us, then, do what we can, offering him the best that we have—surely what we ourselves *are*. He offered himself; who are you who hesitate to offer yourself?

Who will accord to me that such great Majesty condescend to accept my offering? Two mites, Lord, is all I have.* I mean, my body and my soul. If only I could offer them to you perfectly as a sacrifice of praise.* It would be good for me, and far more glorious and expedient, to be offered to you than to be left to myself, for my soul is troubled within me.* Brothers, the Jews

*Rv 5:9;
Heb 9:12*

Ps 110:9
*2 K 16:5;
Ex 29:41;
Nm 28:8*

See Is 53:7

Ps 53:8

Ps 115:12

Mk 12:42
Ps 49:14

Ps 41:7

offered dead victims to the Lord who was going to die; yet now, *I live, says the Lord.*[2] *I desire not the death of a sinner, but rather that he turn back and live.** God does not want my death; and shall I not willingly offer him my life? This is an atoning sacrifice, a sacrifice acceptable to God, a living sacrifice.*

*Ez 33:11

*Nm 5:8;
Rm 12:1

At that offering we read of three persons, and in this offering, too, the Lord looks for three things. At that offering Joseph was present, the husband of the Mother of the Lord, who was thought to be his son;*

*Lk 3:23

the virgin Mother herself was present; and the boy[3] Jesus, who was offered up. May mature[4] self-mastery, physical self-discipline, and humble self-knowledge[5] be present in our offering as well! Yes, in our intention to persevere let us have a mature mind, in our self-discipline a virginal chastity, but in our self-knowledge a youthful[6] simplicity and humility.

---

[2] *Vivo ego* was used as the psalm antiphon at Prime during Lent.

[3] *Puer.*

[4] *Virilis*; also in the following sentence.

[5] *Constantia—continentia—conscientia.*

[6] *Puerilis.*

Of the Ten Precepts
and the Seven Hindrances
Holding Us Back from Them

1. I FIND GREAT CONSOLATION, my broth-
ers, in the Lord's saying, *Whoever is from God hears*
*the words of God.** You, then, will listen readily
because you are from God! I am not unaware that in
another place Scripture says, *From him, and through him,*
*and in him are all things,** but that is quite different from
the condition of those who, according to the Gospel
of blessed John, *are not born from the will of the flesh but*
*from God.** In the letter of this same John you will find
written that *everyone who is born from God does not sin,*
*but his heavenly birth keeps him safe.** He does not sin,
that is, he does not persevere in sin, because the begetting from heaven, which cannot fail, preserves him so
that it is impossible for him to perish. Or perhaps *he*
does not sin means that the *heavenly birth* preserves him
to that point that it is as if he had never sinned at all
because sin is not imputed to him.* In this way, too,
does his *heavenly birth* keep him safe.

But who shall speak of this begetting? Who can say,
"I am one of the elect, one of those predestined to
life, I am numbered among the children?" Who can

*Jn 8:47

*Rm 11:36

*Jn 1:13

*1 Jn 5:18

*Rm 4:8

14

say that, when Scripture says in no uncertain terms, *No one knows whether he is worthy of love or of hatred*?* We have no certainty, but confident hope consoles us; otherwise we would be utterly crucified by anxiety and doubt. This is why certain signs and clear indications of salvation are given so that that there might be no doubt that those in whom these signs reside are counted among the elect.

    That is why I say that those whom God has foreknown he also predestined to be conformed to the image of his Son:* if he denies them certitude in order to keep them alert, he at least gives them the consoling grace of hope. This is why we are always uneasy, why we must be humbled in fear and trembling under the mighty hand of God.* What we are now, this we can know in part; but it is quite impossible for us to know what we will be in the future.* Therefore *let one who is standing take heed lest he fall*,* and let him persevere and progress in that frame of mind which is both evidence of salvation and a sure sign of predestination.

    2. Now the most important of the things that give confidence and the grounds of hope is what I have already said: *Whoever is from God hears the words of God.** Among those who hear, you sometimes find people to whom it seems that nothing that is said applies to them; they will not allow it to enter their hearts, nor throw their behavior into question; they will not even think about what they hear lest they find that it was said with them in mind. If it is indeed the case that God's word is living and active and that it is brought to bear wherever God wills, by his choice, not that of the speaker; and if it is clearly directed against those vices by which people feel they are enslaved, and these people ignore it and turn away the eyes of their hearts, or they minimize their vices by some means and deceive themselves in their misery, then I see in such people no signs of salvation, but I fear the more that

*Qo 9:1

*Rm 8:29

*1 Cor 2:3;
2 Cor 7:15; 1
Pt 5:6
*1 Cor 13:9-12
*1 Cor 10:12

*Jn 8:47

the reason they do not hear God is that they are not *from God.*

But in you, my brothers—thanks be to God!—truly I find *ears that hear,** particularly since the fruit of the word is immediately[1] apparent in the amendment of your lives. Indeed there are times when I sense your spiritual fervor even while I am speaking. The more you suck, the more does the power of the Holy Spirit* fill my breasts; and the more abundantly it is given to be poured out for you, the more quickly you drink it down! That is why I speak to you more often than is the custom in our Order. I know who it is who says, *Whatever you spend in excess I will give you on my return.**

3. Today, my brothers, we celebrate the beginning of Septuagesima, whose name is well enough known in the whole church. Now I say to you, beloved, speaking for myself, that this name excites a great compassion. My spirit is moved within me, sighing for that homeland where there is neither number, measure, nor weight.* How long [must I continue to] receive all the goods of body or of soul in weight, measure, or number? *How many servants in my Father's house have abundance of bread while I am perishing of hunger here?** Because of food for the body Adam was told—and it has come down to me—*in the sweat of your brow you shall eat bread.** It is the same with me. When I work, bread is given me by weight, drink by measure, and food by number.

So much for corporal matters. What of the spiritual? Before I eat, I sigh. Would that my sighs and tears might avail to make me worthy of the smallest fragment of the celestial banquet so that, like a puppy, I may eat of the crumbs that fall from the master's table!* O

*Mt 11:15

*Rm 15:13; 15:19, etc

*Lk 10:35

*Ws 11:20

*Lk 15:17

*Gen 3:19

*Mt 15:27

---

[1] *Sine mora.* See RB 5.1: *Primus humilitatis gradus est obedientia sine mora.*

Jerusalem, city of the great King who satisfies you with the finest of wheat and gladdens you with the stream of a river, in you is neither weight nor measure, but sufficiency and the greatest abundance! Nor do you have number, for all your parts are harmoniously united.* But as for me, who am entirely change and number, when shall I come to that unity I seek? When shall I be satisfied with the appearing of your glory, Lord?* When shall I be inebriated by the richness of your house? When will you give me to drink from the torrent of your delight?* For now the showers falling upon the earth are so scanty that I cannot even swallow my spittle.* *Ps 121:3

*Ps 16:15

*Ps 35:9

*Jb 7:19

4. It is true, my brothers, perfectly true, that everything is now given to us in weight, number, and measure, though a day will come when all these are going to cease. Of number we read that *of his wisdom there is no number,** and in another passage by the same prophet, *in your right hand are pleasures forevermore.** Hear too in the writings of the Apostle of a weight without weight: *beyond all measure*, he says, *an eternal weight of glory.** Hear of the *eternal weight*, but notice that he puts *beyond all measure* first. So too I hear Christ promising a measure without measure: *pressed down, shaken together, and running over.**

*Ps 146:5

*Ps 15:11

*2 Cor 4:17

*Lk 6:38

When will these things come? Truly, at the end of this present Septuagesima, which is the time of our captivity. So we read that after being taken captive by the Babylonians, the children of Israel suffered banishment for seventy years. When these were ended they returned home, restored the temple, and rebuilt the city.* When will our captivity end, my brothers, our captivity which is prolonged so many years, even from the beginning of the world?* When will we be set free from this our slavery?* When will Jerusalem, the holy city, be rebuilt? Surely at the end of this Septuagesima, which is made up of ten and seven because of the

*Jer 25:11-12; 29:10; Ezr 3, 4, etc

*Mt 24:21

*Rm 8:21

Ten Commandments, which we have received, and the seven hindrances, by which our obedience to the commandments is held back.

5. Our first hindrance—a heavy burden—is the compulsions of this miserable body! With its constant demands for sleep, food, clothes, and other such things our body is frequently a hindrance to us in our spiritual activities. Second, we are hindered by the vices of our hearts such as levity, suspicion, the emotions of impatience and envy, hunger for praise, and similar things that we experience in ourselves daily. Take as the third and fourth hindrances prosperity and adversity in this present world, *for a perishable body weighs down the soul, and its earthly habitation burdens the mind that muses on many things.** Therefore beware of the snare of temptations on both sides, and take up the weapons of righteousness for the right hand and for the left.* The fifth hindrance, a very serious and dangerous one, is our ignorance. In many circumstances we have no idea how we should act; we do not even *know how to pray as we ought!** The sixth hindrance is our adversary who *goes around like a roaring lion looking for someone to devour.**

*Ws 9:15

*2 Cor 6:7

*Rm 8:26

*1 Pt 5:8

If only, free from these six tribulations, there were no seventh to touch us with its evil—no danger from false brothers to get to us!* If only it were just evil spirits that attacked us with their suggestions and humans did us no harm with their deadly example, rude opinions, words of flattery* and calumny, and in a thousand other ways.

*2 Cor 11:26

*1 Thes 2:5

You see how necessary it is for us to be sustained in our struggle against these seven dangers by the help of the sevenfold Holy Spirit. It is because of these seven dangers that hinder us from obeying the Ten Commandments that we observe this present Septuagesima in penitential sorrow. Therefore our customary *alleluia*[2] is silenced for a while, and the lamentable story of human transgression is recounted from the beginning.

[2] After at least the time of Pope Gregory the Great, the singing of *Alleluia* was suppressed during the season of Septuagesima.

Of the Threefold Sleep

*T**HE LORD SENT A DEEP SLEEP UPON ADAM.** He also sent it upon himself when he had become the second Adam, yet with a great difference. Adam seems to have fallen asleep from an excess of contemplation and Christ from the affection of compassion. It was truth that sent a deep sleep upon the one, and love upon the other—and each of these is the Lord; for John the Evangelist said, *God is love,** and the Lord himself said, *I am the way, the truth, and the life.**

*Gen 2:21

*1 Jn 4:16
*Jn 14:6

No one who claims the name of Christian doubts that Christ's sleep was of love alone. He lay down as a lion, not vanquished but victorious, laying down his life by his own power and taking upon himself the sleep of death by his own choice. But what are we to say or believe about that deep sleep that God sent upon Adam and then took, while Adam slept, without causing pain, a rib from his side for the fashioning of a woman?*

*Gen 2:21-22

To me it seems that that sleep was a setting aside of the bodily senses in a vision of unchangeable truth and an abyss of divine wisdom; this we can surely infer from his words. On his return he told where he had gone. Like an inebriated man coming from the wine cellar he uttered the great mystery that so long afterward the Apostle applied to Christ and the church. He

said, *This at last is bone of my bones,** and, *For this reason* **Gen 2:23;*
Eph 5:30
a man will leave his father and mother and cling to his wife,
and the two will be one flesh.* Do you think he had been **Gen 2:24;*
Eph 5:31
utterly sound asleep when he arose and burst out with
these words? Could he not rather have said, *I sleep, and*
my heart is awake?* **Sg 5:2*

2. I would say this, without prejudice to others who
might hold another opinion or to anything different
found in the writings of the saints. For I do not think
that "deep sleep" was an ordinary one, like our sleep,
which is sent not by an excess of contemplation, or
by the affection of compassion, but by the defect of
infirmity; generated not by truth or love but by necessity. *Heavy is the yoke on the children of Adam.** Not, **Si 40:1*
in the beginning, on Adam, but as things are now,
on his children. How should it not be heavy for us
wretched folk, for whom life is wearisome, and for
whom—which few seem to notice and scarcely anyone feels—the very capacity for sensation becomes an
insupportable burden unless we are refreshed by peri-
ods of rest. How should there not be toil, sorrow, and
vexation of spirit from all things under the sun when
the heaviest burden is the one that provides the most
pleasure, excitation, and stimulation of the flesh? The
sweetness of intercourse is manifested in the sadness of
separation when wrenching apart is scarcely possible,
bodily corruption being altogether intolerable to an
agent of energy.

It is not just a body, but *a perishable body,* that *weighs*
down the soul.* From this you can infer that the soul of **Ws 9:15*
our first parent was exempt from this burden as long
as he kept his body free from corruption. God placed
the man in a state of freedom so that he might range
between the heights and the depths, advancing to
the heights without difficulty and descending to the
depths without enticement or necessity, penetrating
the heights by natural vigor and purity of heart, and

governing the depths with the authority of a ruler. Finally, all living things were brought to Adam, that God might see what he would call them.* It was not curiosity that led Adam to see them.

*Gen 2:19

3. Reason is not free in us, but is in constant conflict. It is both held captive from the depths by a sort of snare and turned away from the heights as unworthy. As a result we cannot be torn away from the depths without pain or gain admittance to the heights without great and uncommon groaning. On the one hand, those who seek my life* do me violence, and I must cry out, *Wretched man that I am! Who will free me from the body of this death?;** while on the other, *before I eat I sigh,** because *the kingdom of heaven suffers violence, and the violent take it by force.** Yet we must maintain a balance between unity on the one hand and division on the other—as Adam fell into deep sleep in contemplation, and distinguished the animals by giving them names. Likewise we read that Abraham divided the animals, but not the birds, for sacrifice.* And Martha is troubled about many things, when one thing is necessary, plainly only one thing, and that one thing vitally necessary, since this is that best part that will not be taken away.* When fullness comes division will cease, and Jerusalem, the holy city, will be at unity with itself.*

*Ps 37:13

*Rm 7:24
*Jb 3:24
*Mt 11:12

*Gen 15:9-10

*Lk 10:41-42
*Ps 121:3
*Is 11:2

Meanwhile the spirit of wisdom* is not only single but also manifold, establishing in unity what is internal, and by judgment distinguishing the things that are external. The primitive church is commending both to you, for the *multitude of those who believed were of one heart and soul*—the birds were not divided!—while *distribution was made to each as any had need**—the animals were cut apart! Beloved, let us have unity of minds among us; let our hearts be united, loving the one thing, seeking the one thing, clinging to the one thing, and having the same feelings.* In this way external division both avoids danger and incurs no scandal.

*Ac 4:32, 35

*Ph 2:2-3

This means that though each one obviously has his own share of the burden, and that sometimes each will have his own point of view about mundane affairs—for the gifts of grace are diverse and not all the members seem to have the same function*—yet inner unity and unanimity will gather and bind our multiplicity together with the glue of love and the bond of peace.*

*Rm 12:6, 4

*Eph 4:3

SERMON ONE

On the Principle of Fasting, Based on the Lord's Words, *Anoint your head and wash your face* *

*Mt 6:17

1. TODAY, beloved, we enter the holy season of Lent, a season of Christian warfare. We are not the only ones who observe it; it is common to all who are in the unity of the same faith.* Why should all Christians not share in Christ's fast? Why should the members not follow the Head? If we receive good from this Head, why should we not endure the bad?* Or do we wish to reject what is disagreeable but take our share of pleasure? If that were the case we would show ourselves unworthy to share the life of the Head. All that he suffered, he suffered for us. If we are put off by being his collaborators in the work of our own salvation, how will we later show ourselves his coworkers?* Surely it is no great thing for one who is to sit with Christ at the Father's table* to fast with him, no great thing if a member suffer with the Head with whom he will be glorified! Happy is the member who clings to this Head through everything, and follows him wherever he goes!* But if he is cut off and separated, it must follow that he is deprived even of the breath of life.* How

*Eph 4:13

*Jb 2:10

*1 Cor 3:9

*Lk 22:29-30

*Rv 14:4
*Gen 6:17; 7:15

24

will any part that does not remain united to the Head possess consciousness[1] and life? Clearly there will be someone to take possession of the parts exposed to view so they don't remain headless! The root of bitterness will spring up again,* and a poisonous head will again come forth—the head which that valiant woman,* Mother Church, had previously crushed.° I refer to the one who was born anew by her to a living hope,* the one whom his biological mother had given birth to as a child of wrath.*   *Heb 12:15*   *Pr 31:10*   °Gen 3:15   *1 Pt 1:3*   *Eph 2:3*

2. Now if anyone has the eyes of his heart enlightened* and the gift of spiritual intuition he will see a dreadful monster, having the body of a man and the head of a demon. Nor is this all—doubtless *the last state of that person will be worse than the first* since the serpent's head, which had earlier been cut off, will return with seven others even more evil.* Who does not tremble at just hearing this! Shall I take a member of Christ* and make it a member of demons? Shall I be cut off from the body of the Savior and become a limb of Satan? Miserable man! May we always escape that abominable mutation, my brethren!   *Eph 1:18*   *Mt 12:44-45*   *1 Cor 6:15*

For me, it is good to cling to you,* O glorious Head, blessed forever,* on which even the angels desire to look!* *I will follow you wherever you go;*° if you pass through fire I will not be torn away from you, nor will I fear evil, for you are with me.* You bear my griefs* and you grieve over me; you go first through the narrow door of the passion to prepare a broad entrance for the members who follow.   *Ps 72:28*   *Dn 3:26*   *1 Pt 1:12*   °Mt 8:19   *Is 43:2; Pss 65:12; 22:4*   *Is 53:4*

*Who will separate us from the love of Christ?** By this love the whole body grows through its joints and ligaments.* This is the "good soldier" Isaiah mentions.° This is what makes it so good and pleasant a thing   *Rm 8:35*   *Col 2:19; Eph 4:16*   °Is 41:7

---

[1] *Sensus.*

for brethren to dwell together in unity. This ointment that flows down from the Head on to the beard flows even to the skirts of the garment* so that not the smallest thread lacks anointing. On the Head is the fullness of graces of which we all receive;* on the Head is all mercy, an inexhaustible font of divine loving-kindness, and the whole abundance of spiritual ointment. As it is written, *God, your God, has anointed you with the oil of gladness beyond your companions.* That Head, which the Father had anointed so freely, Mary also did not fear to anoint. The disciples were scandalized, but Truth answered for her that she had performed a good work.*

3. Now what does he teach us today in the Gospel? *But you,* he says, *when you fast, anoint your head.* What marvelous condescension! The Spirit of God is upon him because he anoints him and yet, preaching the gospel to the poor,* he says, *Anoint your head.* The Father is well-pleased with the Son, and when the voice sounds from heaven the Spirit descends in the form of a dove.* Do you think, my brothers, anointing was missing at Christ's baptism? The Spirit of the Lord was upon him; and does anyone suppose that he was not anointed by that Spirit? *This is my beloved Son, with whom I am well pleased.* This surely is the fragrance of spiritual oil!* The Father anointed the Son beyond his companions because he was uniquely pleased with him beyond all others. *The Father loves the Son* with a divine affection not experienced by any creature. He anointed him, I say, beyond his companions, heaping upon him all the gifts of goodness, gentleness, and kindness, filling him with compassion and mercy.* Then, when he had anointed him, he sent him to us showing him to be full of grace* and loving-kindness. Thus was our Head anointed by the Father, and nevertheless he asks to be anointed by us: *When you fast,* he says, *anoint your Head.* Does an unfailing

*Ps 132:1-2

*Jn 1:16

*Ps 44:8

*Mt 26:7-10

*Mt 6:17

*Is 61:1; Lk 4:18

*Mt 3:16-17

*Mt 3:17
*Sg 1:3

*Jn 5:20

*Col 3:12;
Ps 102:4
*Jn 1:14

spring ask water from a rivulet? Without a doubt it asks, and asks it again, and more! *The streams go back to the spring whence they flow, that they may flow again.**   *Qo 1:7

4. But it is not because he lacks something that Christ asks back what he has given, but that you don't lose anything you have willingly given to him. Take a river that remains still for a long time; it grows stagnant, so that when a flood occurs it just sloughs off the sudden abundance of water. Even so, if there is no reciprocity the descent of grace stops; for the ungrateful there will be no increase; instead, what they have received will be turned to their destruction. One who is faithful in a small thing is judged worthy of a greater reward. Therefore *anoint your Head*, pouring out on him who is above whatever devotion or delight or affection you have. *Anoint your Head*, so that if there is any grace in you it may be ascribed to him, and you may not seek your own glory, but his.*   *Jn 7:18

He anoints Christ, who is his good aroma in every place.* Remember that this saying was uttered against   *2 Cor 2:14-15 the hypocrites: *Do not make yourselves sad, like the hypocrites.** Yet he does not forbid us sadness of every kind,   *Mt 6:16 but that which is on the face to be seen by other people.* Besides, *the heart of the wise is where there is*   *Mt 5:16 *sadness,** and Paul did not apologize for making his   *Qo 7:4 disciples sad because they were saddened to salvation.*   *2 Cor 7:8-10 The sadness of hypocrites is not like that: it is not in the heart but on the face, *for they disfigure their faces.**   *Mt 6:16

5. Notice, too, that he did not say, *Do not be sad, like the hypocrites*, but, *Do not make yourselves,* that is, *pretend*. We commonly say, "He makes himself sad," or "he exalts himself," or *the one who blesses you leads you astray,** and similar things that are pretence rather   *Is 9:16 than truth. *But when you fast, anoint your head and wash your face.** They disfigure their faces, but you are told   *Mt 6:17 to wash. The face is mentioned because the way of life is seen in the face. The faithful servant of Christ

washes it lest it give offence to the beholder, but the hypocrite disfigures it the more, following strange and unusual customs. He does not anoint his Head when his affections are drawn away from Christ and he finds pleasure in empty flattery. Instead he anoints himself, so that he may spread the fragrance of his own reputation. Certainly it is clear that the hypocrite's head is not Christ, and that one whose mind is caressed not by the testimony of his own conscience* but by adulation cannot anoint his own head, whatever that may be. *Give us some of your oil*, say the foolish virgins.* Why do they say this? Because they have no oil in their lamps. But giving oil in this way is not a prudent thing to do. Why should they do for others what they are unwilling to do for themselves?* Listen to the prophet, to whom God revealed the uncertain and hidden things of divine wisdom:* *Let the oil of a sinner not anoint my head.* The hypocrites buy that oil, as the Lord says: *Amen, I tell you, they have received their reward, for they disfigure their faces that they may appear to be fasting.**

Rm 2:15; 9:1

Mt 25:8

Mt 7:12

Ps 50:8
Ps 140:5

Mt 6:16

See how in a few words he both points out hypocrisy and individualism,[2] and condemns vanity. See how briefly he urges us to practice goodness in the sight of God and of human beings.* *Anoint your head and wash your face*, that is to say, show yourself blameless so that you strive to win for yourself divine grace and in the sight of others seek not your own glory, but that of your Creator.*

Si 25:1

Jn 7:18

6. It is also possible to understand the washed face as a pure conscience and the anointed head as a devout mind. If you look into it, these two words, "washing" and "anointing," seem to be spoken against a double vice that those who fast assault above all. One fasts

---

[2] *Singularitas.*

through vanity, and he is told, *Wash your face*. The other fasts with impatience and rancor, and he must anoint his head. The head is, then, the inner mind. It is anointed by fasting when it takes spiritual delight in it. Does it seem to you strange that we say that the head is anointed by fasting? I say more, it is even fattened! Have you never read what was written, *To keep them alive in famine?** So fasting of the body is anointing of the head, and the abstinence of the flesh is refreshment of heart. Must I speak of the anointing that brings healing to wounds and peace to troubled consciences? Let hypocrites buy *the oil of the sinner** with their fasting; I do not sell my fasting—that is, the oil with which I am anointed. *Anoint your head*, he says, that no murmuring or impatience may come upon you. Not only this, but you must glory in tribulation, as the Apostle says.* You must glory, I repeat, but with no trace of vanity, that your face may be cleansed of the oil of the sinner.

*Ps 32:19

*Ps 140:5

*Rm 5:3

SERMON TWO

How We Should be Converted to the Lord

1. *TURN TO ME WITH ALL YOUR HEART, with fasting, with weeping, and with mourning; rend your hearts and not your garments, says the Lord Almighty.*[1] What does the Lord's commandment that we turn to him mean, beloved? He is everywhere; he fills all things, yet embraces the whole world. Which way do I turn to you, Lord my God? *If I ascend to heaven, you are there; if I descend to hell, you are present.* What are you commanding? In which direction shall I turn to you—above or below? To the right or to the left?

Jl 2:12-13

Ps 138:8

This is a piece of advice, my brothers; it is a secret that he entrusts only to his friends. It is the mystery of the kingdom of God. It is revealed to the apostles in private, for nothing is told the crowds without a parable.* *Unless you turn and become like a little child you will not enter the kingdom of heaven.* What he means by our turning is clear to me. We must turn to the little child that we may learn from him, for he is meek and humble of heart*—it is for this reason a child was given to us.* Clearly he is also great, too, but only in

Mt 13:34

Mt 18:3

Mt 11:29

Is 9:6

---

[1] From the *capitulum* at Terce in Lent.

the city of the Lord, to which is said, *Rejoice and praise, O habitation of Zion, for great in your midst is the Holy One of Israel!** *Ps 47:2; Is 12:6

Why are you puffed up, O human creature? Why do you boast without a cause? Why are you high-minded and why do your eyes survey everything that is lofty?** *Rom 11:20; Jb 41:25 That will not come to good for you. The Lord is lofty, certainly, but such is not your place. His greatness can be praised but not also imitated. His magnificence is high, and you cannot attain it. Even if you do violence to yourself you cannot take hold of it. *The human being shall ascend to a lofty heart, and God shall be exalted.** *Ps 63:7-8 *The Lord is high and looks on the lowly; the lofty he knows from afar.** *Ps 137:6

Be humble—and you have taken hold of it. This is the law of holiness, and because of this law I have waited for you, Lord. What if the way of loftiness were put before you and it was shown to be the way to the salvation of God?—how many things would people do to exalt themselves! How ruthlessly they would jostle each other and trample each other underfoot! How shamelessly they would crawl, striving for the heights on hands and feet to set themselves over the heads of others!** *Ps 65:12

And certainly one who is in competition to surpass his neighbors will encounter many difficulties, will have many rivals, and will suffer many who will speak against him, who are trying to go up on the opposite side. Nothing, however, is easier, for one who wishes to do so, than to humble oneself. This is the word, beloved, that robs us of all excuse so that we may not spread even the thinnest veil over ourselves.

2. But now let us look upon this little child, the master of gentleness and humility, by which means we must be turned. *Turn to me with all your heart*, he says.** *Jl 2:12 My brothers, if he had said, "Turn to me," and nothing more, perhaps we would have replied boldly,

"It is done; give us another commandment." But now, as I understand it, he is urging us to a spiritual turning, which is not completed in one day; if only it might be accomplished in the whole lifetime that we spend in this body! For if the turning of the body were all, it would be nothing. That has the appearance of turning, not the truth, with an appearance of piety but lacking power. Unhappy the person who spends all his time with things outside, ignorant of his own inner self; he thinks himself to be something when he is nothing; he deceives himself. *I am poured out like water, and all my bones are scattered*, says the psalmist in the likeness of such a person.* And another prophet says, *Strangers have devoured his strength, and he knew it not.** Taking a casual view from without, he supposes that all is well with him, not perceiving the hidden worm that gnaws him inwardly. His tonsure remains, he has not laid aside his habit, he keeps the rule of fasting, he says the psalms at the prescribed times; but *his heart is far from me*, says the Lord.*

*Ps 21:15

*Hos 7:9

*Is 29:13;
Mt 15:8

3. Look carefully at the object of your love, your fear, the reason for your joy or your sadness, and you will find a worldly mind under your religious habit, and under the swaddling bands of your conversion a wayward heart. All your heart is in these four affects, and I think it is with reference to them that we should hear what is said about "turning to the Lord with all your heart." Let your love be turned, then, so that you love nothing at all except him, or because of him. Next, let your fear too be turned to him, because all the fear that you feel for anything except him, or not because of him, is wrong. Similarly, let both your joy and your sadness be turned to him. This will only happen if your grief and your joy are in accord with him. What is more perverse than to rejoice when you do evil and to exult in the most wicked things?* The sadness that is in accord with the flesh produces death;

*Pr 2:14

if you grieve for your sin or your neighbor's, you do
well,* and this sadness leads to salvation. If you rejoice   *2 Cor 7:10
at the gifts of grace, this is a holy joy, and true joy in
the Holy Spirit. You must rejoice in the love of Christ
with your brothers in their successes and grieve with
them in adversity, as it is written: *Rejoice with those who
rejoice, weep with those who weep.**   *Rm 12:15

4. This does not mean, though, we should value
lightly the physical turning. As we know, it is no small
support for the spiritual. That is why when the Lord
had said "with all your heart" here, he immediately
added "with fasting,"* for that is of the body. Yet I   *Jl 2:12
would have you warned, my brothers, that that means
not only abstaining from food, but from all fleshly lusts
and all bodily pleasures; indeed you must fast from
vices far more than from food. But there is a bread
from which I do not wish you to fast lest you faint on
the way; if you do not know what it is, I am speaking
of the bread of tears. The text goes on, *with fasting, with
weeping, and with mourning*. It demands mourning of
us by way of repentance for our former way of life;
it demands weeping with desire for future beatitude.
My tears have become my bread, says the prophet, *while
they say to me every day, "Where is your God?"** One   *Ps 41:4
who does not yet mourn the old ways, does not yet
mourn the sins committed, does not yet mourn time
lost, is little pleased by newness of life. If you do not
mourn, clearly you do not feel the wounds of the soul
or the injury to conscience. Nor do you have sufficient craving for the joys to come if you do not beg
for them every day with tears; if your soul does not
refuse comfort* until they come, then you know too   *Ps 76:3
little of them.

5. Then the prophet adds, *Rend your hearts and not
your garments.** By these words he is accusing the   *Jl 2:13
ancient people, the Jews, of hardness of heart and
meaningless superstition. They frequently rent their

garments, but not their hearts. When would those stony hearts, which could not be circumcised, be rent? *Rend your hearts and not your garments.* Who is there among you whose will is obsessed with one particular thing? Let the Spirit rend your heart with his sword,* which is the word of God; let him rend it and speedily shatter it into many fragments. There is no way to turn to the Lord with all your heart except your heart be rent. Until you claim a part in that Jerusalem which is at unity with itself,* you are given many commandments, and if you offend in one, you become accountable for all. The Spirit of God is manifold, says Wisdom,* and you cannot follow his many paths without being rent into many fragments.

*Eph 6:17

*Ps 121:3

*Ws 7:22

Listen to one whom God found to be after his own heart:* *My heart is ready, O God, my heart is ready,*° he says—ready for both adversity and prosperity; ready for what is low and what is lofty; ready for whatever you command. Do you want to make me a shepherd of sheep? Do you want to set me up as a king of the peoples? *My heart is ready, O God, my heart is ready.* Who is as faithful as David in his going out and coming in, and his taking up of the kingship? He used to say of sinners, *Their heart is curdled like milk, but I have meditated on your law.** This is the reason for hardness of heart and obstinacy of mind, that someone does not meditate on the law of the Lord but on his own will.

*Ac 13:22
°Pss 56:8; 107:2

*Ps 118:70

6. Let us rend our hearts, beloved, but keep our garments whole. Our garments are our virtues; love is a good garment, obedience is a good garment. Happy is the one who cares for these garments that he may not walk naked.* *Happy are those whose sins are covered;*° *love covers a multitude of sins.** Let us rend our hearts, as was said before, that we may keep our garments whole, as was our Savior's tunic. The rending of the heart not only keeps the garment whole, but also makes it long and of many colors, like the coat the holy patriarch

*Is 20:3
°Ps 31:1
*1 Pt 4:8

Jacob gave the son whom he loved more than the oth-
ers.* From this comes perseverance in virtue, from this   *Gen 37:23, 3*
the many-colored unity of a beautiful way of life. From
this comes the glory of the king's daughter, in golden
borders, clothed with many colors.*   *Ps 44:14-15*

    We can also take this rending of the heart in another
way: if the heart is wicked it may be rent by confession; if hard, by compassion. Is not an ulcer rent so that
the diseased matter may flow out? Is not the heart rent
to overflow in compassion? Both rendings are expedient, that the poison of sin may not lie hidden in the
heart, and we may not shut off our compassion from
our neighbor's need, that we may receive mercy from
Our Lord Jesus Christ, who is over all, blessed forever.

SERMON THREE

Of Devotion and Fervor
in Fasting

1. I BEG YOU, my beloved, to undertake the Lenten fast with complete devotion; abstinence alone does not commend it to you, but, much more, the mystery. If we have fasted with devotion up until now, at this holy season we should fast with much greater devotion. If we add something to our customary abstinence,* wouldn't it be shameful if we found burdensome what the whole church* is bearing with us? So far, we alone have fasted until the ninth hour; now everyone will fast with us until evening—kings and princes, clergy and people, nobles and common folk, *rich and poor alike.**

    I would say this, however, my brothers, lest any—perhaps remembering that they found a former fast too heavy a burden—be troubled by weakness of spirit and undertake this present fast with less devotion. This is what our enemy strives for with all his strength—to empty our sacrifice of the richness of devotion.* Thus it will be less acceptable to God and our conscience will be less caught up in holy joy.* Weakness of conscience is produced by weakness in endurance. Since we are not ignorant of his cunning designs, I beg that we guard against him with all care. Since *God loves a cheerful giver,** and our conscience is

*See RB 49.5, 8
*Rm 16:23

*Ps 48:3

*Ps 19:4
*See RB 49.6

*2 Cor 9:7; see
RB 5.16

36

raised up by greater fidelity, let us set before ourselves the example of the whole church so that we may fast more devotedly.

2. But why do I speak of our companions in this observance of the fast as if we did not have much better models than they in this matter, even some that are dedicated to it? With what devotion should we enter upon this fast that was transmitted by Moses* **Ex 34:28* as though by hereditary obligation! The Lord used to speak to him face to face,* by a special privilege **Ex 33:11* compared with the other prophets. With what fervor should we embrace the fast that Elijah commended,* **1 K 19:8* he who was snatched up to heaven in a fiery chariot?* **2 K 2:11* Consider how many thousands have met the common fate of death since those days—yet Elijah has escaped its power up to this day, by the Lord's protection. And now, if Moses and Elijah commend this present fast— and although great, they are our fellow servants—how much does our Lord commend it, who himself fasted for the same number of days?* What kind of person— **Mt 4:2* —I don't say monk, but Christian—undertakes with small devotion this fast that Christ himself gave to us? No, we must imitate the example of Christ's fast with much greater devotion because surely he fasted for our sake, not his own.

3. Let us fast, then, beloved, and let us fast with devotion during this holy season of Lent, since we know our Lent does not have just forty days. We must continue this Lent all the days of this miserable life,* while **See RB 49.1* with the help of grace we must fulfill the law of the decalogue which is commended in the four gospels.* **Mt 5:17* Those who think that these very few days are sufficient for repentance are clearly in error, since the whole period of this life is allotted for no other reason. *Seek the Lord*, says the prophet, not just for forty days, but *while he may be found; call on him while he is near.** There will be no more time for calling when **Is 55:6*

that time comes that God will be near to no one, but present to some and extremely distant from others. Meanwhile since he is said to be near, it is evident that we do not yet possess him—and yet he can be easily possessed and found. *Who do you suppose was a neighbor to him who fell among thieves? Surely the one who showed* *Lk 10:36-37 him mercy.**[1] Therefore, my beloved, since during this whole season of mercy he is very near, *seek the Lord while he may be found, call on him while he is near.*

4. During this Lent we must truly seek with greater fervor that which is not just a part but is the entire mystery of this whole season. Therefore if perhaps your zeal has somewhat abated during recent days, it is fitting that you rekindle your fervor of spirit. If only the belly has sinned, let it alone fast, and that will be enough; but if other members have also sinned, why should they not fast as well? Let the eye fast, since it *Lam 3:51 has ravaged the soul.* Let the ear fast, the tongue, the hand, even the soul itself. Let the eye fast from curious glances and from all wantonness, that when well-humbled it may be brought to repentance, the eye that while free wandered wickedly into sin. Let the ear fast that itches for tales and rumors and whatever is idle and of no use for salvation. Let the tongue fast from slander and grumbling, from fruitless, vain, and scurrilous words, and sometimes, too, because of the importance of silence, even from the very things that *See RB 6.8 seem necessary.* Let the hand fast from making useless signs and from all work not explicitly commanded. But also, and much more, let the soul itself fast from vices and from its own will. Without this kind of fast all the rest is disagreeable to the Lord. As it is written, *Is 58:3 on your fast days you do what you want!*

---

[1] *Proximus*, here translated "neighbor," is translated "[very] near" elsewhere in this passage.

Of What Is Written,
*Sanctify a fast, call a solemn assembly**

*Jl 2:15

1. BECAUSE THE SEASON of the forty-day fast is near, I exhort you of your charity to undertake it with complete devotion. I think I should explain how you should fast and what its result should be.

First then, my brothers, by abstaining from what is lawful we are pardoned of the unlawful things we did before. What is the meaning of being forgiven for what we have done if not that by a short fast a perpetual one is warded off! We have deserved hell, where there is never food, no comfort, no end—where the rich man begs for a drop of water and is not worthy to receive it.* That fast is good and salutary, then, that wards off eternal punishment and pardons sins. It is not only the abolition of sins but the uprooting of vices. It not only obtains pardon but wins grace. It not only cancels out sins we have committed in the past but also wards off those we might have committed in the future.

*Lk 16:24

2. I will say only one thing more, which you will understand without difficulty, for, if I am not mistaken, you have often experienced it: fasting gives devotion and confidence to prayer. See how intimately fasting and prayer are joined, for it is written, *Brother helps*

*See Pr 18:19 *brother, and both shall be comforted.** Prayer demands the virtue of fasting, and fasting earns the grace of prayer. Fasting strengthens prayer; prayer sanctifies fasting and offers it to the Lord. What profit do we get from fasting if it remains on earth—which God forbid! Let us lift up fasting, then, on the wing of prayer.

But this wing may not be enough; we must add another to it. *The prayer of the just,* says Scripture, *pierces*
*Si 35:21 *the heavens.** Let our fasting, then, have two wings— prayer and justice—that it may easily pierce the heavens. What is justice but to render to each what belongs to him? Do not, then, pay attention to God alone. You are also indebted to your superiors and to your brothers. God does not wish you to treat as worthless those to whom he attributes great worth. Not without reason does the Apostle say, *Provide good things, not*
*Rm 12:17 *only in God's sight, but in that of humans.** Perhaps you have been in the habit of saying, *It is enough for me if God alone approves what I do. What does the opinion of humans matter to me?* But be assured that he is in no way pleased by whatever you do that gives scandal to his children or is against the will of the one you have to obey as his representative.

*Jl 2:15 *Sanctify a fast, call a solemn assembly.** What does *call a solemn assembly* mean? Maintain unity, cherish peace,
See Eph 4:3; Zec 8:19; 1 Pt 2:17 love the brotherhood. The proud Pharisee kept a fast, he sanctified a fast since he fasted twice a week, and he gave thanks to God; but he did not call a solemn
*Lk 18:11-12 assembly. He said, *I am not like other men,** and so, relying on one wing alone, his fast did not reach heaven. But you, beloved, wash your hands in the blood of
Ps 57:11 a sinner,[1] and take care that your fast has the two wings, holiness and peace, without which no one will

---

[1] See Chrysogonus Waddell, "Shall We Really Wash Our Hands in the Blood of Sinners?" CSQ 44 (2009): 435–45, and especially 443.

see God.* *Sanctify a fast* that a pure intention and devout prayer may offer it to the divine majesty; *call a
solemn assembly* that it may agree in unity; *praise the
Lord with timbrel and dance** that the mortification of
the flesh be done with unity of heart.

3. Now that I have said something about fasting and
about justice it is fitting that I say a few words about
prayer. The more efficacious it is, if done as it should
be, the more skillfully does our adversary usually hinder it. Prayer is gravely hindered by cowardice of spirit
and excessive fear. This often happens when a person
thinks about his own unworthiness so much that he
does not turn his eyes toward divine kindness. But
deep calls to deep,* a deep of light to a deep of darkness,
a deep of mercy to a deep of misery. The human heart
is deep and inscrutable,* but if my iniquity is great,
Lord, much greater is your loving-kindness! Therefore
when my soul is troubled within me,* I remember the
abundance of your mercy* and I am refreshed by it,
and when I enter into my [own] power[2] I will not call
to mind your justice only.*

4. Yet just as there is a danger of prayer being too
timid, so on the other hand there is no less danger, but
rather more, of its being rash. Hear what the Lord says
to the prophet about those who pray thus: *Shout out,
do not cease! Lift up your voice like a trumpet*, and so on.*
Like a trumpet, he says, because the rash ought to be rebuked as by a violent wind!* *They seek me*,° those who
have not yet found themselves. I do not say that I would
take away from sinners their confidence in prayer, but
I want them to pray as people who commit sin, not as
those who act justly. Let them pray with a contrite heart
and humble spirit for forgiveness of their sins, like the
publican who cried, *God, be merciful to me, a sinner*.* I

*Heb 12:14

*Ps 150:4

*Ps 41:8

*Is 29:15;
Jer 17:9 Vulg

*Ps 6:4; Jn 12:27
*Ps 105:7

*Ps 70:16

*Is 58:1

*Ac 2:2
°Is 58:2

*Lk 18:13

---

[2] *In potentias*. Some witnesses have *in impotentias*.

call it rash when a person in whose conscience sin and vice still reign to some extent walks in great matters too wonderful for him,* without consideration for the peril to his own soul.

    A third danger is if his prayer is lukewarm and does not proceed from a lively affection. Timid prayer does not pierce heaven, because immoderate fear binds the soul so that prayer, far from flying upward, cannot even come out. Being lukewarm, it grows weak in its flight and falls because it has no strength. Rash prayer goes up but falls back; it meets resistance, and far from winning grace, it deserves punishment. Prayer that is faithful, humble, and fervent will undoubtedly pierce heaven, and it will certainly not return fruitless.*

*See Ps 130:1

*Jer 50:9

Of the Struggle of the Flesh and the Devil against the Human Spirit, and the Efficacy of Prayer

1. **M**Y LOVING CONCERN for you, brothers, is why I speak to you. It is so compelling that I would speak much more often if I were not prevented by much business. You should not wonder if I am concerned for you, since I find in myself much matter and cause for concern. As often as I think of my own miserable condition and perils of every kind, my soul is troubled within me. I must have no less concern for each of you if I love you as myself. The one who searches hearts knows how often concern for you outweighs concern for myself in my heart. You should not wonder that I have so much concern for you and that great anxiety disturbs me over every one of you when I see you in so miserable a condition and in such great danger. It is clear that we make our own snare, carry our own enemy around everywhere. I am speaking of this flesh, born in sin, nourished in sin, corrupt from its very beginning, but made much worse by its bad habits. This is why it lusts so sharply against the spirit, constantly murmurs, is impatient of discipline, suggests what is

forbidden, and is neither subject to reason nor inhibited by any fear.

2. This the cunning serpent approaches, this he assists, and this he uses to attack us. He has no other desire, no aim or occupation except to shed the blood of our souls. He it is who continually contrives evil, who stirs up the desires of the flesh, who blows on the natural fire of lust with poisonous suggestions, inflames lawless impulses, prepares occasions of sin, and does not cease to tempt the hearts of humans with a thousand harmful tricks. He it is who binds our hands with our own belt and, so it is said, beats us with our own stick, so that the flesh, which was given to help us, becomes for us a ruin and a snare.

3. But what good does it do to point out the dangers without pointing out also some consolation, some remedy that can be applied? The peril indeed is great, and grave is the struggle against an enemy of our own household, particularly as we are strangers and he is a citizen; he dwells in his own land, and we are exiles and pilgrims. Great, too, are the stakes,[1] for we have frequent—no, continuous—fights against the tricks of the devil, the deceiver, whom we cannot see; the subtlety of his nature, combined with his long practice of malice, has made him very clever. It rests with us, however, to refuse to be overcome in this conflict; none of us is overthrown in it against his will. *Your desire, O man, is under you, and you must master it.** The enemy can arouse the impulse of temptation, but it rests with you, if you choose, to give or to refuse consent. You have the capacity, if you choose, to make your enemy your servant so that all things may work together for good. See, the enemy stirs up the desire for food, he puts into the mind vain or impa-

---

[1] *Discrimen.*

tient thoughts, and he arouses the impulse of lust; you alone can refuse your consent, and as many times as you resist so many times will you be crowned.

4. Yet I cannot deny, brothers, that these things are troublesome and dangerous—but if we offer strong resistance in this struggle, we shall have holy tranquility, resulting from a clear conscience. I think, too, that if we refuse to allow those thoughts we frequently find in ourselves to linger but stand up against them with a mighty spirit, the enemy will depart in confusion and not return to that place so readily. But who are we, and what is our strength, that we should be able to resist so many temptations? This surely was what God was looking for, this was what he was working to lead us to, that, seeing our weakness and that we have no other help, we would run toward his mercy with perfect humility. Therefore I ask you, brothers, to have this safe refuge of prayer always at hand. I remember that I spoke of it a short time ago at the end of my sermon.

5. But whenever I speak of prayer, I seem to hear expressed in your hearts some human thoughts that I have also heard frequently from others and sometimes experienced in my own heart. Why is it, seeing that we never cease from prayer, that scarcely ever does any one of us seem to experience the fruit of his prayer? As we come to prayer, so we return; no one responds to us, no one gives us anything, but we seem to have labored in vain. But what says the Lord in the Gospel? *Do not judge by the appearance*, he says, *but judge with right judgment.** What is right judgment but the judgment of faith? *The one made righteous by faith lives.** Follow the judgment of faith, then, and not your own experience, since faith is true but experience is false. What is the truth of faith if not what the Son of God promises: *Whatever you ask for in prayer, believe that you will receive it, and it will come to you?** None of you should think his prayer of small

*Jn 7:24

*Rm 1:17;
Gal 3:11

*Mk 11:24

account, brothers. I tell you that he to whom we pray does not think it of small account. Before it has left your mouth he has ordered it written in his book.* Unquestionably we can hope for one of two things, that he will grant either what we ask, or what he knows is better for us. *We do not know what to pray for as we ought,** but he has pity on our ignorance. He accepts our prayer in his goodness, but does not give us what is not expedient for us or what we should not be given so quickly. Therefore, our prayer will not be fruitless.

6. It shall not be as long as we do as we are instructed in the psalm—that is, if we delight in the Lord. Holy David says, *Delight in the Lord, and he will give you your heart's requests.** But why, O Prophet, do you bid us so absolutely to delight in the Lord, as if we had this delight at our command? We are familiar with delight in food, sleep, tranquility, and other things of the earth; but what reason have we for delighting in God? My brethren, lay people can say this, but not you. Which of you has not often experienced the delight of a good conscience? Who has not savored chastity, humility, and love? This is not the delight of good food or drink or anything of that kind—yet it is delight, and greater than all these others. This delight is divine and not of the flesh; when we delight in these things, plainly we delight in the Lord.

7. But many of you perhaps dispute this, because they rarely experience this emotion that is delightful and sweeter than honey and the honeycomb. For the time being they are disturbed by temptations; they strive more energetically to obtain the virtues, and not for the delight which they experience but for the sake of the virtues themselves, and to please God alone, with all their concentration if not with all their feeling.[2] No doubt a person of this kind fulfills completely

---

[2] *Affectio.*

the prophet's admonition to *delight in the Lord*, since he is not speaking of a feeling[3] but of a practice. The feeling is of happiness, but the practice is of virtue.

Delight in the Lord, he says—strive for this, attempt this—to delight in the Lord—*and he will give you your heart's requests*. Take note that he speaks of a heart's requests that the rational judgment approves. You have no reason to complain, but rather you have reason to occupy yourselves with thanksgiving with all your feelings,[4] since your God has such concern for you that whenever you seek in ignorance what is not to your advantage he does not heed you but changes it for a more advantageous gift. So, too, a father according to the flesh willingly gives his child bread when he asks for it; he does not give him a knife when he asks for it, thinking it unnecessary, but prefers to break the bread he has given him, or order it broken by a servant, so that the child will have no danger or difficulty.

8. Moreover, I think that the heart's requests consist of three things; I don't see anything else that the elect ought to request for themselves. Two of these are transitory—that is, things good for the body and things good for the soul; the third is the happiness of eternal life. Do not be surprised that I said we should seek physical well-being from God, since all physical things are his—just as spiritual well-being is. We must ask him, therefore, and hope for what will sustain us in his service. We must also pray for the things necessary for our souls with greater frequency and fervor—to obtain, that is, grace from God and spiritual virtues. So, too, we must pray with all our piety and desire for eternal life, in which is full and perfect happiness of body and soul.

[3] *Affectu.*
[4] *Affectu.*

9. Therefore, so that we may have our heart's requests in these three matters, we must take heed of three things. In the first, superfluity can creep in; in the second, impurity; and in the third, pride. Sometimes we can seek transitory things from motives of pleasure, virtues from motives of vain show, and some even seek eternal life through confidence in their own merits rather than in humility. I do not mean that grace accepted does not give confidence in prayer, but that no one should base his confidence in making requests on it. These first gifts confer only this: that from the mercy which they bring even greater mercies may be hoped for. So let the prayer for transitory things be restricted to bare necessities; let the prayer for spiritual virtues be free from all impurity and intent only on pleasing God; and let that for eternal life be made in all humility, presuming, as is fitting, only on divine mercy.

SERMON SIX

Of the Pilgrim,
the Dead and the Crucified

*W*E URGE YOU *as strangers and pilgrims to abstain from the desires of the flesh.** Happy are those who conduct themselves as strangers and pilgrims in the present, good for nothing era,* keeping themselves unstained by it!* *Here we have no abiding city, but we seek the one that is to come.** Let us, then, as strangers and pilgrims, *abstain from the desires of the flesh that wage war against the spirit.** Once a pilgrim has entered on a royal road he turns aside neither to right nor to left.* If he should chance to see people quarreling he pays no attention; if he comes upon a wedding, or people having fun dancing, or doing anything else, he passes by because he is a pilgrim and such things do not concern him. He longs for his native land, he makes his way toward it. Having food and clothing he does not wish to be burdened with other things. Happy indeed is the one who thus knows his own home, who complains of his exile, saying to the Lord, *I am a stranger with you, and a pilgrim, like all my forebears.**

This is a big step, but perhaps there is a higher one. Even if a pilgrim does not mingle with the citizens, he sometimes takes pleasure in observing events, hearing of them from others, or himself recounting what

*1 Pt 2:11

*Gal 1:4
*Jm 1:27
*Heb 13:14

*1 Pt 2:11

*Num 20:17;
Dt 2:27

*Ps 38:13

he sees. Even if he is not seriously held back by these things, he is nevertheless delayed and hindered by them; the less he thinks of his true home, the less does desire hurry him on. He can find so much pleasure in these things that not only does he delay and come less speedily; he stays behind altogether so that he does not even arrive late!

2. Who is more separated from worldly activities than a pilgrim? To them the Apostle says, *You have died, and your life is hidden with Christ in God.** A pilgrim can easily be held back from his quest and oppressed by his burden on the pretext of what he needs for his journey; a dead person will not even feel the lack of a tomb! He hears those who heap blame on him as if they are praising him, and those who fawn over him like those who find fault—or rather, he doesn't hear them because he is dead! His death, which keeps him thus unstained, or rather, which separates him inwardly from this world, is altogether happy. Christ has to live in a person who does not live in himself. That is what the Apostle says: *I live, yet not I, for Christ lives in me,** as if he were saying, "I have died to all else; I do not feel, I do not notice, I am not concerned; if these things are truly of Christ, they find me alive and ready. If I can do nothing else, at least I feel pleasure at what I see being done for his honor, and displeasure at what is done for any other reason." This is a very large step.

3. But perhaps we can find something still higher. Where shall we seek it? Where do you suppose, but in him of whom we were just speaking, who was caught up to the third heaven?* What keeps us from speaking of a third heaven if you can find some step above those? Hear him then from his lofty height, not glorying in himself but saying, *Let me not glory except in the cross of our Lord Jesus Christ, through whom the world has been crucified to me and I to the world.** Note that he says not only *dead* to the world, but also *crucified*, which is a

*Col 3:3

*Gal 2:20

*2 Cor 12:2

*Gal 6:14

dishonorable kind of death. I have been crucified to it, he says, just as it has been crucified to me. Everything the world loves is, to me, a cross: pleasures of the flesh, honors, riches, the empty praise of human beings. As for the things the world reckons a cross—I have been attached to them, I cling to them, I embrace them wholeheartedly. Is this not greater than the first and second steps? A pilgrim, if he is wise and not forgetful of his pilgrimage, passes by, although with suffering, and is not much involved in worldly matters.* A dead **2 Tm 2:4* person spurns the blandishments of this world just as much as its hardships. To him who was taken up to the third heaven, the cross is everything to which the world clings, and he clings to the things which seem to the world a cross.

We can also understand the Apostle's words to mean that the world has been crucified to him as a result of his reflecting upon it, and he to the world by compassion. He saw the world bound to the cross by its vices, and he himself was crucified to it by his feelings of compassion.

4. Let us all consider for ourselves what step each of us is set on, and let us be zealous to advance from day to day, because *from strength to strength the God of gods will be seen in Zion.** Especially in this holy season, **Ps 83:8* I beg, let us endeavor to live in all purity. A certain short number of days has been set; otherwise in our human frailty we might lose hope. If we were told, *Be careful at all times to maintain the purity of your way of life,* who would not lose hope? But now we are bidden to amend *the negligences of other times** in a few days so **RB 49.3* that we may taste the sweetness of perfect purity, and that from now on the vestiges of this holy Lent may be radiant in our way of life.[1]

---

[1] *Conversatio.*

Let us try then, my brothers, to use this holy season with all devotion, and now more than ever to repair our spiritual armor. Now is our Savior going out with the entire world as with an army to meet the enemy. Happy are they who fight bravely under such a leader!* The King's household indeed fights all year and is continually ready for war; once, however, at a certain time, he assembles his whole realm in a universal army. Happy are you who are deemed worthy to be his servants! To you the Apostle says, *You are no longer strangers and aliens, but you are citizens with the saints and servants of God.** What will they do, who have undertaken to fight throughout the year, when those who are untrained and previously idle take up spiritual arms? Surely they must press on with their usual battle, more than usual, so that a great victory may result, for the glory of our King, and for our salvation.*

*See RB Prol. 3

*Eph 2:19

*Ph 1:19

On the Birth Day of Saint Benedict [into Heaven]

1. **N**OW that you have all come together to hear a saving word, I am very much afraid, my brothers, that some may receive it unworthily, and that is not how the word of God is to be received. I know that if the earth, which receives the rain that often falls upon it, fails to produce fruit, it may be rejected and all but cursed. For myself, I would prefer to bless, if I could, rather than curse. Or rather, it is not my blessing but your heavenly Father's, which he allows you to receive from my mouth, that I hope will remain with you always, and be incapable of being changed into a curse.

2. We celebrate today our glorious teacher Benedict's birth into heaven, and I owe you the customary solemn sermon for and about him. You must embrace and honor his most illustrious name with perfect delight, for he is your guide, he is your teacher and lawgiver.

I, too, rejoice in the commemoration of this blessed father, although I cannot hear his name without blushing. Along with you, I must imitate him in his renunciation of the world and his profession of monastic discipline. But, unlike you, I share with him the name of abbot. He was an abbot, and so am I. There are *abbots*, and then there are abbots![1] One name [for both of us], but in the second of us only the shadow of the great name! One ministry, but—it pains me to have to say it—how different the ministers, and how unlike one another the practice of the ministry! I cringe to think what will happen to me in the future, blessed

[1] O abbas, et o abbas!

53

Benedict, if I am as far behind in following your holy path then as I find myself to be now!

But I don't need to go on to you about this. I know that I am speaking to people who know me. I ask only that you relieve my embarrassment and fear by brotherly compassion.

3. Since this charge has been entrusted to me, even though I have nothing of my own to set before you I shall ask Saint Benedict for three loaves to feed you with. May his sanctity, his righteousness, and his piety restore you.

Remember, my beloved, that not all those in the Lord's procession spread out their garments.* In that procession, I say, which with the Lord's permission we are soon to celebrate, as the people met him as he was going to his passion seated on an ass,* they did not all spread their garments on the road, but some cut branches from the trees.* This was no great thing; what they had freely received, they freely gave!* Yet even these were not altogether idle, not to mention that they were not driven from the procession. My brethren, holy beast of Christ, you who can say with the prophet, *I have become as a beast before you, and I am always with you,** you on whom Christ is seated—since *the soul of the righteous is the seat of wisdom,** and the Apostle proclaims Christ as the power of God and the wisdom of God*—if I have no garments to spread before your feet, I will try to cut branches from the trees so that nothing may be wanting to so great a procession, and I may do my duty.

4. Blessed Benedict was a tree, tall and fruitful, *like a tree planted near running waters.** Where are the running waters? In the valleys, surely, because *the waters will flow between the hills.** Does anyone fail to see these torrents falling down the steep places of the hills and always diverted into a low place in the middle of the valley? Just as surely, so *God resists the proud, but gives grace to the*

*Mt 21:8

*Jn 12:14

*Mt 21:8
*Mt 10:8

*Ps 72:23
*Pr 12:3 (LXX)

*1 Cor 1:24

*Ps 1:3

*Ps 103:10

humble.* Set your foot safely there, whoever of you is
Christ's beast. Be supported by this branch, and enter
on the valley path. It is certain that on the mountain
is where the ancient serpent has set his chair, *biting the
horse's heels so that its rider falls backward.** Choose, then,
the valley for walking, choose the valley for planting.

We do not choose hills for planting trees because
they are usually dry and stony. The valleys are fertile.
There plants flourish, there is the full ear, there is the
yield of a hundredfold, according to the text, *the valleys will abound with grain.** Everywhere you hear valleys praised, everywhere humility is proclaimed. Plant
where waters run, because an abundance of spiritual
grace is there and the waters above the heavens praise
the name of the Lord—that is, they produce heavenly
blessings, that he may be praised.

Let us stay in this valley, beloved, and let us stay
with our roots buried so that we may not dry out. We
should not be moved by any breeze—as Scripture says,
*If the spirit of the powerful rises against you, do not leave
your place.** No temptation will prevail against you if
you do not occupy yourselves with things too great
and marvelous for you, but endure with strong roots,
rooted and grounded in humility.*

Thus *planted near running waters*, this holy confessor
of the Lord yielded his fruit in its season.*

5. There are people who produce no fruit, people
who produce fruit but not their own, and people who
produce their own fruit but not in due season.

There are *trees without fruit,** like the oak, the elm,
and other trees of the wood; no one plants trees of this
kind in the garden because they do not bear fruit, or
if they do, it is not fit for human consumption, but for
pigs. Such are the children of this age, who spend their
time in reveling and drunkenness, in dissipation and
greed, in debauchery and licentiousness. These things
are the food of the pigs the true Jew is forbidden to

*Jm 4:6

*Gen 49:17

*Mk 4:28;
Ps 64:14

*Qo 10:4

*Ps 130:1;
Eph 3:17

*Ps 1:3

*Jude 12

*Dt 14:8
eat and to which no Christian should adhere.* As the flesh of pigs adheres to our flesh when we eat it to become one flesh, so those who transgress the Lord's command unite themselves to unclean spirits and by adhering to them become one evil spirit with them.

*Dt 14:8
We are forbidden to offer such an animal in sacrifice because it represents unclean and impure spirits.* Abandoning all that is pure, these find filth alone pleasing and delight to take part in a continued feast of vice and crime. So too in the gospel that accursed Legion, when cast out of the man, sought an animal *Mk 5:9-13 like themselves, and were not denied it.* For such as these the unfruitful trees do bear fruit—you can al*Mt 3:10ready see the ax laid at their roots!*

6. The trees that bear fruit but not their own are hypocrites, like Simon of Cyrene carrying a cross not *Lk 23:26; Mt 27:32 his own.* Lacking religious intention, they are under constraint, driven to do what they do not love by love of the glory they desire.

Now as regards the words *in its season* some declare that they wish to bear fruit before its due time. Do we not fear for our trees when they put forth shoots earlier than they should and come into flower unseasonably? There are those whose fruit is less than good because it is too early. At the beginning of their conversion these presume to want to bear fruit immediately for the benefit of others, hastening to plough with a firstling ox and shear a firstling sheep, against *Dt 15:19 the demands of the law.*

Would you know how careful our holy teacher was to avoid this? I put this branch too before you: for three years he remained unknown to humans and *Gregory the Great, Dial 1.1.4 known only to God.* He brought forth much fruit, as you yourselves see, but *in its season*. He did not believe that it was the time for bearing fruit when he was weighed down with such a great temptation of the flesh that he almost gave way, indeed almost gave up.

I will not pass over that branch, for though it is roughened with the prickles of the thorns on which the blessed one[2] of the Lord cast himself,* yet it is altogether profitable. It is profitable to the Lord's beast because of the pits of temptations, to keep it from falling into them by consenting, but rather to resist, striving courageously and waiting for the Lord so that it may not fall into despair. Set your foot here, beast of Christ, and learn. No matter how sharply temptation may rage, believe that you are not therefore abandoned by God. Remember that Scripture says, *Call on me in the day of trouble; I will deliver you, and you shall honor me.** *Gregory the Great, Dial 1.2.2*

Ps 49:15

7. As I was saying, blessed Benedict did not think when he was still tossed about by such temptations that it was the time to bear fruit; the time did come, however, and he produced fruit *in its season*. Three of these I touched on before, his sanctity, his righteousness, and his piety. His miracles demonstrate his sanctity, his teaching demonstrates his piety, and his life demonstrates his righteousness. You see, O beast of Christ, boughs green with foliage, covered with flowers, and laden with fruit. Walk on them to make straight paths for your feet.*

Heb 12:13

How am I to present his miracles to you? Am I to make you wish to work miracles? No, rather that you be supported by his miracles, have complete confidence in them, and rejoice that you are under the protection of such a shepherd and that you have been counted worthy of having so great a patron. He is *a mighty one in heaven** who was powerful on earth, exalted in the greatness of his glory according to the greatness of his grace. Branches are known to produce according to the extent of the roots, and, as the saying goes, "on as many roots as the tree rests, with so many branches is the tree dressed."

2 Mc 15:3

---

[2] Latin, *Benedictus*.

Thus, since we have none of our own, the miracles of our patron should be a great consolation to us. His teaching instructs us and guides our feet into the way of peace. The righteousness of his life strengthens us and gives us life, so that we are roused to do what he taught as we know that his teaching was no different from his actions.* His living and active word was the template of his work, making what he said totally persuasive and showing that what he persuaded was doable.

8. This, then, is how his sanctity comforts, his piety informs, and his righteousness confirms. His piety was so great that he not only benefited those present at the time but was even concerned for those to come! This tree bore fruit not only for those who existed then—its fruit increases and lasts even to the present time! Clearly he was beloved by God and people, and not only must his presence have been a blessing, as is the case with many who are loved only by God because now known only to God, but his memory, too, is blessed now. As even to today he brings us a threefold expression of the love of God, so he feeds the Lord's flock with this threefold fruit, feeds it by his life, by his teaching, and by his prayer for them.

You too must be fruitful, being always aided by him, beloved, when you are in a position to go and bear fruit. What should you go from? Surely from your-selves—as it is written, *turn away from your desires.** We read of the Lord that he went forth to sow his seed.* See, here we have his seed, just as before we had his fruit. Let us be like him, brethren, since he has come to give us his likeness and show us his path.

*Si 18:30; RB 7:19
*1 Cor 15:44

9. But perhaps the Lord himself is also a tree, and we should take from him branches to walk upon. No, not perhaps—truly he is that tree, that heavenly plant, yet he is planted in the earth, as it is written, *truth has sprung from the earth.** I take this branch from him to give to you, so that, just as he emptied himself, you

*Ps 84:12

may have within yourselves this mind—except that it is not so much I who give it to you as it is the Apostle, in whose writings you read, *Have this mind in you that was also in Christ Jesus, who, though he was in the form of God, thought it not robbery to be equal with God, but emptied himself. Taking the form of a servant, he was made in human likeness, and found in human form.*   *Ph 2:5-7

So you, beloved brethren, empty yourselves, humble yourselves, sow yourselves, lose yourselves. *It is sown a physical body, it is raised a spiritual body.** Lose your lives,   *1 Cor 15:44
and you will keep them for eternal life.*   *Jn 12:25

Do you want to know how the Apostle himself did what he taught? He says, *If we are beside ourselves, it is for God; if we are in our right minds, it is for you.** What does   *2 Cor 5:13
that have to do with you? *I have become like a broken vessel.** Someone who never does anything for himself   *Ps 30:13
loses himself in style! That is because his whole intention and whole desire is aimed at pleasing God and bene-fiting his brothers. But the one who sows in the flesh is unhappy, for from the flesh he will reap corruption.* In   *Gal 6:8
another place Scripture says: *Happy those who sow upon all waters.** What does *upon all waters* mean? Perhaps it   *Is 32:30
means upon the waters of which we read, *and you wa-ters above the heavens, let them praise the name of the Lord!**   *Ps 148:4-5
These are the angelic powers and the people of heaven. Thus clearly *we have become a spectacle to angels and men.**   *1 Cor 4:9

10. Let us, then, sow a good example to people by our works done openly, and let us sow great joy for the angels by our hidden sighs and other things of that kind that are known only to them. *For there is joy among the angels of God over one sinner who repents.**   *Lk 15:10
Hence the Apostle said, *providing good things, not only in the sight of God, but also before humans.** He said *in the*   *Rm 12:17
sight of God—that is, in the sight of those who stand before God's face. They are greatly pleased when they see you praying in secret, meditating on some psalm, or doing some other such thing.

You, too, beloved, sow like that and be fruitful like that. Sow like that, too, as many have sown before you. Be fruitful, because they have sown for you! O race of Adam, how many have sown in you, and what precious seed! How shamefully you will perish, and how deservedly, if such seed—and the work of the sowers—should perish in you! To what destruction will you be handed over by the farmer if everything should perish in you? The whole Trinity has sown on our land; the angels and apostles have sown, the martyrs, confessors, and virgins, all have sown. God the Father has sown, uttering a good word from his heart: *The Lord will give goodness, and our earth will yield its fruit.** The Son, too, has sown, for he it is who goes forth to sow his seed.* The Father does not go forth, but the Son proceeds from the Father and comes into the world that he who has first a thought of peace in the Father's heart might become our peace in his mother's womb.* The Holy Spirit too sowed, because he too came, *and divided tongues as of fire appeared to the disciples.** Thus the whole Trinity sowed, the Father bread from heaven, the Son truth, and the Holy Spirit love.*

11. The angels sowed, too, when they stood while others fell. Lucifer, no longer "lucifer," but darkness-bearer and the end of day, said, I *will sit on the mountain of the covenant, and I will be like the most high.** O brash and rash one! A thousand thousands serve him, and ten thousand times ten thousand stand before him*— and will you sit? *Cherubim*, the prophet says, *were standing;** they did not sit. How have you toiled that you should sit? *Are they not all ministering spirits for the sake of those who are heirs of salvation?**—and will you sit? What have you sown, that you should now reap?* It is not for you, not for you, but for those for whom it has been prepared by the Father.* Why do you envy them? Certainly they will sit down. The very worms of the earth, I say, will sit in judgment,* and you will

Pss 44:2; 84:13
Lk 8:5

*Jn 16:28;
Jer 29:11*

Ac 2:3

*Ws 16:20;
Jn 1:17; Rm 5:5*

Is 14:13-14

Dn 7:10

Ez 10:3

Heb 1:14
Lk 19:21-22

Mt 20:23

Mt 19:28

not only stand but you will stand to be judged. *Do you not know*, the Apostle says, *that we shall judge angels?**   *1 Cor 6:3

*Those who went forth weeping, bearing their seed, shall come home with joy, carrying their sheaves.** There are two   *Ps 125:6 sheaves you seek, honor and tranquility. You strive after the right to sit in a lofty place; but not so, not so:* you shall not reap because you have not sown.   *Ps 1:4 Those who have sown [by undergoing] hardships and contempt shall reap honor and tranquility. For their double share of shame and disgrace they shall receive double on their land.* That is why someone said, *Look*   *Is 61:7 *upon my humiliation and my hardship.**   *Ps 24:18

You heard today in the gospel the Lord promising his disciples, saying, *You will also sit on twelve thrones, judging the twelve tribes of Israel.** See the tranquility of   *Mt 19:28 sitting and the honor of judging! Even the Lord himself was unwilling to attain these except through humiliation and hardship. Hence he was condemned to a most shameful death, examined with tortures, and filled with insults, but surely so that the enemy, both he and those who imitate him and pass along the way, might be clothed with shame.*   *Jb 8:22

[The Lord] it is, O wicked one, he it is who will sit on the throne of glory like the Most High, and most high with him.* This is surely what the holy angels   *Mt 19:28; thought when the wicked one fell. They took no part   Is 14:14 in his apostasy and so left us an example that as they chose to serve, so we should do also.* Those who flee   *Lk 10:18; from hardship and snatch at honor know that they are   Jn 13:15 imitating him who sought a lofty seat; if his crime is not enough to frighten, let his punishment be so! Everything has come out other than he thought—that he might be *formed to play in* [the great sea]*—and   *Ps 103:26 eternal fire has been prepared for him.* To prevent   *Mt 25:41 this, the holy angels sowed the seeds of wisdom for us—those who had earlier held firm when the others transgressed.

12. The apostles also sowed this for us when, departing from those who followed the wisdom of this world, which is foolishness with God,* and the wisdom of the flesh, which works death and is an enemy to God,* they held to the Lord alone.* Those who were offended by him when they heard of the sacrament of the body and blood were no longer with him.* When the disciples were asked whether they would go away they answered, *To whom shall we go? You have the words of eternal life.**

My brethren, we must imitate this wisdom, because there are many still who walk with Jesus until it comes to eating his flesh and drinking his blood, that is to say, sharing in his sufferings—for that is the meaning of his words and of the sacrament. Then they are offended and turn back, saying, *this teaching is hard.** Let us be wise like the apostles and say, *Lord, to whom shall we go? You have the words of eternal life. We do not forsake you, and you will give us life. One does not live by bread alone, but by every word that comes from the mouth of God.** The world is not alone in possessing delight—there is much more delight in your words! So the prophet says, *How sweet are your words to my taste, sweeter than honey to my mouth!** To whom, then, should we go? *You have the words of eternal life*, Lord, and they are above everything that the world can offer. Not only life itself, but the promise of eternal life* and the hope of the righteous: this is gladness, such gladness that nothing one could desire can be compared with it. This is the wisdom the holy apostles sowed for us. The martyrs clearly sowed fortitude. Then the confessors sowed justice and pursued it throughout their lives. The difference between martyrs and confessors is that between Peter, who left everything at once, and Abraham who put his worldly goods to good use. The former were made perfect, having lived a long life in a short time, but the latter dragged out a long and manifold martyrdom. As for the holy virgins, it is clear that they sowed temperance, for they trampled lust under foot.

*1 Cor 3:19
*Rm 8:6-7;
2 Cor 7:10
*1 Cor 6:17

*Jn 6:61-68

*Jn 6:68

*Jn 6:60, 66

*Jn 6:68;
Ps 79:19; Mt 4:4

*Ps 118:103

*2 Tm 1:1

ON THE ANNUNCIATION OF THE LORD

SERMON ONE

On the Verse of the Psalm,
That Glory May Dwell in Our Land

1. *T*HAT GLORY *may dwell in our land, mercy and truth have met, righteousness and peace have kissed.** *This is our glory*, says the Apostle, *the testimony of our conscience**—not a testimony like that of the proud Pharisee, who, mistaken, and by a mistaken judgment, gave testimony to himself.* His testimony was not true, but the Spirit himself gives testimony to our spirit.*

    Now I think that this testimony consists of three things. First of all, you must believe that you cannot have remission of your sins except by God's goodness; then, that you cannot have any good work at all unless he grants it to you; and finally, that you cannot earn eternal life by any works unless that too is given you freely. *Who can make clean one conceived of unclean seed, except the one who alone is clean?** Surely what is done cannot be undone—yet if God does not impute it, it will be as if nonexistent. The prophet also, reflecting on this, says, *Blessed is the one to whom the Lord has not imputed sin.** It is certainly true that no one has good works by means of himself. If human nature could not stand while it was still unimpaired how much less can it rise of itself now that it is corrupt? Certainly all things tend toward their source, as far as they can, and

*Ps 84:10-11

*2 Cor 1:12

*Lk 18:11-12

*Rm 8:16

*Jb 14:4

*Ps 31:2

63

in it [that is, human nature] there is always a downward tendency. So it happens that we, having been created out of nothing, always fall into sin, which is nothing, if left to ourselves.

2. Moreover, we know of life eternal that *the sufferings of this present time are not to be compared with the glory to come*,* not even if one person were to endure them all. Human merits are not such that we have a right to eternal life and that God would be doing us an injury if he did not bestow it! Let me pass over the fact that all our merits are God's gifts, and therefore we are more indebted to God than God to us—what are all merits in comparison with such great glory? Who is worthier than the prophet to whom God gives such signal testimony as to say, *I have found a man after my own heart*?* Yet he had to say to God, *Do not enter into judgment with your servant*.* No one so deceives himself that, if he chooses to think correctly, he will not discover that *with ten thousand he cannot oppose one who comes to him with twenty thousand*.*

3. What I have just said is by no means enough, but it is a beginning and can be taken as the foundation of faith. So if you believe that your sins cannot be wiped out except by him against whom only you have sinned, and to whom sin does not belong, you are right.

But in addition you must believe this: that sins are forgiven you by him. This is the testimony that the Holy Spirit* gives in our hearts when he says, *Your sins are forgiven you*.* Thus the Apostle testified that people are justified by faith as a gift.* So if you believe that you cannot possess merits except through him, this is not enough, until the Spirit of truth* testifies to you that you have them through him. Likewise you must have the testimony of the Spirit with regard to eternal life,* because you can attain it only by a divine gift. He forgives sins, he bestows merits, and no less does he reward us.

*Rm 8:18

*Ac 13:22
*Ps 142:2

*Lk 14:31

*Jn 1:19
*Mt 9:5
*Rm 3:24, 28

*Jn 15:26

*Mt 19:16

4. Furthermore, these testimonies have been made exceedingly believable. I hold a very powerful argument for the remission of sins: the Lord's passion. The voice of his blood is far stronger than the voice of Abel's,* and it proclaims the remission of all the sins in the hearts of the elect. He was handed over for our sins,* and we cannot doubt that his death is more powerful and effective for good than our sins are for evil. Nevertheless his resurrection is for me the most potent proof of good works, because *he rose for our justification.** Further, his ascension is testimony to our hope of reward, because he ascended for our glorification.

*Gen 4:10; Heb 12:24

*Rm 4:21

*Rm 4:25

We have these three ideas in the psalms. The prophet says, *Happy is the one to whom the Lord imputes no sin,** and in another place, *Happy is the one whose help is from you,** and again, *Happy is the one whom you have chosen and brought near; he will dwell in your courts.** This is true glory, indwelling glory, because it comes from him who dwells in our hearts through faith.* The children of Adam, seeking the glory which is from one another, did not desire the glory that is from God alone;* thus, pursuing the glory which comes from without, they had glory, not in themselves, but rather in others.

*Ps 31:2

*Ps 83:6

*Ps 64:5

*Eph 3:17

*Jn 5:44

5. Do you wish to know the source of the glory that dwells in us? I will tell you in a few words, because my intention is to hasten on to the mystical meaning.[1] I had set before myself the task of tracing this alone in the prophet's words, but what the Apostle said about the glory within and the testimony of our conscience* struck me first and turned me back to the moral aspect.

*2 Cor 1:12

This glory dwells here in our land if mercy and truth meet and righteousness and peace kiss.* The truth of

*Ps 84:10-11

---

[1] *Mystica intentio.*

our confession must come to meet the mercy that goes before it, and in all other respects we must pursue the holiness and peace *without which no one will see God*.* When someone feels compunction, mercy is going before him, but he will not advance until the truth of his confession runs to meet it. *I have sinned against the Lord*, David said to Nathan the prophet, when he was charged with adultery and murder. *And the Lord has put away your sin*, said the prophet.*

*Heb 12:14

*2 Sm 12:13

Truly *mercy and truth have met*, and this is to turn you away from evil. Indeed, that you may now do good, you must praise him with timbrel and dance,* so that the very mortification of your flesh, the fruits of penitence, and the works of righteousness* may be done in unity and concord—since the unity of the Spirit is the bond of perfection*—and you may turn neither to the right nor to the left.* There are people whose right hand is the right hand of iniquity. The Pharisee, whom I mentioned earlier, was not like other men;* he gave testimony to himself, as I said, but his testimony was not true.* No doubt one in whom *mercy and truth have met, righteousness and peace have kissed*, may glory safely; but let him glory in him who gives testimony to himself, in the Spirit of truth.

*Ps 150:4

*Ti 3:5

*Eph 4:3;
Col 3:14
*Dt 5:32;
Pr 4:37

*Lk 18:11

*Jn 5:31; 8:13

6. *That glory may dwell in our land, mercy and truth have met, righteousness and peace have kissed.** If *a wise son is the glory of his father*,* since no one is wiser than Wisdom himself, then clearly Christ, the power of God and the wisdom of God,* is the glory of the Father. Because in many and various ways it had been foretold of him by the prophets* that he would be seen on earth and would live with humankind,* how that was to come about, and how all that had been said of him through all the prophets would be fulfilled*—that glory would dwell in our land—the psalmist indicates in these words: that the Word might become flesh and dwell among us* *mercy and truth have met, righteousness and peace have kissed.*

*Ps 84:10-11
*Pr 13:1, according to an ancient version
*1 Cor 1:24

*Heb 1:1
*Bar 3:37

*Lk 24:44;
Ac 3:18

*Jn 1:14

This is a great mystery, my brethren, and we must carefully look into it, lest we fail to understand it and lack the words to express our understanding. I am saying, however inadequately, what I think, though I may seem to have given an occasion to the clever.* **1 Tm 5:14*

Beloved, I seem to see the first man arrayed in these four virtues from the very beginning of his creation and, as the prophet recalls, clad in the garment of salvation.* In these four is the wholeness of salvation, and salvation cannot exist without them all, particularly since virtues cannot exist if they are separated from each other. **Is 61:10*

The man had, then, received mercy as his guardian and attendant, to go before him and to follow him, to protect and keep him safe everywhere. You see what nourishment God prepared for his little child, what kind of attendant he gave to man who was born but recently.

He needed a teacher as well, however, for he was a free-born and reasoning creature, and was not to be guarded like a beast of burden but brought up like a child. No better teacher could be found for him than Truth himself, who could bring him in the end to the perception of the highest truth.

Meanwhile, lest being wise he might find a way to do evil and commit sin as one who knows the good and fails to do it,* he was given righteousness also, by which he could be ruled. And the kindly hand of the Creator added peace as well, by which he might be cherished and delighted—indeed a twofold peace, that there should be no disputes within nor fears without,* that is, that flesh should not lust against the spirit,* nor should any creature cause him alarm. He freely gave names to every animal, and the serpent, because he could not succeed by violence, attacked him by treachery. What did he lack, when mercy guarded him, truth taught him, righteousness ruled him, and peace cherished him? **Jm 4:17*

*2 Cor 7:5, though with adverbs transposed
*Gal 5:17

7. But then—it grieves me to have to say it!— to his own great harm and folly the man went down from Jerusalem to Jericho.* He fell among thieves, by whom we read he was first of all stripped. Is he not stripped who, when the Lord comes in, bewails the fact that he is naked?* Nor could he be clothed again or receive the clothing taken from him, unless Christ put off his own. Just as he could not live spiritually except by the physical death of Christ, so he could not be clothed again except by Christ's stripping. And see, the clothing of the second, the new man, was divided into four parts, like the clothing which the first, the old man, had put off.

*Lk 10:30

*Mt 22:11-12

But perhaps you seek the seamless tunic,* which is not divided, but is won by lot? I think it is the divine image, which, not being sewn, but engrafted and imprinted on nature, can be neither divided nor cut. Humankind is made in the image and likeness of God,* possessing freedom of choice in the image and virtues in the likeness. The likeness perishes—*surely humankind passes as an image.** The image can burn in hell but not burn up, can blaze up but not be destroyed. Therefore it cannot be torn, but perhaps it can be won by lot. Wherever the soul goes, the image will be there likewise. The likeness is not like it but either endures in a good person or, if the soul sins, is pitiably changed, like senseless beasts.*

*Jn 19:23-24

*Gen 1:26; 9:6

*Ps 38:7

*Ps 48:13

8. But because we have said that the man was stripped of the four virtues, let us say how it was fitting that he was stripped of each one individually. Man lost righteousness when Eve obeyed the serpent's voice, and Adam the woman's, rather than God's.* Still, something remained for them to hold on to. The Lord indicated this by his investigation.* Yet they cast this away too by turning to evil words to make excuses for sins.* The first part of righteousness is not to sin, and the second is to condemn sin by penitence.

*Gen 3:1-7

*Gen 3:9-13

*Ps 140:4

He lost mercy as well when Eve was so inflamed with desire* that she spared neither herself, nor her husband, nor the children to be born, but delivered them all together to the terrible curse and necessity of death. In addition, Adam threw in the teeth of divine wrath the woman in whose presence he had sinned, as if wanting to divert the arrow to behind his back! The woman saw the tree, that it was pleasant to look upon and sweet to the taste,* and she had heard the serpent say that they would be as gods.* *A threefold cord is difficult to break,* one made up of curiosity, pleasure, and vanity. This is all the world has to offer, the desire of the flesh, the desire of the eyes, and the pride of life.* Lured and enticed* by these, our cruel mother cast aside all mercy. So too Adam, who was so lacking in compassion for the woman that he sinned with her, was unwilling to pity her or endure punishment for her.

Dn 13:8 Vulg [Susanna 8]

*Gen 2:9; 3:6
*Gen 3:5
*Qo 4:12

*1 Jn 2:16
*Jm 1:14

The woman was deprived of the truth as well, first distorting what she had heard, *you shall die*, to *lest perhaps we die*, and at length believing the serpent when he altogether denied it and said, *you shall surely not die.** Adam too was deprived of the truth when he was ashamed to acknowledge it, making any excuses that occurred to him to cover himself. Truth himself said, *Those who are ashamed of me before humans, I shall also be ashamed of them.**

*Gen 2:17; 3:3, 4

*Lk 9:26, after an ancient version

They straightaway lost peace, because *there is no peace for the wicked, says the Lord.** Had they not found a contrary law in their members* that began to shame them with the novelty of nakedness? *I was afraid*, he said, *because I was naked.** You were not so wretched, nor were you so frightened a short time ago; you were not looking for leaves, although your body was naked, just as it is now.

*Is 48:22; 57:21
*Rm 7:21, 23

*Gen 3:10

9. Hence—to follow the parable of the Prophet, who recorded that they met and were reconciled in a kiss—serious strife seems to have arisen among the virtues. If Truth and Righteousness rained blows on

the wretched man, Peace and Mercy, being free of this zeal, thought it better to spare him. These latter two are paired just as the former two were.

So it happened that as the former continued in their vengeance, attacking the transgressor from this side and that and heaping the threat of future punishment on present troubles, so the latter withdrew to the Father's heart, returning to the Lord who gave them. He alone was thinking thoughts of peace* when everything seemed full of affliction. Peace was not inactive, nor was Mercy silent, but they spoke in a holy whisper, beating, as it were, at the entrails of the Father, *Will the Lord cast us off forever, and never again be favorable? God will not forget to show mercy, will he, or in his anger shut up his compassion?** And although the Father of compassion might seem to dissemble long and greatly so as to satisfy the zeal of Righteousness and Truth, the pertinacity of those who prayed to him was not fruitless, but was heard at an acceptable time.*

10. Perhaps an answer such as this may have been given to those who demur: "How long will your prayers go on? I am in debt to your sisters, Righteousness and Truth, whom you see ready *to take vengeance on the nations.** Let them be summoned, let them come, and let us confer together about this saying." The heavenly messengers come quickly, and as they see the misery of humans and their cruel punishment, let the prophet say, *The messengers of peace weep bitterly.**

Who seek the things that belong to Peace more faithfully than messengers of peace? Truth arose from their deliberation on the agreed day, but she rose to the clouds, not clearly and openly but in some darkness, and clouded over still by the zeal of indignation. It happened as we read in the prophet, *Lord, your mercy is in heaven and your truth reaches even to the clouds.** The Father of lights* sat in their midst, and each spoke what was most expedient for each side.

*Jer 29:11

*Ps 76:8, 10

*Pss 31:6; 144:15

*Ps 149:7

*Is 33:7

*Ps 35:6
*Jm 1:17

Who do you think was worthy to take part in that conversation and to report it to us? Who heard it and will describe it? Perhaps it cannot be described, and no human may speak of it.* Here, in any case, is what the whole dispute seems to have been about:

"The rational creature is in need of compassion," says Mercy, "since he has become pitiable and truly deserving of pity. *The time has come to have mercy on him*,* indeed the time has passed."

Truth says the contrary: "*The word you have spoken must be fulfilled, Lord*.* Adam had to die entirely, with all who were in him, on the day he transgressed by tasting the forbidden fruit."

"Why," says Mercy, "why have you brought me to birth, Father, when I am to die so soon? Truth herself knows that your mercy perishes and is no more, if you never have pity."

Similarly, she who speaks on the other side says, "Who does not know that if a transgressor escapes the prescribed sentence of death your truth perishes, nor will it remain forever, O Lord?"*

11. See, one of the cherubim suggests that they should be sent to King Solomon, because all judgment, Scripture says, was given to the Son.* In his sight *Mercy and Truth have met*, just as we said before when we were recalling the words of the complaint. "I confess," says Truth, "that Mercy has good zeal; now only if it were based on intelligence!* Why is she now judging that the transgressor should be spared rather than her sister?" "But you," says Mercy, "spare neither. On the contrary, you so fiercely vent your rage on the transgressor that you engulf your sister too! Why do I deserve this? If you have anything against me, tell me! If not, why do you persecute me?"*

This is a great problem, my brothers, and a perplexing debate. In such circumstances who would not say, "It would have been better for us if that man

*2 Cor 12:4

*Ps 101:14

*Lk 22:37

*Ps 118:89-90

*Jn 5:22

*Rm 10:2

*Ac 9:4; 22:7;
Jn 18:23

*Mt 26:24
had not been born"?* That was the situation, beloved, such indeed it was. There seemed to be no way that both Mercy and Truth could be preserved. And when Truth added that the merits of her case turned back against the judge himself—that at all costs the Father's word must not be made ineffective, his living and ac-

*Heb 4:12
tive word* emptied of all meaning—then Peace said, "Spare us, I beg you, spare us words of this kind. A quarrel of this kind does not befit us: it is a dishonorable disagreement of virtues."

12. Then the Judge bent down and wrote with his

*Jn 8:6
finger on the ground.* The words were the words of Scripture, which Peace herself reads in the hearing of everyone—if indeed she can get close enough. This one says, "I perish if Adam does not die," and this one says, "I perish if he does not win mercy. Let there be a good death, and each possess what she asks."

Everyone was astonished at the word of wisdom and the beauty of both the argument and the verdict. It was clear that no grounds for their complaints remained; what each asked would be possible: that he should die, and that he should win mercy.

*Lk 1:34
"But how will this come about,"* they ask. "Death is very cruel and bitter; death is terrible and dreadful to hear about. How can it be made good?" But he says, "The death of the wicked is very evil, but the death of

*Ps 33:22 Vulg; Ps 115:15
the saints can be made precious.* Indeed, how will it not be precious if it is the door to life, the gate of glory?"

"It will be precious," they say; "but how will this come about?"

"It can be brought about," he says, "if a person not deserving of death dies out of love. Death cannot hold a blameless person, but, as it is written, the jaw of Leviathan will be pierced, the dividing wall will

*Jb 41:1-2; Eph 2:14; 1 Cor 15:26; Lk 16:26
*Sg 8:6
be destroyed, and the great chasm that is fixed between life and death will be removed.* Love is strong as death*—no, rather, stronger than death; if a strong

man enters his court,* he will bind him and seize his
property; by his very passing he will make the depths
of the sea a way so that the delivered may pass over."*

*Lk 11:21;
Mt 12:29

*Is 51:10

13. The saying seems good, inasmuch as it is sure and
worthy of full acceptance.* But where could there be
found an innocent person willing to die, not because
he deserved to, not for any evil he had done, but out
of his own gracious purpose?* Truth takes the world's
measure, and *no one is free from filth, not even a child
whose life has lasted one day on earth.** But also, Mercy
traverses the whole of heaven and finds among the angels, I won't say wickedness, but less love. Evidently this
victory was due to another, than whom no one has
greater love, so that he would lay down his life* for his
unprofitable and unworthy servants. The fact that he
no longer calls us servants* is a mark of boundless love
and extreme respect. We, however, even if we did all
that we were commanded to do, what else should we
say than that we are unprofitable servants?*

*1 Tm 1:15; 4:9

*See Eph 1:9

*Jb 14:4 after an
ancient version

*Jn 15:13

*Jn 15:15

*Lk 17:10

But who would presume to agree with him about
this? Truth and Mercy return on the agreed day, greatly
troubled, without finding what they sought.

14. Then Peace consoled them separately. "*You,*" she
said, "*know nothing, nor do you understand. There is no one
who does good, no, not one.** May he who gave counsel bring help." The King understood what she was
saying, and said, "*I repent that I have made man.** The
penalty is binding upon me, and I must bear the punishment and do penance for the man I have created."
Then he said, "*See, I come. This cup cannot pass away except I drink it.*"* And immediately summoning Gabriel,
he said, "Go, say to the daughter of Sion, *Behold your
King.*"* He made haste and said, "*Zion, deck the bridal
chamber, and receive your King.*"[2] Then Mercy and Truth

*Jn 11:49-50;
Pss 13:1; 52:4

*Gen 6:7

*Heb 10:7;
Mt 26:42

*Mt 21:5

---

[2] Antiphon *Adorna* for Candlemas.

went before the King who is to come, as it is written, *Mercy and Truth go before your face.* Righteousness prepares a throne, according to the saying, *Righteousness and Judgment are the preparation of your throne.** Peace comes with the King, so that the prophet might be found faithful* who said, *Peace shall be in our land when he comes.*[3] This is the source of what the angelic chorus sang at the Lord's birth, *Peace on earth to people of good will.**

But then, too, *Righteousness and Peace have kissed,* which does not seem very different. But if there is any righteousness that comes from the law,* there ought first to be a sting rather than a kiss, driving on by fear rather than urging by love. But this righteousness does not contain reconciliation, as does now the righteousness that we recognize comes from faith.* Otherwise why was it that Abraham, Moses, and the other just ones of that time could not receive the peace of eternal beatitude at their deaths or enter the kingdom of peace, except that righteousness and peace had at that time not yet kissed?

Therefore, beloved, we must pursue righteousness* with burning zeal. *Righteousness and Peace have kissed* and formed an indissoluble bond of friendship, so that whoever bears the mark of Righteousness may be received by Peace with a joyful countenance and glad embraces, sleeping and resting in the selfsame.

*Ps 88:15

*Si 36:18

*Lk 2:14

*Rm 10:5

*Rm 10:6

*1 Tm 6:11

---

[3] Mi 5:5 as in the responsory *Bethlehem* on the third Sunday of Advent.

On the Annunciation of the Lord

SERMON ONE

Alternate Version

THIS IS A GREAT MYSTERY,* my broth-   *Eph 5:32*
ers, and who can understand it? Yet I will say
something, since it is my duty to say what I
experience.[1] The first man was arrayed in the four virtues at his creation, wherefore he said that *he has clothed
me with the garment of salvation.** Nothing less than that   *Is 61:10*
would suffice for the fullness and completeness of his
salvation, nothing more was necessary. Adam was first
given mercy to protect him; while he preserved mercy,
no doubt it would preserve him, because mercy merits
mercy. Thus the Lord's mercy would go before him
and follow him* as his guardian and attendant.   *Pss 58:11 Vulg; 22:6*

But it was not right that [mercy] should guard
so noble a creature, stamped with the image of his
creator, like some dumb animal, devoid of reason.
Therefore he was given truth to teach him so that
he might someday attain recognition of the supreme
truth. But because *one who knows the good and fails to
do it commits sin,** lest, as some say, he should be wise   *Jm 4:17*
to do evil,* he was given righteousness to guide him.   *Jer 4:22*

One thing was lacking to his perfect salvation—that
is, peace. Yet even this was not lacking, for so great was
his interior peace that he felt no disturbing emotions

---

[1] *Sentio.*

75

Rm 7:23
at all, no lust, no curiosity, no experiencing the law of sin.* His exterior peace was such that, as a man, he feared no wild beast nor any other creature. For he gave names to every wild beast, and no enemy dared to try his strength against him to attack him by treachery.

What, then, did he lack, when he was guarded by mercy, taught by truth, guided by righteousness, and nurtured by peace?

7. That man, to his great undoing, went down from *Lk 10:30ff.* Jerusalem to Jericho and fell among thieves,* who first of all stripped him. For this reason at the coming of the *Mt 22:11-12* Lord he confessed that he was naked.* He could only be reclothed and receive these garments again if Christ would lose his own. Just as he could not live again spiritually except by Christ's physical death, so he could not be reclothed except by Christ's being stripped.

Therefore for the sake of the four parts of his clothing which the first and old man had lost, the garments *1 Cor 15:45-46* of the second,* the new man, so we read, were divided *Jn 19:23* into four parts.* But what was the seamless robe that *Jn 19:24* was not divided but won by lot?* It is the image of God, not patched together, but grafted into and imprinted on nature, so that it cannot in any way be divided and separated from it.

Man was created in the image and likeness of God— in his image because of freedom of choice, in his like- *Gen 1:26; 9:6* ness because of the virtues.* The likeness can burn in hell, but it cannot be destroyed; for that reason it is not torn, but as it happens,[2] wherever the soul ends up it will be there too. He does not bear the likeness of God with himself in a malicious way but is rather *Ps 48:13* compared to senseless beasts and becomes like them.*

---

[2] *Forte.*

8. But because we have said that the first man was stripped, it is fitting that we tell how he was stripped. The man lost mercy by disobedience when he condemned to a terrible curse and the necessity of death not only himself but all his posterity, his children as yet unborn. Eve was so inflamed with desire* that she spared neither her husband, nor us, nor even herself. *A threefold cord is difficult to break** and the three are the desire of the flesh, the desire of the eyes, and worldly ambition,* by which the woman was lured and enticed.* She saw the tree, that it was pleasant to look upon—that is, curiosity; and was good to eat—that is, pleasure. Third, the serpent found her and said, *You will be like Gods,** which is vanity. Enticed by these, our cruel mother cast aside all mercy. *If one is evil to himself, to whom will he be good?** So the first man—for the two, Adam and Eve, were in a certain way one, not two—lost mercy.*

*Dn 13:8 Vulg; Susanna 8

*Qo 4:12
*1 Jn 2:16 according to an ancient version
*Jm 1:14

*Gen 3:6; 2:9; 3:5

*See Si 14:5

*Gen 2:24

Further, the man lost truth when God came and called, *Where are you?** In the first place he did violence to the truth when he was ashamed of it and was unwilling to confess where he was. Truth himself said, *Of one who is ashamed of me, I will also be ashamed.**

*Gen 3:9

*Lk 9:26 after an ancient version

In the second place he clearly spoke against the truth; he lied against his own head.* *Lord, I heard your voice and I hid myself.*[3] Not so, wicked one, not so;* you have lost the whole truth. You might more truly have said, *I heard the voice of the serpent, or of the woman, and I hid myself.* The sound of the divine voice did not strip you and make you hide yourself; it was because you obeyed the words of your wife,* for *one who does evil hates the light.**

*Dn 13:55, 59 Vulg; Susanna 55, 59
*Ps 1:4

*Gen 3:17
*Jn 3:20

---

[3] Gen 3:10 as in the responsory *Dum deambularet* in Septuagesima.

He lost a first part of righteousness when he obeyed the voice of his wife rather than that of God. Yet one part remained by which he could, as with a horn, defend his nakedness; and though God signified how he might keep it, the unhappy man threw even that away. The first part of righteousness is to refrain from sin; the second part is to condemn sin by confession and repentance. Therefore the Lord tried to draw a confession from them, but they both turned *to making excuses*

*Ps 140:4 Vulg

*in their sins.**

When these three virtues had been driven out, Peace could not remain, since *there is no peace for the*

*Is 48:22

*wicked, says the Lord.** Because he cast aside the rest, she became angry, and the unhappy man was cast out of

*Gen 3:23-24

paradise* and exposed to every misery.

9. When the virtues had been thus spurned and banished, they considered what they should do. And see, Truth counsels them, saying, "You, Peace and Mercy, return to God the Father; Righteousness and I will

*Dn 13:22 Vulg;
Susanna 22

pursue Adam, that he escape not our hands;* for unless you pray while we pursue him, he would be extremely cast down and would perish." So Peace and Mercy re-

*Qo 12:7

turn to the Lord who gave them,* while Righteousness and Truth pursue the unhappy exile to avenge the injuries done to the four of them. They bear him here and there, to the point of utter destruction with cruel

*Ps 7:3

punishment, *while there is no one to redeem or save* him.*

*2 Cor 7:5

*There are combats without and fears within.** His physical weariness increases and, nevertheless, his conscience burning, he earnestly demands more interior things. Righteousness did not rest and Truth gave no pause in inflicting many ills and uttering ever more bitter and intolerable threats.

But could Mercy forget her own nature, or the given discord be pleasing to Peace? Of course not! They were in the Father's heart; they importune him

*2 Tm 4:2

in season and out of season,* beating upon his kind

spirit with pitiable prayer, asking for peace and pardon
with tearful voices. Mercy sighed and won his pater-
nal affection with her humble whispers: *How long, O
Lord? Will you be angry forever, and your zeal be like a fire?
Will the Lord cast us off forever, and never again be favorable? Will God forget to show mercy, or will he in his anger
shut up his mercies?**   *Pss 78:5;
76:8, 10

While Mercy uttered these and other like words
first, Peace in the same way added, *Hear, O Lord; be
appeased, O Lord—listen and act. You are the father of mer-
cies, gracious and merciful, exalted above evil.** And also, *Let*   *Dn 9:19; 2 Cor
there be peace in your strength.* What can he do, whose   1:3; Jl 2:13
nature is goodness, whose characteristic is always to
have mercy and to spare?[4]

And [the Lord] said to Mercy, *Can a mother forget the
child of her womb? Even if she should forget, yet I will not
forget you.**   *Is 49:15

10. Truly, as I am a debtor to you,* so am I to your sis-   *Rm 1:14
ters, Righteousness and Truth, who are on earth. Now
is the time to call them, and, when you come together,*   *1 Cor 1:20
we will take counsel as to what is to be done. If you can
come to some agreement with them, they will have to
give way to your importunity and do what you ask.

So they came, and seeing what was happening on
earth, the messengers of peace wept bitterly.* They came   *Is 33:7
together and spoke to Truth and Righteousness but
could scarcely draw a reply from them. Righteousness
did not consent to curtail vengeance for a while but said
to Truth, *Go up to the festival yourselves; I will not go up,**   *Jn 7:8
that you may be more circumspect and may better ob-
serve. Then Truth altogether refused to enter heaven but
promised that she would go to the clouds; indignation
clouded her mind, and she raged against the unhappy
man with great fury. Thus were the words of the psalm

---

[4] See Ps 121:7; *Prayer of the Roman Liturgy for the day of death or of burial.*

fulfilled, *Your mercy is great above the heavens, and your truth reaches even to the clouds*; and again, *Lord, your mercy is in heaven and your truth reaches even to the clouds.**

*Pss 107:5; 35:6

*Jm 1:17

Then, with the Father of lights* sitting in their midst, Mercy, inspired by the counsel of Peace, said, *Lord, you brought me, Mercy, to birth; but now is the time to have mercy,** because the man, a noble creature, has plunged himself into misery. Otherwise, where are your mercies, Lord? And Truth replied, Let it be done, Lord, according to the next words, *as you swore in your truth.** And, as she always had a ready tongue, she added, "Lord, you yourself told Adam, *On the day that you eat the tree of knowledge of good and evil you shall die.** Let what went forth from your lips not be fruitless, *for the truth of the Lord abides forever.** I indeed would have perished if your words had not been fulfilled.* So deal with my sister that I do not perish on her account."

*Ps 101:14

*Ps 88:50

*Gen 2:17

*Pss 88:35; 116:2

But Mercy, as was her wont, turned the Father's mind toward herself by her humble and submissive voice, her tearful and pitiable face. Speaking from the same quarter she repeated what Truth had said, "I also am your daughter, Father, if you judge fairly, and you need not cast me away because of her. Truth herself knows, and your fatherly affection knows, that if you have no mercy, I, Mercy, must perish. If such is your mind, Father, why did you bring me to birth if I am to perish so soon?" Truth said the same thing.

Peace, modest as ever, humbly suggested to the Father that Mercy should be heard. Truth was scornful, yet Peace was solicitous for the one who scorned her. Then Truth cried out in opposition, "If you wish to spare someone, my sisters, should you not spare your sister rather than the transgressor?" Mercy replied, "If you were to inveigh so fiercely only against the transgressor, it would seem more tolerable; but now you rise up against your sister just as much."

So they spoke, by turns and with anger. When Truth said, "You two sisters are united against me; I have no one remaining on earth united with me," do you not think that she clung to her Father with anxious uncertainty, for he was father of both and desired to be father of both?

11. Meanwhile, one of the Cherubim suggested that she be sent to King Solomon, his son, because *the father judges no one, but has given all judgment to the son.** Truth did not refuse but said that she would willingly approach him, because, she said, "He is truth." Peace and Mercy agreed no less willingly, because he is peaceable*—not only that, but Peace itself.° In his sight *Mercy and Peace have met.*

*Jn 5:22

*1 Ch 22:9
°Mi 5:5

To which Truth said, "The Father said that Adam would die on the day he tasted the forbidden tree;* if this be unfulfilled, I, Truth, perish—and you also, as the Father's Word." But Mercy replied, "You speak freely, Truth, to incline the mind of the Judge to your side. I call to you, O God, not in the learned words of human wisdom, but with my whole heart;* if the Father does not have mercy, I, Mercy, perish!"

*Gen 2:17

*1 Cor 2:13;
Ps 118:145

12. He bent down and wrote with his finger on the ground,* and when Peace urged him, he said, "*I think thoughts of peace,*"[5] and one said, "If Adam does not die, I perish," and the other said, "Nevertheless, I perish if he does not obtain mercy." If death could be good, each could have what she is asking. One is arguing for verity, not severity, and one for piety, not depravity.

*Jn 8:6

But when they asked how death could be good, being a matter so harsh and full of bitterness, he said, "*The death of the wicked is very evil*, but precious is the death of the saints.* Ask therefore whether any

*Pss 33:22;
115:15

---

[5] Jer 29:11 as in the Introit *Dicit Dominus* for the 33rd Sunday of the Year.

death can be found that is not from necessity but from choice, so that a righteous person* would die not for his evil deserts but out of his own good pleasure.* Such a one will purify death, and make it possible for death henceforth to be good."

Rm 5:7

Eph 1:9

13. Truth makes the circuit of the world, and *no one is free from filth not even a child whose life has lasted one day on earth.** Mercy makes the circuit of heaven,° but she does not find wickedness in the angels, does she?* Everyone flees from death, everyone wishes to live.

Jb 4:18 according to an ancient version
°*Si 24:5*
Jb 4:118

14. They return anxiously on the appointed day, and, in vain, Peace whispers in their wearied ears, "*You know nothing, nor do you understand. There is no one who does good, no, not one.** May he who gave counsel bring help." The King understands what they are saying to one another, and says, "*I repent that I have made man*,"* that is, "the penalty is binding upon me." Then he says, "*See, I come.** Summoning Gabriel he says, "*Go and say to the daughter of Sion, Behold, your king is coming.*"* He comes and says, "*Zion, deck your bridal chamber*."[6]

Pss 13:1; 52:4

Gen 6:7

Heb 10:7
Mt 21:5

Then Mercy and Truth went before the King who is to come, as it is written, *Mercy and Truth go before your face.* Righteousness also prepared his throne, according to the saying, *Righteousness and judgment are the preparation of your throne.** Peace came with the king, so that the prophet who said, *Peace shall be in our land when he comes*[7] might be found faithful. Hence the angelic chorus sang at the Lord's birth, *Peace on earth to people of good will.*

Ps 88:15

Then Righteousness and Peace kissed, which were at first somewhat distrustful. But the former righteousness, that is, the righteousness that comes from the law, could reconcile no one to God,* nor had it a kiss so

Rm 10:5; 5:10

[6] Antiphon *Adorna* for Candlemas.

[7] Mi 5:5, as in the responsory "Bethlehem" on the Third Sunday of Advent.

much as a sting or a goad, as it is written, *The sting of death is sin, and the power of sin is the law.** At the coming of the Savior *Righteousness and Peace have kissed*, for the righteousness that comes from faith,* freely given, possesses reconciliation. This is why Abraham and all the rest, although they were the most righteous of people, could not attain to eternal life and the peace of God which passes all understanding* when they died, since Righteousness and Peace had not yet given each other a kiss. Now we can follow Righteousness in safety, for *Righteousness and Peace have kissed*, and as we are brought through death by Righteousness, we shall straightaway be graciously received by Peace.

*1 Cor 15:56

*Rm 10:6

*Ph 4:7

Of the Sevenfold Spirit

1. ON TODAY'S FEAST of the Annunciation of the Lord, my brothers, we must
reflect on the simple story of our restoration as a very pleasant plateau. The angel Gabriel is
entrusted with a novel task, and the Virgin manifests
a novel virtue; she is honored by a novel salutation.
Gen 3:16   The ancient curse of women is removed, the new
Lk 1:28   mother receives a new blessing. She who does not
know worldly desire[1] is filled by grace, so that, by the
Spirit's coming upon her, she who declines to admit a
Lk 1:34-35 husband may give birth to the Son of the Most High.
The antidote comes in to us by the same gate of salvation through which the serpent's poison entered and
infected the whole of the human race.

We can easily gather countless flowers of this kind
from these meadows, but I am looking into the middle
of an abyss of fearful depth, an abyss that cannot be
sounded, the mystery[2] of the Lord's incarnation; it is
an unfathomable abyss. *The word became flesh and lived*
*Jn 1:14   among us.** Who can trace this, who can attain to it,
who can understand it?

---

[1] *Concupiscentiam nescit.*
[2] *Sacramentum.*

The well is deep,* and I cannot drink from it, yet
the vapor exhaled by wells sometimes moistens cloths
lying above them.* Therefore, although I am afraid
to intrude, being conscious of my own weakness, yet
frequently I stretch out my hands to you, Lord,* as
though over the mouth of this well, for *my soul is to
you like earth without water.* And now, if there is anything my shallow thought has drunk in when a mist
rises from below, I will take care to communicate it
ungrudgingly, poor as it is, as though wringing out a
linen cloth, or pouring out tiny drops of heavenly dew.

    2. I ask, then, why it was the Son who became flesh
rather than the Father or the Holy Spirit, since the
whole Trinity is not only equal in glory but is one
and the same substance? But *who has known the mind
of the Lord, or who has been his counselor?* The mystery
is very deep, and we must not pronounce judgment
upon such things rashly. It seems, however, that the
incarnation of either the Father or of the Holy Spirit
could not have avoided the confusion of a plurality of
sons since the one would be called the Son of God
and the other the Son of Man. It also seems especially
fitting that one who was, in fact, uniquely the Son
should become a son so that there would be no ambi-
guity in the name. Then there is the singular glory of
our Virgin, and Mary's surpassing prerogative, that she
has merited to have one and the same Son in common
with God the Father. Clearly this prerogative would
have been lost if the Son had not become flesh.

    As for ourselves, we could not be given another
similar chance for the hoped-for inheritance. He who
was the only-begotten became the first born among
many brothers and sisters;* he will without doubt
share his inheritance with those he has called to adoption.* If they are siblings, they are also joint heirs.°
Therefore this Jesus Christ, the faithful mediator,* has
joined in one person the substance of God and man in

*Jn 4:11

*Jn 20:5-7

*Ps 87:10

*Ps 142:6

*Rm 11:34

*Rm 8:29

*Gal 4:5; Eph 1:5
°Rm 8:17
*1 Tm 2:5

a mystery[3] that cannot be put into words, so that in the very act of reconciliation, by his deep counsel, he did not desert true justice but gave each what was due to each, honor to God, and mercy to the human creature. This was the best form of reconciliation between an offended Lord and his guilty servant, that zeal for the Lord's honor should not crush the servant with too severe a sentence, nor, on the other hand, would God be deprived of due honor when he condescended extravagantly to his servant.

3. Listen, then, and diligently mark the distinction made by the angels at the birth of this Mediator. *Glory*, they say, *to God in the highest, and on earth peace to people of good will.** Thanks to this remark, Christ, the faithful reconciler, did not lack the spirit of fear,[4] by which he always showed reverence to his Father, always deferred to him, and always sought his glory; nor did he lack the spirit of godliness by which he showed mercy and compassion to people. He also possessed the needed spirit of knowledge by which fear and godliness are clearly distinguished.

*Lk 2:14

Notice that in the first sin of our parents, three actors were present, but clearly the three lacked three things. I am speaking of Eve, the devil, and Adam. Eve did not possess knowledge; as the Apostle says, she was deceived and became a transgressor.* Truly the serpent, who is described as more cunning than any other animal,* did not lack knowledge, but this evildoer, who, it seemed, was a murderer from the beginning,* had no godliness. Perhaps Adam seemed godly when he did not make his wife sad, but he wholly forsook the fear of the Lord when he obeyed the voice of the serpent rather than that of God. Would that the

*Is 11:3

*Gen 3:1

*Jn 8:44

---

[3] *Sacramentum.*

[4] Bernard mentions three "spirits" found in Is 11:2-3 (Vulg). See section 5 for the whole text.

fear of the Lord had prevailed in Adam, as we read expressly of Christ, that *the spirit* not of godliness but *of fear has filled him.** In all things and through all things we must prefer the fear of the Lord to our neighbors' godliness, and he alone is the one who must lay claim to the whole human being.

*Is 11:3

By these three things—fear, godliness, and knowledge—our Mediator has reconciled humans to God; by counsel and might he has set us free from the hand of the enemy. By his counsel he has deprived the enemy of his former rights, the authority given him to lay hands on the innocent. By his might he prevailed, lest [the enemy] be able to retain the redeemed by violence when he came back victorious from hell and all life arose with him.

4. Furthermore, he feeds us with the bread of life and understanding, and he gives us the water of saving wisdom* to drink. The understanding of things spiritual and invisible is the soul's true bread, strengthening our heart* and giving us vigor for every good work° in every spiritual exercise. Carnal people, those who do not perceive what is of the Spirit of God—these things seem to them foolish*—may groan and grieve, saying, *My heart is withered because I forgot to eat my bread.** Look, this is pure and perfect truth, that it does not profit a person to gain the whole world and bring about the loss of his own soul.* But how can a miser grasp this? Whoever tries to persuade him sees no fruit of his labor. Why? Because it seems to him foolishness. What is truer than that the yoke of Christ is pleasant?* Put this before a worldly man, and see if he does not consider it a stone rather than bread. Certainly the soul lives on the understanding of this kind of inner truth, and this food is spiritual. *A man does not live by bread alone, but by every word that comes forth from the mouth of God.** Yet until the truth becomes palatable to you it does not easily pass into you. When you begin

*Si 15:3

*1 Thes 3:13
°Ti 3:1

*1 Cor 2:14

*Ps 101:5

*Mt 16:26;
Mk 8:36

*Mt 11:30

*Mt 4:4

to take pleasure in it, it is no longer food but drink. It enters your soul without difficulty, for the spiritual food of understanding is dissolved by the drink of wisdom. Then the limbs of the inner person—that is, the affections—are not burdened but helped as they labor in dryness.

5. Therefore, of everything necessary for saving people the Savior lacked nothing. He it is of whom Isaiah sings, *A shoot shall come out from the root of Jesse, and a flower shall rise from his root. The spirit of the Lord shall rest on him, the spirit of wisdom and understanding, the spirit of counsel and might, the spirit of knowledge and godliness. And the spirit of the fear of the Lord shall fill him.** Notice this carefully, that he says this flower will rise from the root, not from the shoot. Even if the new flesh of Christ had been created out of nothing in the Virgin, as some people have thought, the flower could be said to have risen not from the root but perhaps from the shoot. What has now come forth from the root is beyond all doubt proved to be of common stock from a common origin. But because the Spirit rested on him, [Isaiah] declares there was no contradiction in him. Because the Spirit is not altogether on top in us, he does not rest. As the flesh lusts against the spirit and the spirit against the flesh,** the new man, the true man, in whom there is nothing like this, frees us from the conflict—he who took to himself the true origin of our flesh but did not take the old leaven* of lust.

*Is 11:1-3

*Gal 5:17

*1 Cor 5:7

Of Mary and the Adulteress and Susanna[1]

1. **W**HAT A WEALTH of mercy is yours, O Lord our God! How great you are in righteousness, how prodigal of grace! *There is none like you,** most abundant in giving, most fair in recompense, most kind in setting free. With kindness you look down on the humble,* with justice you pass judgment on the innocent, and with mercy you save even sinners.

 *Ps 39:6

 *Ps 112:6

My beloved brothers, these are the things set before us on the table of this wealthy Householder by the testimonies of Holy Scripture, more abundantly today than usual, if we pay close attention. Clearly the season of Lent and the most holy day of the Lord's Annunciation coming at the same time present us with this abundance. Today in our hearing, the Redeemer's indulgence absolved the woman taken in adultery,* today he set free the innocent Susanna,* today also he filled the Blessed Virgin with the singular gift of

 *Jn 8:3-11

 *Dn 13
 [Susannah]

---

[1] This sermon was preached in a year when the Feast of the Annunciation fell on the Saturday after the third Sunday in Lent, on which day are read the story of Susanna and the gospel story of the woman taken in adultery. This occurred in the year 1150.

his freely given blessing. How great is the feast when mercy, justice, and grace are put before us equally!

Is not mercy the food of humankind? It is altogether health-giving and brings healing. Is not justice the heart's bread? It strengthens the heart, as solid food* for nourishment. Happy, indeed, are those who hunger for it, for they will be filled.* Is not the grace of its God the soul's food? It is perfectly sweet, providing every pleasure and suiting every taste;* even more, it contains them all alike and not only pleases but refreshes and heals.

*1 Thes 3:13;
Heb 5:12
*Mt 5:6

*Ws 16:20

2. Let us approach this table, my brothers, and take a small taste of every dish. "*In the law Moses commanded us to stone such a one*,"* say sinners of the sinful woman, say Pharisees of the adulteress. Because of the hardness of your hearts [Moses] said this.* *Jesus bent down.*° *Lord, bend down your heavens, and come down.** He bent down, and having turned toward mercy—he did not think as the Jews did—he *wrote with his finger*, not now on tables of stone, but *on the ground.** Nor did he do this only once, but here also the Scriptures mention two occasions, as with Moses and the two tablets.* Perhaps he wrote of truth and grace and, writing again, seemed to make an impression on the earth, according to the Apostle's words, *The law was given through Moses; grace and truth came through Jesus Christ.** Consider whether perhaps he could have read from the tablet of truth what he used to confute the Pharisees: *Let anyone who is without sin among you be the first to cast a stone at her.**

*Jn 8:5
*Mt 19:8;
Ez 11:19
°Jn 8:6
*Ps 143:5

*Jn 8:6

*Ex 31:18

*Jn 1:17

*Jn 8:7

It is an abbreviated word,* but living and active, and sharper than a two-edged sword.* How seriously their rocky hearts were pierced by this word, how violently their stony foreheads were bruised by this one small stone,* and their slinking away in blushing confusion made evident. The adulteress deserved to be stoned— but let those be eager to punish her who do not themselves merit punishment! Let them presume to

*Rm 9:28
*Heb 4:12

*1 Sm 17:49

exact punishment from the sinful woman who do not deserve to receive the same punishment! Otherwise let those nearer to themselves begin with themselves; let them first give sentence and exercise vengeance on themselves! This is Truth.

3. Yet something is lacking. If this Truth refutes her accusers, yet he does not absolve the accused woman. Let him write again, let him write words of grace, let him pronounce them, and let us listen. *Has no one condemned you, woman? No one, Lord. Neither will I condemn you. Go, and sin no more.*[2] O voice of mercy, O saving utterance of joy! *Let me hear of your mercy in the morning, for in you have I hoped,* Lord.* Only compassionate hope finds a place with you; not even the oil of mercy, unless you put it in the vessel of faith. But it is, at any rate, a treacherous trust[3] deserving only condemnation, when we openly sin in hope. (It should not, though, be called trust, but a kind of insensibility and dangerous pretense. For what trust is there for one who expects no perils; what remedy for fear, where fear is not felt, nor is there any reason to fear? Trust is a consolation, but no one needs consolation who rejoices when he does evil and rejoices in most wicked things.)*

So, brethren, let us ask to be told how many iniquities and sins we have, let us desire to be shown our misdeeds and trespasses. *Let us examine our ways** and our endeavors, and let us weigh all the dangers with vigilance and attention. Let everyone say in his dread, *I shall go to the gates of hell,** unless we breathe in the mercy of God alone. This is the authentic trust of the one who forsakes himself and relies on the Lord his God. This, I say, is authentic trust, which is not denied mercy. The

Ps 142:8

Pr 2:14

Lam 3:40

Is 38:10

---

[2] Jn 8:10-11, as in the Communion *Nemo* on Saturday after the third Sunday of Lent.

[3] *Fiducia*, here and in the following passage.

*Ps 146:11

prophet bears witness that *the Lord takes pleasure in those who fear him, in those who hope in his mercy.** Nor does a small amount suffice for us—of fear in ourselves, in

*Ps 85:5; Jl 2:13;
Is 55:7
*Mk 14:55

him reason to trust. He is kind and gentle, abounding in mercy, ready to repent of evil, great in forgiving.* Let us rely even on our enemies, who found nothing in him* of which to make a false accusation. He has compassion, they say, toward the sinful woman and does not allow her to be killed when she is handed over to him. He will thus be considered an open flouter of the law, since he pardons one whom the law condemns. All the scheming of your wickedness will be flung back upon your own head, O Pharisee! You spoil your case, you who evade the judgment. Now she who is pardoned without harm to the law is left with no accuser.

4. But let us consider, my brothers, where these Pharisees depart from. Do you see two old men—for

*Jn 8:9

they began to go away, beginning with the elders*— hiding in Joachim's orchard?[4] They are looking for Susanna, his wife; let us follow them, for they are full of a wicked plot against her. *Consent to us,* say the old men, say the Pharisees, say the wolves who a little earlier had been frustrated in the act of gobbling up a sheep[5] of

*Dn 13:30

Christ's flock. *Consent to us, and lie with us.** You who have grown old in evil days, at one moment you accused her of adultery, at another you urged adultery. This is the extent of your justice; that which you censure in public you practice in private. Thus it was that

*Jn 8:9

you went out one by one* when the one who is aware of all that is hidden so strongly smote your consciences, saying, *Let whoever is without sin among you be the first to*

*Jn 8:7

*cast a stone at her.** Rightly, then, does Truth say to his

---

[4] The next two sections of Bernard's sermon incorporate quotations from Daniel 13 in the Vulgate, Susanna in modern versions.
[5] *Ovicula.*

disciples, *unless your righteousness exceeds that of the scribes and Pharisees, you will not enter the kingdom of heaven.** *Mt 5:20

*Otherwise we will testify against you,** the old men say. *Dn 13:21
Offspring of Canaan and not of Judah, Moses did not command this in his law.* Did he who decreed that *Jn 8:5
you should stone an adulterous woman order you to accuse a chaste one? Did he who commanded that an adulteress be attacked with stones also command that witness be borne against the innocent? On the contrary, in fact, just as he ordered that the adulterous woman should not go unpunished, so he ordered that neither should the false witness. You who boast in the law dishonor God by breaking the law.* *Rm 2:23

5. *Susanna groaned and said, "I am trapped on every side.* It is death on every side, physical death this way, spiritual death the other. *If I do this thing, it is death for me; if I do not, I cannot escape your hands."** O Phari- *Dn 13:22
sees, neither the adulterous woman nor the chaste one escapes your hands; neither the saint nor the sinner evades your accusations. You overlook your own sins* *Ws 11:23
when you discover those of others; and if anyone has none of his own, you always thrust your own offense on him!

What does Susanna do, between one death and an-other, death of the soul and death of the body, trapped on very side? *Better for me to fall into the hands of men than to forsake the law of my God.*[6] She knew that it is a fearful thing to fall into the hands of the living God.* *Heb 10:31
Humans, when they kill the body, have nothing more they can do to the soul; that one is to be feared who has the power to destroy both body and soul in hell.* *Lk 12:4-5

Why is Joachim's servant so slow? Let him rush in through the side door for he has heard the uproar in

---

[6] Dn 13:23 as in the responsory *Angustiae* for the month of November.

the orchard, an uproar as of large wolves, and the bleating of Christ's little sheep among them. He does not allow her, the innocent one, to be devoured by them; he does the right thing and rescues her from their very jaws, for she did not deserve to be snatched away.

Rightly, then, as she is being led off to execution, *does her heart have confidence[7] in the Lord*, whom she fears more than she fears any human being, and whose law she puts before both life and reputation. *Never has any such thing been said about Susanna.* Her parents were righteous, and her husband the most honorable of all the Jews. Rightly then does she obtain just revenge from the just Judge* against the unjust, she who hungered so strongly for justice* that for its sake she made light of the death of the body, the disgrace of her family, and the inconsolable grief of her friends.

*2 Mc 12:5
*Mt 5:6

6. And we, brothers, if we hear from Christ, *Neither will I condemn you,** if we do not want to sin against him, if we want to live a godly[8] life in him, we must endure persecution,* not returning evil for evil or abuse for abuse.* One who does not maintain patience will lose righteousness, that is, will lose life, that is, will lose his own soul. *Vengeance is mine, I will repay, says the Lord.**

*Jn 8:11

*2 Tm 3:12;
1 Cor 4:12
*1 Pt 3:9

*Rm 12:19

Thus indeed it is. He will repay—if you leave vengeance to him, if you do not take judgment out of his hands, and if you do not return evil for evil.* He will work judgment—for one who suffers wrong.* He will judge with equity—for the meek of the earth.* Now, if I am not mistaken, it is a cause of worry to you that pleasures are slow in coming. Do not be astonished—pleasures there are! They will not burden

*Ps 7:5
*Ps 102:6
*Is 11:4

---

[7] *Fiducia.*
[8] *Pie vivere.*

you, however satisfied you may be, nor will they be
scorned by those who are glutted.

7. *The angel Gabriel was sent by God to a town of Galilee called Nazareth.** Do you wonder why Nazareth, a
small town, should be made illustrious by the messenger of such a king, and such a messenger? A great
treasure is hidden in this little town—hidden, I say,
from humans, not from God. Is Mary not God's treasure? Wherever she is, his heart is there also.* His eyes
are on her; everywhere he looks upon the lowliness of
his handmaiden.*

Is the Only-Begotten of God the Father familiar
with heaven? If he is familiar with heaven he is familiar with Nazareth too. How should he not be familiar with his homeland? How should he not know his
heritage? He claims heaven from his father, Nazareth
from his mother, as he testifies that he is both son and
Lord of David.* *The heaven of heavens belongs to the
Lord, but the earth he has given to the children of men.**

Let us allow him, then, the necessary possession of
both, since he is not only Lord but also Son of Man.
Hear then how as Son of Man he claims the earth but
also is related to it as a bridegroom. *The flowers have
appeared on our earth.** No one disputes that Nazareth
means *flower*. The flower from the root of Jesse* loves
his flowery homeland, and the flower of the field and
the *lily of the valleys* feed gladly among the lilies.*

Beauty, sweetness, and the hope of fruit, a threefold
gift, commend the flowers. God regards you, too, as
a flower, and he is well pleased with you* if you do
not lack the beauty of an honorable way of life,[9] the
fragrance of a good reputation, and the intention of
gaining a future reward. The fruit of the Spirit is eternal life.*

*Lk 1:26

*Mt 6:21

*Lk 1:48

*Mt 22:42-43
*Ps 113:16

*Sg 2:12
*Is 11:1

*Sg 2:1, 16

*Mt 3:17

**Gal 5:22;
Rm 6:23*

---

[9] *Conversatio.*

8. *Fear not, Mary, you have found grace with the Lord.*[10] How much grace? Full grace, unique grace. If unique, it cannot be general, can it? It is both, surely: because full, both unique and general. You have received the general grace uniquely!

Both unique and general, I say, for you alone found grace for everyone. Unique, for you alone found it in its fullness; general, for all may receive it from that fullness. *Blessed are you among women and blessed is the fruit of your womb.** The fruit is uniquely of your womb, but it comes to the hearts of all through you. Thus in time past all the dew fell on the fleece, and all fell on the threshing floor—but it was not all on any part of the threshing floor in the same way it was on the fleece.*

Lk 1:42

Jgs 6:37-40

In you alone is that wealthy, that very wealthy, King poured out;* lofty, lowly, immeasurable, diminished, and made lower than the angels;* true God and incarnate Son of God. But what is the result of this? Surely that we may all be enriched by his poverty, lifted up by his lowliness, enlarged by his diminution; and as we cleave to God by his incarnation we may begin to be one spirit with him.*

Phil 2:7

Heb 2:9

1 Cor 6:17

9. But what are we saying, brothers? Into what vessel can grace most effectively be poured? If, as we said above,[11] faith can hold mercy, and patience justice, what can we present as the vessel most fit for grace? Balm is very pure and needs a strong vessel—and what is as pure, or as strong, as lowliness of heart? Rightly is grace given to the lowly,* rightly has God looked upon the lowliness of his handmaiden.* By what right, you ask? Certainly because a humble soul lacks all human merit; therefore the fullness of divine grace can freely flow in.

Jm 4:6

Lk 1:48

---

[10] Lk 1:30 as in the Antiphon *Ne timeas.*
[11] See sections 1 and 3 of this sermon.

But for such as us this humility will have been ascended by degrees.* First, the human heart, which still finds pleasure in sin, does not change its wretched habits at the suggestion of something better, nor is it capable of receiving grace, being hindered by its vices. In the second place, when it already intends to mend its ways and not to repeat its former misdeeds, its former sins themselves, although they seem to have been in some degree cut off, do not admit grace as long as they remain within. They remain until they are washed away by confession, until they are removed and fruits worthy of repentance take their place.*

But take care[12] that ingratitude, more dangerous, does not succeed your vices and sins. I mean, what is so clearly opposed to grace? In the course of time we grow cool after the ardor of our conversion, our love gradually grows cold, lawlessness abounds,* and we who began in the Spirit end up in the flesh!*

Then, before we know it, what we know about the gifts bestowed on us by God seems unimportant* and we become irreverent and ungrateful. We forsake the fear of the Lord,* abandon religious solitude, and are full of words, curiosity, and jokes; we are slanderers and complainers; we spend our time on trifles; we avoid work and discipline as far as we can without being caught, as if we can do these things without immediately incurring guilt.

No wonder grace deserts us when it is driven away by obstacles such as these! So then, if anyone is glad that the word of Christ, the word of grace, dwells in him,* as the Apostle says; if anyone is devout and solicitous; if anyone is fervent in spirit,* let him take care lest he trust in his own merits and rely on his own

*RB 7:5-6

**2 Thes 2:7;
Lk 3:8*

*Mt 24:12
*Gal 3:3

*1 Cor 2:12

*Jb 6:14

*Col 3:16
*Rm 12:11

---

[12] *Vae tibi.*

works. Grace will not enter such a spirit. He is full of himself, and grace finds no place for itself in him.

*Lk 18:11-14
10. Have you considered that Pharisee who was praying?* He was not greedy, dishonest, or an adulterer. He was not without the fruits of repentance, was he? He fasted twice a week, he gave a tenth of all that he possessed. Maybe you think that he was ungrateful. But hear what he says: *God, I thank you.*

True, but he was not empty. He had not been emptied. He was not humble, but proud. He was not eager to know his shortcomings but exaggerated his merit. This was not unalloyed fullness, but a swelling! The one who pretended to fullness returned empty.

*Ph 2:7
On the other hand, the Publican, who emptied himself,* who took trouble to present an empty vessel, brought back more abundant grace.

So, brothers, if we desire to find grace, let us keep free of vices so that we may also worthily repent of our past sins. Let us not be anxious but present ourselves as devoted to God and truly humble. Surely he looks joyfully upon souls of this kind, with the loving look of which Wisdom says, *God's grace and mercy are*
*Ws 4:15
*with his saints, and he looks upon his chosen ones.** And perhaps for this reason he calls four times to the soul he looks upon, saying, *Return, return, O Shulammite!*
*Sg 6:12
*Return, return, that we may look upon you,** that it may not persist in habitual sin, nor in awareness of sins, nor in the lukewarm mess and torpor of ingratitude, nor in the blindness of elation. He has deigned to summon and rescue us from this fourfold peril, who became for us wisdom from God the Father, and righteousness,
*1 Cor 1:30
and sanctification, and redemption,* Jesus Christ our Lord, who with the Father and the Holy Spirit lives and reigns, God through all the ages of eternity. Amen.

On the Procession and the Passion

1. **N**OT WITHOUT REASON does the church, having the Spirit alike of her Bridegroom and of her God, by a singular and wonderful connection of ideas add a procession to the passion today. The procession gives rise to applause, the passion to sorrow. Since we are debtors to both the wise and the foolish, let us see what the connection contributes to each.

Let us see first how it affects worldly people, since *what is spiritual is not first, but what is natural.** Let the worldly soul see, let it see and understand, that *the end of joy is grief.** This is why the one who began to do and to teach all things when he appeared in the flesh took care to demonstrate openly in his own person, declaring not only by words but by example, what he had foretold by the prophet, that *all flesh is grass, and all its glory is like the flower of the grass.** That is why, knowing that the day of his ignominious passion was at hand, he arranged to be exalted by the glory of the procession.

Who then should now trust in the doubtful glory of this world, seeing that, even after such exaltation, such humiliation came upon the one who is Creator of time and Maker of the universe, who committed no sin? In the same city, by the same people, and at the

*1 Cor 15:46

*2 Cor 4:11

*Is 40:6

99

same time, he was one moment honored by the glory of a procession and divine praises, and the next examined with insults and abuse and *counted with the transgressors.** This is the end of transitory joy; this is the result of temporal glory. For this reason the prophet wisely prays that he may sing his glory to the Lord and not regret it;* that is, that he may hold a procession that is not followed by a passion.

2. Beloved, to you, as people comparing spiritual things with spiritual,* we depict the procession as representing the glory of our heavenly homeland and the passion as the way to it. If in the procession you think of the joy that is to come and the exceedingly great gladness when we will be caught up in the clouds to meet Christ in the air;* if with all your heart you desire to see that day when Christ the Lord will be received in the heavenly Jerusalem,* the head with all his members, bearing the triumphal sign of victory, not now applauded by throngs of people but by angelic hosts, with the people of each testament crying out on all sides, "*Blessed is the one who comes in the name of the Lord*"*—if, I say, you think where this procession is hastening, learn from the passion the route it takes. This present tribulation is the path of life, the path of glory, the path to the inhabited town,* the path of the kingdom, as the thief cried from the cross: "*Remember me, Lord, when you come into your Kingdom.*"[1] He saw going into his kingdom the one he asked to remember him when he arrived there. Therefore he too reached it; and if you want to know how short the way is, he merited to be in paradise with the Lord that same day.* The glory of the procession makes even the suffering of the passion bearable, for *nothing is difficult for a lover.*[2]

*Is 53:12

*Ps 29:13

*1 Cor 2:13

*1 Thes 4:17

*Heb 12:22

*Mt 21:9

*Ps 106:4

*Lk 23:43

[1] Lk 23:42, as in the antiphon *Memento mei.*
[2] Cicero, *Orator* 10.33.

3. You need not be surprised that I say that this present procession represents heaven, given that one and the same person is received in each, even if in quite different ways and by different people. In this procession Christ sits on an unreasoning beast; in the other it will have become a reasoning beast, for *you will save humans and beasts, O Lord.** And likewise, *I became like a beast before you*, and *I am always with you.** See if Scripture is not talking of the procession when it goes on, *You have held my right hand; you guided me with your counsel, and received me with glory.** Not even the chick will be missing there, for although the heretic[3] may complain—not allowing the children to come* and withholding the baptism of children—the One who was born as a child* and chose a vanguard of children—I mean the Innocents*—does not exclude children from grace even today. To supply the gift of grace which is not possible to them by nature corresponds well with his loving kindness and is not impossible for his majesty. In heaven the crowd of people will not strew branches of trees and common clothing, but the sacred creatures will let down their wings,* the twenty-four elders will cast their crowns before the throne of the Lamb,* and all the angelic virtues will ascribe and attribute to him the whole of their glory and beauty.*

4. And now, since we have spoken of the beast and the garments and the branches of trees, I would like to consider more carefully the threefold homage that I see being shown to the Savior in this procession: the first by the beast on which he sits, the second by those who strew their garments, the third by those who are said to cut branches from the trees.

*Ps 35:7
*Ps 72:23

*Ps 72:24

*Mt 19:14

*Is 9:6
*Mt 2:16-18

*Ez 1:24

*Rv 4:10

*Ex 28:2, 40, and so on

---

[3] Henricianus, *Epist.* 24, and Colonienses, *Serm. Sup. Cant.* 66.9–10.

Do not all the rest contribute out of their abundance and pay homage to the Lord without troubling themselves, while only the donkey gives himself as homage? Am I to be silent, that you may avoid exaltation, or shall I say more, that you may have consolation? Are you not the beast on which Christ sits, according to the bidding of the Apostle, glorifying and carrying God in your bodies?* Worldly people spend in homage to the Lord not their bodies, indeed, but what is close and is necessary to their bodies, when they give alms from their earthly goods. Bishops cut branches from trees for the sake of the word when they preach of the faith and obedience of Abraham, the chastity of Joseph, the meekness of Moses, and the virtues of the other saints. Truly they give from full storehouses,* and what they have received without payment they are bidden to give without payment.* Yet all, if they are intent on being faithful to their service, are in the procession of the Savior and enter the holy city with him, for the prophet foresaw that three were to be saved: Noah, who cut branches to make an ark; Daniel, who by inferior food and the hardship of abstinence became like a beast carrying the Savior; and a third, Job, who managed this world's goods well and warmed the sides of the poor with the fleece of his sheep.* I think you can easily see to which in this procession Jesus is closest, to which of the three ranks salvation is nearest.

*1 Cor 6:20 Vulg

*Ps 143:13
*Mt 10:8

*Ez 14:14;
Gen 6:14;
Dn 1:18-16;
1 Jn 3:17;
Jb 31:19-20

Of the Passion, the Procession, and the Four Ranks in the Procession

1. **I** MUST SPEAK rather briefly today because of lack of time. The procession we are about to celebrate serves us in many ways but also prevents me from saying very much. Today we are going to celebrate a procession, and soon afterward we will hear the passion. What is the meaning of this strange connection, and what did our forebears have in mind when they added the passion to the procession? The procession is rightly presented anew today because it took place today, but why was the passion that took place on [the following] Friday added? Perfectly rightly was the passion added to the procession so that we may learn to trust in none of the happiness of this world, being aware that *the end of joy is grief.** Let us not be foolish then, lest our prosperity be our downfall, and let us not forget adversity on the day of prosperity and vice versa.* The present age is a mixture of both, not only for those in the world, but for those of spiritual mind too. We see that what happens to people in the world is sometimes pleasant, sometimes unpleasant, and to spiritually minded people things are not always sad, not always happy, but it is *evening*

*Pr 14:13

*Si 11:25 Vulg

and morning, one day, and likewise, *you visit him in the* *Gen 1:5; Jb 7:18* *morning, and suddenly test him.** Truly for as long as this present age abides, it ebbs and flows.

2. Besides, after this age there will be two ages, separate and distinct, such that in one there will be nothing but *weeping and gnashing of teeth*, and in the other only *Mt 8:12; 13:42;* *thanksgiving and the voice of praise.** *God will wipe every* *Is 51:3* *tear from the eyes of the saints, and there will be no more mourning, nor crying, nor any pain.*[1] In the meantime, just as those who love the world suffer many hardships, so not all things fall out favorably for the servants of God. *Sir 11:7* In the day of adversity let them remember prosperity* lest they become weak and impatient, like the one of whom we read in the psalm, *he will praise you when you* *Ps 48:19* *do well for him.** On the day of prosperity let them not forget adversity, lest they exalt themselves and say in *Ps 29:7* their abundance, *we will never be moved.** As prosperity in worldly matters slays the worldly who lack wisdom, so an abundance of spiritual prosperity can slay the spiritual who lack learning and therefore are really unspiritual.

1 Cor 2:15 *Those who are spiritual judge all things.** How it hap- *Pr 1:32* pens that prosperity slays those without wisdom* and not the wise we read in another place: *The heart of the wise is where there is sadness, and the heart of fools is where there is mirth.* Rightly then does it say, *better to go to* *Qo 7:7, 3* *the house of mourning than to the house of feasting.** True, adversity may break many, yet prosperity uplifts many more,[2] as it is written, *a thousand may fall at your side—* your left side, of course, which signifies adversity—*and* *Ps 90:7* *ten thousand*—that is, many more—*at your right hand,** which signifies prosperity. Then because there is peril on both sides, Wisdom prays, saying, *Give me neither*

---

[1] Rv 21:4 as in the responsory *Absterget Deus*.
[2] *Extollit*. The idea is that prosperity "lifts up" in pride.

riches nor poverty,[3] lest riches lift me up in pride or poverty cast me down to impatience.

3. As the Lord took care to demonstrate patience in the passion, so he showed humility in the procession. In the passion, *like a sheep he was led to the slaughter, and like a lamb silent before its shearer, so he did not open his mouth; when persecuted he did not threaten*, but he prayed the more, saying, *Father, forgive them, for they know not what they do.** What happened in the procession? The people were ready to go out to meet him, and he who knew what was in people did not hide himself.* For this he too was prepared, not with chariots and horses,* not with silver bridles and saddles covered with gold, but he was lowly, seated on the back of an ass, with the apostles' garments upon it—which I think were not the best in the area.

4. Knowing that the passion would soon follow, what meaning did he intend the procession to have? Perhaps so that the passion, being preceded by the procession, would be all the more bitter for that reason. It was by the same people, in the same place, at the very time—with a few days in between—that he was first received in such triumph and afterward crucified. How different is *Away with him! Away with him! Crucify him!* from *Blessed is he who comes in the name of the Lord, Hosanna in the highest!** How different is *The King of Israel!* from *We have no king but Caesar!** How unlike one another are green branches and the cross, flowers and thorns! See how the one before whom the garments of others were spread is stripped of his own, and lots are cast for them.* How bitter to you are our sins, which need such bitterness to wash them away!

*Ac 8:32 [Is 53:7]; 1 Pt 2:23; Lk 22:43; 23:34

*Jn 12:13; Mt 25:6; Jn 2:25

*Ps 19:8

*Jn 19:15; Mt 21:9

*Jn 12:13; 19:15

*Mt 27:35 [Ps 21:19]

---

[3] Pr 30:8 as in the responsory *Verbum iniquum*.

5. Now as I come to the procession, I seem to see four groups within it; perhaps they can all be found in our procession today. Some go ahead and prepare the way; they are the ones who prepare a way into your hearts for the Lord, who guide you and direct your steps into the way of peace.* Others follow;° these are the ones who, knowing their own lack of wisdom, follow in a spirit of devotion and keep always in the footsteps of those who have gone before. There are disciples too, like servants, keeping to his side; they are the ones who choose the best part,* who live in cloisters only for God, clinging always to God and considering his good pleasure. Then there is the beast on which he sits; it represents those who are hard of heart and have souls like those of beasts. But there was no larger number of such animals there than was needed. They are more a bother than an honor, and the procession is no more glorious because of them. They do not know how to sing, but make a loud roar. They need the rod and the spur the whole time. Yet the Lord will not abandon them as long as they are willing to bear discipline. To them he says, *Serve the Lord in fear,* and, *Embrace discipline, lest at any time the Lord be angry, and you perish from the path of righteousness.** After a beast refuses to bear discipline, what remains for the Lord to do but throw him out with indignation? Immediately he strays from the path, running toward the thorns and thistles by which the word of God is choked; these are the riches of this world and the pleasures of the flesh.*

6. If some such are here for whom the discipline is heavy and all things burdensome, who must often be prodded and urged forward, I beg them to change from beasts into human beings, if they can, and be counted among some of the others, that they may be either with those who go ahead, or with those who keep by his side, or with those who follow. And if

*Mk 11:9; Mt 3:3; Lk 1:76, 79
°Mt 21:9

*Lk 10:42

*Ps 2:11, 12

*Gen 3:18; Lk 8:7, 14

they do not do so, I beg them to stay where they are* and bear patiently for the time being the things that belong to their salvation, even if these are somewhat unpleasant, until God is pleased to look on their humility* and move them on to something better.

But do you want me to console our beast a little? We know that he cannot sing. He is not among those who can say, *Your statutes have been my songs in the place of my pilgrimage.* But still, he is the one who is nearer the Lord than any other. Those who keep with the Lord on one side or the other are not as near as the beast on which he sits. Hear this from the prophet: *The Lord is near to the brokenhearted.* When a mother knows that her child is sick she cherishes it more and embraces it more frequently. No one should be offended by, no one be scornful of, someone who chooses to be Christ's beast. Anyone *who puts a stumbling block before one of these little ones* offends gravely the one who, like a mother, cherishes them in his bosom until they are grown strong. Thus the blessed Benedict has urged us to bear weaknesses of character with the greatest patience.*

7. There are four kinds of people, then, in the Lord's procession: there are the wise and good, who go ahead, and there are the simple and good, who follow. (I add "good" because the wise who are not good are wicked, according to the saying, *They are wise in doing evil,* and the simple who are not good are foolish. In the Lord's procession neither the wicked nor the foolish has a place.) Then there are those who cling to him: they are the contemplatives. Those who carry him and are burdened by him, these are the hardhearted* and are not devoted in the least.

But look, they are all in the Lord's procession—but none of them sees his face! Those who go ahead are busy preparing the way; they are anxious about the sins and temptations of others. Those who follow cannot

*1 Cor 7:24

*Lk 1:48

*Ps 118:54

*Ps 33:19

*Mt 18:6

*RB 72.5

*Jer 4:22

*Is 46:12; Ez 3:7

*Ex 33:23

see his face at all, but, as was said of Moses, they see his back parts.* The beast on which he sits never lifts its eyes to see but is always facing the ground.

Those who cling to him can sometimes see, but fleetingly and not continuously, nor can they see him fully while they are on the path. Nevertheless, compared to the rest, they come closest to seeing him face-to-face, in accord with what Scripture said of Moses, that [God] spoke to the rest of the prophets in visions *Nm 12:6-8; Ex 33:11 and dreams, but to Moses he spoke face-to-face.* As to the full sight, not even Moses could obtain the vision of his face in this life, because, as he himself said, *Ex 33:20 *no one shall see me and live.* I shall not be seen, he said, in this life; no one shall see my face on this path and in this procession.

May he in his great loving-kindness grant us so to persevere in his procession while we are alive that in that great procession, in which he is to be received by the Father with all those who belong to him, and will *1 Cor 15:24 hand over the kingdom to God his Father,* we may *Rv 11:12 be worthy to enter the holy city* with him who lives and reigns world without end.

Of the Five Days:
the Procession, the Supper, the Passion, the Burial, the Resurrection

WHEN GOD MADE all things by weight, number, and measure,* but particularly at the time when *he was seen on earth and lived with humankind*,* whatever he did, spoke, or suffered among us was so arranged that not the smallest detail, not one iota,* was devoid of sacramental content or passed without mystery. He showed this in what we celebrate today, the procession, and more clearly in the four days that are coming, the days of his supper, passion, burial, and resurrection. These are extraordinary days, and of greater significance than others.

    On the first day he condescended to accept human glory and to enter Jerusalem, not on foot as was his custom, but borne on a dumb beast, with an enormous celebration and *the joy of all the earth*.* This prepared for the passion, for the envy of the priests was greatly incited by it. When the crowds were about to come to take him by force and make him king, we read that he fled and withdrew.* Yet now he was there even without being sought, to be received and proclaimed by

*Ws 11:21

*Bar 3:37

*Mt 5:18

*Ps 47:3;
Lk 19:27-28

*Jn 6:15; 5:13

*Jn 12:13

*Jn 8:59; 7:1;
11:54
*Jn 13:1;
Mt 7:29

*Heb 4:15

*Col 2:9;
Mt 3:15;
Ph 4:12

*1 Cor 1:24;
Rm 1:16

*Pr 1:32

*Ps 19:8

*Mt 21:3

them as King of Israel*—yes, there is no doubt that he incited their souls to this proclamation!

Now we must look at the passion. At one point Jesus went out and hid himself from the Jews, being unwilling to go about openly in Judea because *the Jews were seeking to kill him*.* Knowing that his hour was coming, of his own accord, *as one having authority*,* he offered himself for suffering. It was fitting that our high priest be tempted in every respect as we are, yet without sin,* so that as truly human he might either avoid or accept human success and failure as occasion demanded, giving us in himself a beneficial example of the one or the other. If temperance inclines to the refusal of popular praise and worldly prosperity, justice allows them under certain circumstances. Persecution and temporal adversity must sometimes be prudently avoided with regard to time and place, but when necessary they must be courageously borne with.

2. And in the midst of these two conditions—I mean prosperity and adversity—all human life is whirled around. Likewise, the whole of virtue consists in these four well-known types. It was fitting for one in whom the whole fullness of virtue dwelt to fulfill all virtue so that he might make known to everyone that he knew how to abound and how to suffer need.* He was not the wisdom of God for those whose own prosperity might slay them, nor the power of God for those whose turning away might destroy them.* Scripture speaks of both: prosperity slays, not everyone, but fools, and turning away destroys, not just anyone, but the petty.*

With what modesty does he seem to have accepted this glory, coming to his triumphal encounter on an ass, not with chariots and horses!* And he said, *If anyone says anything to you, say, The Lord needs them*.* Great is his need, the need for their salvation. He had come to save humans and animals, God multiplying his mercy.* This condescension nurtures the beginnings of our monastic way of life[1] so that by the slave girl we might bring forth our first child.*

*Ps 35:7 Vulg

*Gal 4:22-24

By the Lord's command this child has been set free who formerly was held back because either unable or unwilling to do good—or, bound more strongly by both, neither willing nor able. But this child does not know how simply to give thanks to the Lord. He is persuaded that what he does pleases the Lord, and he takes comfort in thinking he is making the Lord in some sense indebted to him! But as time goes on he will be moved to give attention to what he owes and will fear that perhaps he may be found ungrateful for such favors, saying, *I am a worthless servant,* and *You have no need of my goods.** This is true and faithful affection. This is the child of the free woman, with whom the child of the slave girl cannot share the inheritance.* This is what happens in the procession.

*Lk 17:10;
Ps 15:2

*Gal 4:30

3. Moreover before the passion the loving house-holder took care to offer his servants a meal. Here too the kindness and generous love of the Savior appeared.* *Having loved his own, he loved them to the end,* and he said, *With desire have I desired to eat this Passover with you before I suffer.** It was necessary. Satan was seeking them, that he might sift them like wheat.* He had to anticipate the meal. If they defected even just a little after they had eaten, what would they have done had they been hungry? So he refreshed not only their bodies but also their hearts, as much as possible. Not physical suffering but a spiritual temptation was approaching, which he would bear alone until he passed through it. As this victim alone could be effectual, so it alone was sufficient; it was not fitting that Peter, James, or John should suffer with Christ for the salvation of

*Ti 3:4

*Jn 13:1;
Lk 22:15

*Lk 22:31

---

[1] *Conversatio.*

*Mt 27:38

humanity. Yes, two others were crucified with him,* two bad men. But just as afterward it would be impossible to suspect them of anything again, theirs was in no way an efficacious sacrifice.

4. With what loaves did he feed the apostles at the supper? I think there were five. *My food*, he said, *is to do the will of my father**—food indeed, but food of the heart. What so strengthens and confirms the human heart, what so comforts and sustains it in every necessity, as the carrying out of the divine will, ingested as it were into the stomach of the soul—that is to say, the conscience? Only one whose heart is dry, inasmuch as he has forgotten to eat his bread,* is unaware of the loaves of the heart—the discourse of divine encouragement, the consolation of the promises, and the tears of those who pray. Above all, the Lord's flesh is true food, the food of life, the living bread from heaven.*

*Jn 4:34

*Ps 101:5

*Jn 6:55, 51

If you look diligently you will find none of these lacking in the Lord's festive supper. While his disciples were still reclining at table, he rose from supper, girded himself with a towel, poured water into a basin, washed his disciples' feet, and dried them.* There is no will of flesh and blood here; it is the will of the Father and our sanctification.* Then, *If I do not wash you*, the Lord said to Peter, who was strongly objecting, *you have no share with me*.* We know who said, *One who comes to me I will not cast out; I have come down from heaven, not to do my own will, but the will of him who sent me*.*

*Jn 13:4-5

*Jn 1:13; 1 Thes 4:3

*Jn 13:8

*Jn 6:37-38

Following his custom, after the action he added an exhortation that fit the situation. In speaking (his long discourse has survived) he was concerned to comfort and encourage them, because of his imminent passion, with many promises concerning his resurrection, the coming of the Paraclete, their strengthening, and finally his taking them up to himself. Soon afterward he went to prayer, and being in agony he prayed until the third hour. There, he appeared to weep not only with his eyes but with all his limbs, so that his whole body, that is, the church,* was purified by the tears of his whole body. Concerning the sacrament of his Body and Blood, everyone knows that this great and unique nourishment was first revealed on this day, commended and commanded on this day to be frequently done afterward.

5. There follows the day of the passion on which, just as he had saved an entire human being,* he made himself wholly a saving victim,* exposing his body to great torments and injuries and his soul to be affected by two kinds of the most human compassion: one, for the inconsolable grief of the holy women, and the other for the despair and dispersion of the disciples.* It was in these four things that the Lord's cross consisted, and all of them he suffered for us—he who surrounded us with such compassion.

But the things concerning him had an end, as he told the lamenting women,* an end rapid and renowned: first, rest, and then, resurrection. We recall that we too must pass through many tribulations if we are hastening to enter into that rest.* At first, while we are in tribulation, it seems best to us to long for that rest, as though we were never to desire anything more. But even that rest will not be rest for us because of the desire for glory, the desire for resurrection. *Henceforth, now says the Spirit, let them rest from their labors.* Those who die in the Lord rest from labor,* but they do not rest from crying out! At last the souls of the slain shall cry out under the throne of God.[2] Even if they have nothing to trouble them, they do not yet have all they could desire until the resurrection follows the rest, and Easter follows the Sabbath. Amen.

*Mt 26:44; Lk 22:43; Col 1:24

*Jn 7:23
*Lv 10:14; 2 Mc 3:32

*Lk 23:27; Mt 26:31-35

*Lk 22:37; 23:27

*Ac 14:22; Heb 4:3

*Rv 14:13

[2] Antiphon and responsory for the feast of the Holy Innocents; see Rv 6:9.

Of the Lord's Passion

STAY AWAKE, BROTHERS! Do not let the mysteries of this time pass through you fruit-lessly. Blessing abounds here. Offer yourselves as clean vessels to be filled. Show that you have devout souls, alert minds, well-balanced emotions, and pure consciences to receive such great gifts of grace. Indeed the special way of life[1] that you have professed and also the common observance of the church whose chil-dren you are ask such care of you. Truly, during this holy week all Christians should live in a holy way, show modesty, cultivate humility, and array themselves in seriousness—either more than your usual practice or contrary to it!—so that they are seen to suffer in some degree with the suffering Christ.

Who is so bereft of religious sense as not to feel the prick of repentance? Who is so arrogant as not to humble himself? Who is so wrathful as not to grant forgiveness? Who is so indulgent as not to fast? Who is so shameless as not to practice restraint? Who is so steeped in wickedness as not to repent during these days? And rightly so. For the passion of the Lord is at hand, which even today shakes the earth, splits the rocks, and opens tombs!* His resurrection is near, when you celebrate a solemn festival to the Lord most high.*

*Mt 27:51-52
*Nm 29:12

---

[1] Conversatio.

114

Would to God your swift and eager spirits might bring
you even to the great things that he has done!* Noth- *Ps 70:19
ing better can happen in the world than what God has
done during these days; nothing can benefit the world
more than that each year it should celebrate his memorial by a perpetual observance with the soul's desire
and gush forth the memory of his abundant goodness.

Both [the passion and the resurrection] are for our
sake, because in each is the fruit of salvation for us, and
in each is the life of our spirit.

Wonderful is your passion, Lord Jesus, which has
averted the passions of all of us, atoned for all our sins,
and is never found ineffectual for any deadly disease
of ours. What is so deadly as not to be destroyed by
your death?

2. In his passion, my brethren, we do well to notice
three things in particular: the work, the manner, and
the cause. We praise his patience in the work, his humility in the manner, and his love in the cause.

His patience was unique, because when sinners
ploughed on his back,* when all his bones were *Ps 128:3
stretched on the wood to be counted,* when the *Ps 21:18
mighty fortress that protects Israel* was pierced every- *Ps 120:4
where, when they dug his hands and feet,* like a lamb *Ps 21:17
he was led to the slaughter, and like a sheep before its
shearers he did not open his mouth.* He made no *Is 53:7
complaint against his Father by whom he had been
sent, nor against the human race for which he restored
what he did not steal,* nor even against his very own *Ps 68:5
people, from whom he received so many bad things in
return for so much goodness. Some people are pun-
ished for their sins and bear it humbly, and this is ac-
counted to them as patience. Others are beaten, not so
much to be purified as to be tested and rewarded, and
we commend their patience in this as greater. How
can the patience of Christ not be judged the greatest? *Ps 77:54;
In his own country* and by those to whom he had 104:11

particularly come as Savior he was subjected to the cruelest of deaths—he who not only was totally without sin, whether personal or contracted, but possessed nothing at all that could be improved upon. All the fullness of divinity dwells in him not in appearance but bodily;* in him God reconciles the world to himself,* not just in a manner of speaking but actually; he is full of grace and truth,* not in collaboration[2] but on his own, that he may do his work. *His work is strange to him,** says Isaiah, because it was both *his work* that the Father had given him to do,* and it was *strange to him*, that such a one should bear such things. There you have his patience in his work.

*Col 2:9
*2 Cor 5:19
*Jn 1:14

*Is 28:21
*Jn 17:4

3. Now if you look carefully at the manner, you will not only recognize that he is gentle but also that he is humble of heart.* *In his humiliation justice was denied him,** and he made no reply to the great blasphemies and the false accusations that were leveled against him.* *We saw him*, [Isaiah] said, *and he had no appearance*; he was not *the most handsome of men* but *the reproach of people*, like a leper, *the most abject of men, a man of sorrows*, struck down and humiliated by God so that he had no form or comeliness.* O most abject and most exalted! O humble and sublime! O reproach of people and glory of angels! No one was higher than he, no one more lowly! At the end he was smeared with spittle, filled with insults, condemned to a shameful death, and *numbered among the transgressors.** Will humility of this description, or rather beyond description, merit nothing? As is his unique patience, so is his wonderful humility, both without precedent.

*Mt 11:29
*Ac 8:33

*Mt 27:14
and parallels

*Is 53:2-4; Ps
44:3; Ps 21:7

*Mt 26:67; Lam
3:30; Ws 2:20;
Is 53:12

4. The cause wonderfully commends both—it is of course love. *Because of his great love with which God loved us*, to redeem a servant the Father did not spare the

---

[2] *non cooperative.*

Son,* nor did the Son spare himself. It is truly great because it passes measure, exceeds the limit, and rises above all description. *No one has greater love than this, to lay down one's life for one's friends.** You had greater, Lord, when you laid it down for your enemies. While we were still enemies, we were reconciled to you and to the Father through your death.* What other love can you imagine that is, that has been, or that can be like this love? *Scarcely will one die for a righteous person**—but you suffered for the unrighteous, dying for our trespasses, you who came to justify sinners freely,* to make slaves your brothers, captives your joint heirs, and exiles kings.

Eph 2:4; Rm 8:32

*Jn 15:13

*Rm 5:8, 10

*Rm 5:7
*Rm 4:25; 3:21

Nothing else illustrates this patience and humility more than his giving up his soul to death and bearing the sins of many,* even praying for transgressors that they not perish.* *The saying is sure, and worthy of full acceptance:** he was offered because he willed it.° Not only was he offered and willed it, but he was offered *because* he willed it. He alone had the power to lay down his life;* no one took it from him. When he had taken the vinegar, he said, *It is consummated.** Nothing was left to be done; there is nothing more for me to look for. *And bowing his head,* having become obedient unto death, *he gave up his spirit.** Who, when he wishes to, falls asleep so easily? There is great weakness in death, but to die thus is great strength. *God's weakness is stronger than human strength.**

*Is 53:12
*1 Tm 1:15
*1 Tm 4:9
°Is 53:7

*Jn 10:18
*Jn 19:30

*Ph 2:8; Jn 19:30

*1 Cor 1:25

Human insanity can strike itself to death with its own most heinous hands, but this is not to lay down a life; it is to use force against it and to cut it short violently, rather than to lay it down at will. O wicked Judas, plainly you had the unhappy ability not to lay down your life but to hang it up; that wicked spirit of yours did not die when you betrayed him but when you tightened the noose.* You did not let it go, you lost it. *Only he delivered up his soul to death,** as only he

*Mt 27:5
*Is 53:12

returned to life by his own power. Only he had the power to lay it down who alone could take it up again of his own free will, having power over life and death.

5. Worthy is such immeasurable love, worthy such wonderful humility, such unconquerable patience. Worthy is so holy, so spotless a victim, and so accept-able. *Worthy is the lamb that was slain to receive power,** to do what he came to do, to take away the sins of the world.*

I say that the sin that prevailed on the earth* is threefold. You are already thinking of what I am going to say: the desire of the flesh, the desire of the eyes, and the pride of life.* It is *a threefold cord* that *is not easily broken.** Many drag this cord of vanity—no, are dragged by it; but that prior group of three rightly prevails in the elect. How can the remembrance of patience not keep all passion at a distance? How can the consideration of humility not utterly drive out the pride of life? The worthy love that engages the mind in meditation and claims for itself the whole will quenches the vice of curiosity altogether. The passion of the Savior is a bulwark against these things.

6. But it may be more profitable for you to hear of another threefold sin I am going to tell you about, and how the virtue of the cross wipes it out. First is original sin, second personal, and third individual sin. That greatest transgression, which we contract from the first Adam, in whom we all sinned,* is called *original*, and because of it every one of us dies. It is greatest because it takes possession not only of the whole human race but also of every member of that race, so that no one evades it, not even one. It extends from the first human being to the last, and in each one this poison is diffused from the sole of the foot to the top of the head.* Else, why is *a heavy yoke upon* everyone and *all the children of Adam,* that is, *from the day when they come out of their mother's womb to the day*

Rv 5:12

Jn 1:29
Gen 7:19

1 Jn 2:16
Qo 4:12

Rm 5:12

Is 1:6

of their burial in the mother of all?* We are begotten in *Si 40:1*
unclean places, fostered in darkness, and brought forth
in pains.* We are a burden to our pitiable mothers *Jb 14:4 after an
ancient version;
Gen 3:16*
before our birth, and we rend them like a viper when
we are born; it is strange that we are not equally rent
ourselves. Our first cry is one of woe, and rightly so,
because we have entered the vale of woe, so that the
words of Job, that holy man, can be fitly said of all of
us: *A mortal, born of a woman, living but a short time, is
filled with many miseries.** *Jb 14:1*

How true is what we are taught not by words but
by blows! *A mortal*, he says, *born of a woman*—nothing is more abject! And so that mortals do not soothe
themselves with the pleasure of the bodily senses that
they drink in from the things they perceive, at their
very entrance they are fearfully reminded of their
departure by the words *living but a short time*. And so
they do not suppose that the short space that is left
them between their coming in and their going out is
at their own disposal, it is said to be *filled with many
miseries*—many and manifold miseries, I say, miseries
of the body, miseries of the heart, miseries when they
sleep, miseries when they are awake, miseries at every
turn. Even he who was born of the Virgin, or, more
correctly, made of a woman*—but one blessed among *Gal 4:4*
women*—one who said to his mother, *Woman, here* *Lk 1:28*
is your son—even he, *living but a short time* on earth, *Jn 19:26*
nevertheless was *filled with many miseries*. In that short
time he was beset with plots, examined with insults,
struck with injustices, abused with torments, and he
had reproaches heaped upon him.

7. Do you doubt, then, that this obedience was
enough to remove all the guilt of the first trespass?
But *the free gift is not like the transgression. The sin of
one brought condemnation, but the free gift following many
offenses is unto justification.** Indeed that original trans- *Rm 5:15, 16*
gression was grave, for it not only tainted the person

but also the nature. Yet personal transgression is more grave for everyone, for when the reins have been slackened we make our members totally available as *weapons of wickedness for sin*,* now no longer shackled only by another's offense, but by our own as well.

*Rm 6:13

But gravest of all is the unique sin committed against the Lord's majesty when the impious killed the righteous One unrighteously and laid sacrilegious hands on the very Son of God,* a cruel homicide— no, deicide, if this can be said! What are the first two compared to this? At this the whole fabric of the world grew pale and was afraid, and everything nearly turned back into the ancient chaos.

*Mt 26:50

Let us imagine that one of the leading men of a kingdom laid waste the king's realm in hostile devastation; now suppose that another, who sat at table and in council with the king, strangled the king's only son with treacherous hands. Does not the first seem innocent and harmless compared to the second? Just so is every sin compared to this one, yet he who made himself sin bore this sin, that with sin he might condemn sin.* By this all sin, both original and personal, is blotted out, and even this unique sin is destroyed by itself.

*2 Cor 5:21; Rm 8:3

8. I now come to the main point, for the two minor points have been dealt with. The point is this: *He bore the sin of many, and prayed for the transgressors** so that they would not perish: *Father, forgive them, for they do not know what they are doing.** Your word flies, Lord, and it cannot be recalled. It will not return to you empty but will accomplish the purpose for which you sent it.* *See now the works of the Lord, the wonders he has done on the earth!** He was scourged, crowned with thorns, pierced with nails, fastened to the cross, filled with insults—yet unmindful of all his pain he said, *Forgive them*. From this came many miseries of the body, many mercies of the heart, pain, compassion, the oil of gladness, and drops of blood falling down on the ground.*

*Is 53:12

*Lk 23:34

*Is 55:11
*Ps 45:9

*Heb 1:9; Lk 22:44

Many are the Lord's mercies,* but many, too, are the   *Ps 118:156
Lord's miseries. Will the miseries prevail over the mercies, or will the mercies superabound over the miser-
ies? May *your ancient mercies* prevail, Lord, may wisdom   *Ps 88:50;
prevail against evil!*   Ws 7:30

Great is their iniquity,* but is not your loving-   *Gen 4:13 Vulg
kindness greater, Lord? *Much, in every way.* Is evil a   *Rm 3:2
repayment for good? For they have dug a pit for my life.*   *Jer 18:20
Clearly they have dug a pit of impatience, supplying
the most skillfully devised occasions for anger. But
which of these pits is equal to the abyss of your clemency? By repaying evil for good* they dug a pit: but   *Ps 34:12
love is not irritable, it is not hasty, it never ends,* it   *1 Cor 13:5, 8
does not fall into a pit, and it heaps up good for the
evils repaid. God forbid that flies that will die should
spoil the sweetness of the ointment* that flows out of   *Qo 10:1
your body, because in your breast *is mercy, and with him
is plentiful redemption.* The flies that are going to die   *Ps 129:7
are the miseries, they are the blasphemies, they are the
insolence and insulting that a perverse and provoking
generation* repays you.   *Ps 77:8

9. But what about you? In the very raising of your
hands, when the morning sacrifice had passed over to
the evening holocaust, in the very power, I say, of the
incense that mounted to the skies, covered the earth,
and spread out over hell, you cried out to be heard for
your reverent submission,* *Father, forgive them, for they*   *Heb 5:7
do not know what they are doing? O how bountiful you
are to pardon!* *O how abundant is your sweetness, Lord!°*   *Is 55:7
O how far are your thoughts from our thoughts!* O   °Ps 31:19
how secure is your mercy even upon the ungodly!   *Is 55:9

What a marvel! He cries out, *Forgive them,* and the
Jews cry out, *Crucify him.* Smoother than oil are his words,*   *Lk 23:24, 21
*and these are darts.** What patient and compassionate love!   *Ps 54:22
Love is patient—it is enough. *Love is kind*—it is more   *1 Cor 13:4
than enough. *Do not be overcome by evil*—love is abundant—*but overcome evil with good*—it is superabundant.   *Rm 12:21

Not only patience but God's kindness led the Jews to repentance* because the love that is kind also loves those it tolerates, and loves them with a burning love. The love that is patient turns a blind eye, waits, succors the transgressor; love that is kind draws, leads, turns him from the error of his way, and at the last covers a multitude of sins.* O Jews, you are stones, but you strike a softer stone, from which reechoes the sound of goodness, and from which issues the oil of love! Lord, how you will give from the torrent of your delights drink to those who desire you,* when you thus drench those who crucify you with the oil of mercy!

10. That this most powerful passion is able to deal with all kinds of sins is clear.* But does anyone know if it applies to me? It does apply to me, because it could not apply to anyone else. Not even to an angel? But an angel has no need of it. Not to the devil? But he does not rise again. And being made neither in the likeness of angels, nor—heaven forbid!—in the likeness of demons, but *in human likeness, and found in human form, he emptied himself, taking the form of a slave.** He was a son, and he became like a slave. Not only did he take the form of a slave, that he might be subservient, but he even took the form of a wicked slave, that he might be beaten,* and a slave of sin° that he might destroy its penalty when he was without fault. *In human likeness*, [Paul] said, not in the likeness of a single human, because the first man was created neither in sinful flesh nor in the likeness of sinful flesh. Christ plunged pressingly and profoundly into every human misery, and the subtle eye of the devil did not detect this great mystery of loving kindness.* He was found in the condition, the whole condition, of a human, nor did any mark of singularity appear in him with respect to what he owed to nature. Just as he was found, so was he crucified. He revealed himself to a few, so that some would believe; from others he was

*Rm 2:4

*Jm 5:20

*Ps 35:9

*Heb 9:28

*Ph 2:7

*Mt 25:26;
Lk 12:47
°Rm 6:17

*1 Tm 3:16

hidden, because *if they had known, they would not have crucified the Lord of glory*.* For this reason he added ignorance to this unique sin—that he could pardon the ignorant under some semblance of justice.

*1 Cor 2:8

11. That old Adam who fled from the face of God left an inheritance of two things, labor and sorrow, labor in acting and sorrow in suffering.* He knew nothing about this in the paradise that he had received *to till it and to keep it*,* to till it with delight and to keep it faithfully for himself and his children. Christ the Lord looked at the labor and sorrow to deliver them into his own hands*—or rather to deliver himself into their hands, stuck in deep mire* and the waters reaching even into his soul.* *See*, he says to his Father, *See my abjection and my labor*,* that *I am poor and in labors from my youth*.* He underwent labor, his hands served in labors.* See what he says of sorrow: *O all you who pass by the way, look and see if there is any sorrow like my sorrow*.* Surely he has borne our infirmities and carried our sorrows*,* a man of sorrows, poor and sorrowful, tempted in all things without sin.* In life he had suffering action and in death he bore active suffering, while working salvation in the midst of the earth.*

*Gen 3:8;
Jon 1:3;
Ps 9:28, 35
*Gen 2:15

*Ps 9:35
*Ps 68:2
*Ps 69:1
*Ps 24:18
*Ps 87:16
*Ps 81:6

*Lam 1:12
*Is 53:4
*Is 53:3; Ps
68:30; Heb 4:15
*Ps 73:12

Therefore will I remember as long as I live* the labors he bore in preaching, the weariness in going about, the temptations in fasting, the nights of wakefulness in prayer, the tears of compassion. I will also call to mind his sorrows, the insults, the spitting, the blows, the taunts, the reproaches, the nails, and other such things that passed through him and over him in plenty. This gives me courage, this makes me like [him]—but only if I imitate him as well so as to follow in his footsteps.* Otherwise the righteous blood that has been shed on earth will be required of me, and I will not be free of that so singular enormity of the Jews, because I would be ungrateful for his great love, because I would bring reproach on the spirit of grace,

*Pss 41:7; 145:2

*Jb 23:11 and
following

*Mt 23:35;
Zec 9:11;
Mt 26:28

*Rm 8:29

*Mt 19:27;
Rv 14:4

*Ps 125:2
*Ps 148:5

*Mt 8:20

*Jn 1:14

because I would defile the blood of the covenant, because I would trample the Son of God.*

12. Many people suffer labor and sorrow, but they do so of necessity, not of their own will, and these are not conformed to the image of God's Son.* Some suffer willingly, but they have no part or share in this discussion: the lover of luxury stays awake all night, not just patiently but even willingly, to fulfill his own pleasure; the robber, bearing arms, stays awake in order to seize his prey; the thief stays awake to break into a stranger's house. All these and those like them are far from the labor and sorrow that the Lord has in mind. People of good will, who with a Christian will have replaced riches with poverty, or even spurned what they did not have as if they had it, leaving everything for him as he left everything for them, follow him wherever he goes.* Such faithful imitation is to me the strongest evidence, because the Savior's passion and the likeness of his humanity pass over to my use. This is the savor and the fruit of his labor and sorrow.

13. See what great things his majesty has done for you.* Of everything in heaven and under heaven he spoke, and they were made.* What is easier than to speak? But when he remade you whom he had made, was it done only with a word? He was seen on earth and spoke with humans for thirty-three years; he bore those who uttered calumnies at his deeds, who set traps for his words; he had nowhere to lay his head.* Why was this? Because the Word had descended from its fine subtlety and taken on a coarser covering. It became flesh* and so made use of coarser and slower work. As a thought clothes itself in a physical sound without any diminution of itself, neither before nor after it is spoken, so the Son of God took flesh, suffering neither commixture nor diminution, neither before nor after taking flesh. He is not seen when he is with his Father, but here our hands have handled

the Word of life, and what was from the beginning we have seen with our own eyes.* This Word, because it had united in itself pure flesh and a holy soul, freely controlled the actions of his body, both because he was wisdom and righteousness* and because he had no law in his members at war with the law of his mind.* My word is neither wisdom nor righteousness, yet it is capable of both, and they can be either absent from it or present with it, but being absent is easier. We seem more at home with serving the vices of our flesh than with regulating its actions and sufferings because our whole life is inclined to evil from youth,* and we surround ourselves with pleasure in the midst of scourges and swords right up to the moment of death.

14. Happy those whose thinking[3]—the word is ours—directs all their actions toward righteousness, so that their intention is pure and its operation true! Happy those who order their physical sufferings according to righteousness, so that whatever they undergo they undergo for the sake of the Son of God, and instead of murmuring in their heart their mouth keeps voicing thanksgiving and praise!*

Those who bear themselves like this take up their mat and go to their home.* Our mat is our body in which we formerly lay idle, slaves to our desires and lusts. Now we carry it since we are constrained to obey our spirit, and we carry our death, because our body is dead because of sin.* We walk, we do not run, because *the body which suffers corruption weighs down the soul, and the earthly habitation presses down the mind that ponders many things.* We walk even into our own home. Into what home? *Into the mother of all,* because *the graves are their homes forever.*

*1 Jn 1:1

*1 Cor 1:30

*Rm 7:23

*Gen 8:21

*Is 51:3

*Mk 2:11

*Rm 8:10

*Ws 9:15

*Si 40:1;
Ps 48:12

---

[3] *Cogitatio.*

We who walk under this burden, how shall we run, do you suppose? How shall we fly? Clearly, on the wings of the wind.* The Lord Jesus has embraced us through our labor and sorrow;* let us cleave to him then with borrowed embraces, through righteousness, his righteousness. By directing our actions toward righteousness, and by holding our passions in check for the sake of righteousness, let us say with the bride, *I held him, and would not let him go.** Let us also say with the patriarch, *I will not let you go, unless you bless me.**

What remains now, except a blessing? What is there after the embrace, except a kiss? How should one who thus cleaves to God not now be free to exclaim, *Let him kiss me with the kiss of his mouth?** Feed us meanwhile, Lord, with the bread of tears, and give us tears to drink in full measure,* until you lead us to the good measure, pressed down and shaken together, which you will give into our bosoms, you who are in the Father's bosom, God over all, blessed forever.*

*Ps 17:11
*Ps 9:34
*Sg 3:4
*Gen 32:26
*Sg 1:2
*Ps 79:6
*Lk 6:38; Jn 1:18; Rm 9:5

Of Baptism, the Sacrament of the Altar, and the Washing of Feet

1. THESE ARE THE DAYS we are bound to observe, days full of holiness and grace by which even the minds of the wicked are provoked to repentance. So great is the power of the sacraments we recall during these days that they can rend even hearts of stone, and they are enough to soften every breast though it be hard as iron. Until today we have seen not only the heavens suffering at Christ's passion, but the earth shaken, rocks split asunder, and tombs opened in the confession of sins.* Indeed, just as with material foods the flavor of some is present at once while others require preparation to bring it out, so it is with spiritual foods; those readily apparent do not need our ministry, while those shut inside demand careful consideration. A mother does not give a child a whole nut, but she breaks it open and takes out the kernel. So I, too, beloved, if I could, should open for you the sacraments that are shut inside. But because I cannot, I hope that mother Wisdom may break open those nuts—those nuts, I say, that the priestly scepter brought forth, the scepter of power that the Lord sent forth out of Zion.* The sacraments are many, and an hour is not enough for exploring all of them. Perhaps, too, some of you are not strong enough to grasp them all at once. Therefore I will speak about what the Lord

*Mt 27:51-52

*Ps 109:2

127

himself presents concerning three sacraments appropriate to this season.

2. A sacrament is a sacred sign or a sacred rite [*secretum*]. Many things are done simply for their own sake, but others in order to represent other things, and these are called signs and are indeed so. Let us take an example from everyday life. A ring is given purely as a ring and has no significance; but if it is given as a token of some hereditary office it is a sign, so that the one who receives it may now say, "In itself, the ring has no value, but it denotes the hereditary office I was seeking."

This is what the Lord did as he approached his passion. He wanted to invest his disciples with his grace and wanted this invisible grace to be communicated to them by a visible sign. This is what all the sacraments were instituted for. This is what sharing in the Eucharist is for, and the washing of feet, and, finally, baptism itself, the beginning of all sacraments in which we are planted together in the likeness of his death* and whose threefold immersion lends its form to the Triduum we are about to celebrate.

*Rm 6:5

There are different signs when it comes to outward things. To stay with the example with which we began, there are different kinds of investiture corresponding to the office with which we are being invested. For instance, a canon is invested with a book, an abbot with a staff, a bishop with both a staff and a ring. In the same way, the different graces are transmitted by the various sacraments. With what grace are we invested in baptism? Surely the cleansing of transgressions.* *Who can make clean one conceived of unclean seed if not you who alone are clean,** and who have no sin, O God? Formerly the sacrament of this grace was circumcision, so that the knife would cut away the corrosion of original sin which had its origin in our first parents. At the Lord's coming, however—the Lamb all gentle and mild, whose yoke is easy and whose bur-

*2 Pt 1:9
*Jb 14:4

den is light*—it was changed for the better so that
the deep-seated corrosion might be dissolved by water
with the anointing of the Holy Spirit, and that affliction might come to an end.

3. But perhaps someone may ask, "If what we contracted from our parents is erased in baptism, why
do our evil desires persist, the fuel and incentive for
sin?" There is no doubt that the law of sin was passed
down to us by our first parents. We are all begotten in
the context of a sinful act of will. Therefore, although
unwillingly, we feel an itching, certain forbidden and
brutish stirrings of concupiscence. I have often said to
you, and it should not slip from your minds, that we
all fell in the fall of the first man. We fell over a heap
of stones, we are in the mire where we have been not
only befouled but also wounded and badly shaken. We
can be washed quickly enough, but a complete cure
needs a long treatment.

Baptism washes us because it erases the record of
our condemnation.* This grace is conferred on us
so that concupiscence may no longer harm us if we
withhold our consent. Thus the bloody matter, so to
call it, of our old sore is removed, while the condemnation and response of death,* which formerly flowed
from it, is taken away.

*Col 2:4

*Lk 24:20

But who can curb such wild passions? Who can
bear the itching of this sore? Have confidence, because grace comes to your aid even in this, and, that
you may be free from care, you have the sacrament of
the Body and precious Blood of Christ as your ves-
ture. This sacrament is at work in us in two ways—it
diminishes our sensuality, and in more serious sins it
altogether takes away consent. If any of you feel the
passion of anger, envy, lust, or any other such thing,
less often or less sharply, let them give thanks for the
Body and Blood of the Lord, and let them rejoice
because the worst sore yields to healing.

4. But what shall we do, since we cannot be without sin in this body of sin and at this evil time?* Shall we despair? Far from it! *If we say*, says blessed John, *that we have no sin, we deceive ourselves, and the truth is not in us. If we confess our sins, God is faithful who forgives our sins and cleanses us from all iniquity*.* Now to keep us from uncertainty about the remission of sins we commit day by day we have his sacrament, the foot washing. Do you ask how I know that it is the sacrament of this remission? Chiefly because the Lord himself made this promise to Peter, saying, *What I am doing you do not know now, but later you will know.** "But he said nothing about a sacrament," [someone might say], "but only, *I have given you an example, that you also do the same.*"*

Truly, he had many things to say to them, but they could not bear them then.* He neither wanted to leave them anxious and mistrustful, nor to say anything they would not grasp then. But do you want to know that this was done as a sacrament and not merely as an example? Listen to what was said to Peter: *If I do not wash you, you will have no part with me.** So something that is necessary for salvation is hidden, something without which Peter himself would have no part in the kingdom of Christ and of God. See if Peter was not terrified at the frightening words of such a great threat, and if he did not acknowledge the mystery of salvation when he answered, *Lord, not my feet only but also my hands and head!** And how do we know that this washing is to wash away sins that are not unto death* and that we cannot wholly avoid before death? Clearly from the answer given him when he offered his hands and his head too for washing: *One who has bathed needs to wash only the feet.** One who has no serious sins has bathed; his head—that is, his intention—and his hands—that is, his work and his way of life—are clean. Feet, however, which are the dispositions of the soul, cannot be entirely clean while we are

*Rm 6:6; Ps 36:19

*1 Jn 1:8

*Jn 13:7

*Jn 13:15

*Jn 16:12

*Jn 13:8

*Jn 13:9

*1 Jn 5:16

*Jn 13:10

walking in the dust of this world, because the mind yields sometimes to vanity, sometimes to pleasure or curiosity, more than it should, and suddenly: *In many things we all offend.**

*Jm 3:2

5. Yet let no one underestimate these things or consider them unimportant. It is impossible to be saved with them, and it is impossible that they should be washed away except by Christ and with Christ. Let no one, I say, sleep in pernicious security, turning to words of malice to make excuses for sins, for, as Peter heard from him, unless Christ washes them, we will have no part with him.* Yet we must not be too anxious about them, for he will pardon easily, and even gladly, if only we acknowledge them. In matters of this kind, which are almost inevitable, negligence is culpable and anxiety excessive! For this reason in the prayer he himself taught he wanted us to pray every day for those sins.* We have spoken of concupiscence because, although he has taken away condemnation—since, according to the Apostle, *there is no condemnation for those who are in Christ Jesus**—yet to humble us he allows it still to live in us and to afflict us heavily, so that we may feel what grace does for us and always return for his help. Likewise he deals with us with gentle forbearance in the matter of those slight sins, in that they are not taken away completely, but in them God may teach us that since we cannot avoid the little ones we may be certain that we do not overcome the greater ones by our own powers. Thus may we always fear God and be careful not to lose his grace, which we so many times feel to be necessary for us.

*Jn 13:8

*Mt 6:12-13

*Rm 8:1

Of the Reproaches of the Jews

*Rv 5:5

*Ws 7:30; 8:1

*Lk 11:21
*Heb 2:14

*1 Cor 15:55

*Mk 15:29

*Mk 15:32

*Pss 139:4;
140:4; 63:6

*Jn 11:50
*Jn 7:18; 11:51

*T*HE LION OF THE TRIBE *of Judah has prevailed.** Wisdom has conquered evil, reaching mightily from one end to the other and ordering all things sweetly*—yes, mightily, on my behalf, and sweetly, [in dealing] with me.[1] On the cross he has conquered the blasphemies of the Jews, in the courtyard he has bound the strong man fully armed,* he has triumphed over the very dominion of death.* Where are your reproaches, O Jew? Where, O devil, are the vessels of captivity? *Where, O death, is your victory?** The accuser is confused, the spoiler is despoiled of his prey. *This is power of a new kind!*[2] Death, until now the victor, is astounded! What do you say now, O Jew, who yesterday were wagging your impious head before the cross?* Why were you loading with insults the sacred head of humanity, the Christ? *Let the Christ, the King of Israel, come down from the cross!** O venomous tongue, O evil word, O mischievous speech!* Is it not what you said just a moment ago, Caiphas: *It is better that one man should die for the people, and that the whole nation not perish?** But because that was not a lie, you did not say it of yourself, nor did you speak on your own.*

[1] *Pro me fortiter, suaviter mihi.*
[2] From the Epiphany hymn *Hostis Herodes.*

132

*If he is the King of Israel, let him come down from the cross.** These are clearly your own words, or rather his who is a liar from the beginning.* Why does it seem important that he should come down? If he is a king, should he not rather go up?* Do you not remember, ancient serpent, how you once withdrew in confusion when you presumed to say *throw yourself down*, and *all these I will give you if you will fall down and worship me?** Has what you have heard so slipped away from you, Jew—that the Lord has reigned from the tree—that you reject your king because he stays on the tree? But perhaps you have not heard, because this announcement was not intended for the Jews, but for the nations: *Say among the nations, The Lord has reigned from the tree.*[3]

2. Rightly then did the Gentile governor inscribe the title of his kingship on the tree, and the Jew could not, as he wished, destroy the words of the title,* much less prevent the Lord's passion and our redemption. *Let him come down*, they say, *if he is the King of Israel*. Instead, since he is the King of Israel, let him not abandon the title of his kingship, let him not set aside the scepter of dominion, *whose dominion is upon his shoulders*,[4] as Isaiah foretold. *Do not*, the Jews said to Pilate, *do not write, The King of the Jews, but, This man said, I am King of the Jews*. And Pilate said, *What I have written I have written.**

If Pilate has written what he has written, shall Christ not finish what he has begun? *He has begun, and he will save us.*[5] But they say, *He saved others, himself he cannot save.** Indeed, if he comes down he will save no one. Since no one can be saved except the one who perseveres to the end,* how much more so for

*Mt 27:42
*Jn 8:44

*Rm 10:6-7

*Mt 4:6, 9

*Jn 19:19-22

*Jn 19:21-22

*Mt 27:42

*Mt 10:22

---

[3] Ps 95:10 and hymn *Vexilla Regis* for Passiontide.

[4] Is 9:6 as in the introit *Puer* for Christmas.

[5] Hos 6:2 (Bernard: *Ipse enim coepit et salvabit nos*; Vulg: *quia ipse cepit, et sanabit nos*).

the one who would be Savior? Yet he does save others since he is salvation, while at the same time, being salvation, he has no need to save himself. He works our salvation, not allowing the least part of the saving victim to be overlooked at the evening sacrifice.* He knows, wicked one, what you are thinking. He will not give you any chance to take from us our perseverance, which is our only crown. He will not make fall silent the tongues of preachers encouraging the fainthearted* and saying to each one, "Do not desert your post," something that, no doubt, would follow if they could respond that Christ had deserted them.

The human frame of mind and thought are prone to evil.[6] Without reason, evil one, have you prepared the arrows in your quiver* and compounded the disciples' sighs with the insults of the Jews. The ones despair, the others upbraid, but neither will harm the Christ. He has chosen another time to comfort his disciples and silence his enemies.

3. Meanwhile he gives an example of patience, he commends humility, fulfills obedience, and brings charity to its goal. These gems of virtue adorn the four arms of his cross: at the top is charity, on the right obedience, patience is on the left, and at the foot humility, the root of all virtues. With these the perfection of the Lord's passion has enriched the victory of the cross: humility before the blasphemies of the Jews and patience when wounded, being pierced by tongues within and nails without. Charity too was made perfect in him,* for he laid down his life for his friends,° and his obedience was complete when *he bowed his head, gave up his spirit, and became obedient even to death.**

The one who said, *if he is the King of Israel, let him come down from the cross*, was trying to despoil the church

Margin notes:
*Ps 73:12; 2 K 16:15; Ezr 9:4
*1 Thes 5:14
*Ps 10:3
*1 Jn 2:5
°Jn 5:13
*Jn 19:30; Ph 2:8

---

[6] *Sensus hominis et cogitationes*; Gen 8:21.

of these gifts and deprive her of Christ's glory. [He wanted] that neither the model of obedience, nor the stimulus of love, nor the example of patience and humility [should prevail], but rather that those words of the gospel, sweeter than honey and the honeycomb— *No one has greater love than this, to lay down one's life for one's friends,* and to the Father, *I have finished the work that you gave me to do,* and likewise to the disciples, *Learn from me, for I am meek and humble in heart,* and, *I, if I am lifted up from the earth, will draw all things to myself*—should be utterly obliterated.*

Jn 15:13; 17:4;
Mt 11:29;
Jn 12:32

This is what the cunning* of the poisonous serpent deplores—that bronze serpent lifted up in the desert that heals the wounds he caused of those who would look upon it.* Besides, who else do we suppose caused Pilate's wife to send to him, saying, *Have nothing to do with that just man; I have suffered many things today in a dream because of him?** He was already afraid then, but now he is even more afraid; the enemy feels himself deprived of vigor by the power of the cross. He has come to regret it, but it is too late, and so those whom he had urged to crucify [the Lord] he now urges to persuade him to come down from the cross. So they say, *If he is the King of Israel, let him come down from the cross, and we will believe in him.**

2 Cor 11:3

Nm 21:8-9

Mt 27:19

Mt 27:42

This is the cunning of the serpent, this is the practice of spiritual wickedness.* The godless one had heard the voice of the Savior saying, *I was sent only to the lost sheep of the house of Israel,** and he knew how much zeal he seemed to be showing for the salvation of that people. Therefore he wickedly manipulated the tongues of blasphemers, suggesting that they say, *Let him come down, and we will believe,* as if nothing could now stand in the way of his coming down since he desired their belief so very much.

Eph 6:12

Mt 15:24

4. But who is it who schemes, and for whom does this double-dealer prepare his traps? Surely one

against whom no enemy makes headway, and whom
the child of iniquity has no power to harm.* The one
who knows the hearts of all* is unmoved by empty
promises, just as the meekest of all was unmoved by
blasphemy and reproach. Evil counsel was directed
against him, not indeed that they should believe in
him, but that our faith in him, if any existed, should
altogether perish. We read, *The works of God are perfect.**
How can we keep praising God if he left the work of
salvation imperfect?

But let us hear what Christ replies to these words
through the prophet. Do you ask for a sign, O Jew?*
*Look for me on the day of my resurrection.** If you are
willing to believe, I have already shown you greater
works.* I have multiplied the signs, I brought perfect health yesterday and the day before; today I have
greater things to accomplish. Is it not greater that evil
spirits come out of haunted bodies, as you have seen,
and paralytics leap off of their mats, than that the nails
you drove in spring from my hands and feet? But this
is time to suffer, not to act, and as you tried in vain
to anticipate the hour of my passion, so you will not
prevent it.

5. But if a wicked and adulterous generation asks
for a sign, none will be given it except the sign of
the prophet Jonah:* not a sign of coming down but
a sign of resurrection. And if the Jew does not ask,
let the Christian understand it and rejoice. *The Lion
of the Tribe of Judah has prevailed.** The lion's whelp is
raised by its father's voice. The one who did not come
down from the gibbet came forth from the closed
tomb. Whether this be greater let our enemies judge,
those who secured his tomb with such care, sealing
the stone and setting guards.* This stone, about which
the holy women were asking one another, was very
large;* when the Lord's resurrection occurred, the
angel rolled it back and sat on it, as has been written.*

*Ps 88:23
*Lk 16:15

*Dt 32:4

*Mt 12:39;
1 Cor 1:22
*Zep 3:8

*Jn 10:38;
1 Cor 1:22

*Mt 12:39

*Rv 5:5

*Mt 27:66

*Mk 16:3-4
*Mt 28:2

It is certain, then, that his body, restored to life, came forth from the closed tomb, his body that had come into life from the closed womb of the Virgin at his birth, and that had come to his disciples with the doors shut.* But there is a place from which he was unwilling to come forth with the doors shut, the prison that is hell. He burst the iron bars, he smashed every bolt, so that he might freely lead out his own whom he had redeemed from the hand of the enemy, and that the throng of those made white, who had washed their robes and made them white in the blood of the Lamb,* might march out of wide open gates— white in the blood truly, because the whitening water had also issued with it and in it, and the one who saw this bears witness.* They are surely *white in the blood*, the blood of the young Lamb, milky white, radiant and ruddy, as you have it in the Song of Songs: *My beloved*, says the Bride, *is radiant and ruddy, distinguished among thousands.** This is why the witness of the resurrection appears in a white robe and with a countenance like lightning.*

    *Jn 20:19, 26

    *Rv 7:14

    *Jn 19:34-35

    *Sg 5:10

    *Mt 28:3

6. If his coming forth from a closed tomb already seems sufficient to refute the calumnies of the Jews who said to him mockingly, *If he is the King of Israel, let him come down from the cross*—for they were more anxious to close the tomb and seal it than to drive in nails—*if then the lion of the tribe of Judah has prevailed* in this appearance and demonstrated a greater deed than they were asking for, to what can the miracle of his resurrection now be compared? We read of the resurrections of some people that preceded his*—or rather of their restoration to life—but his rising you celebrate because you recognize that it surpasses the others in two ways. Others were raised only to die again; [but] *Christ, being raised from the dead, dies now no more; death will no more have dominion over him.** Those having died have to be restored to life again; [but] *in that*

    *Mt 27:52

    *Rm 6:9

*he died to sin, he died once for all; in that he lives, he lives
to God,* he lives in eternity. Deservedly, then, is Christ
the first fruits* of those who have arisen; he has arisen
no more to fall,* he who alone attains immortality.

*Rm 6:10
*1 Cor 5:20, 23
*Am 5:2

7. The unique glory of this resurrection is made
known in another way. Who of all the others ever restored themselves to life? This is beyond description,
that one who sleeps wakes himself from death! It is
exceptional; no one does it, not even one. The prophet
Elisha restored a dead person to life, but someone else,
not himself.*

*2 K 4:35

See how many years he lay in a tomb, he who had
not power to raise himself, hoping to be raised by another—by him in fact who conquered the realm of
death in his own person. This is why we say that while
others have been restored to life, Christ has arisen. He
alone came forth from the tomb, a victor by his own
power—indeed, in this too, *the Lion of the tribe of Judah
has prevailed*. How much he can do! Or better, what
will he prove unable to do, the living one who says to
the Father, *I have risen, and I am still with you,*[7] who, so
powerful, was counted among the dead yet was free
among the dead?*

*Ps 87:5-6

8. He did not put off his resurrection beyond the
third day, that the prophet who said, *after two days he
will revive us, and on the third day he will raise us up,*
might be found trustworthy. It is fitting that as our
head went before, so the limbs should follow. He redeemed humanity on the gibbet on the sixth day, the
very day on which he had made humanity in the beginning;* the following day he kept the Sabbath in
the tomb, for he had finished the work he had undertaken; on the third day, which is the first of days, the

*Hos 6:2

*Gen 1:26, 31

---

[7] Ps 138:18 as in the introit *Resurrexi* for Easter Sunday.

new human being[8] appeared, the victor over death, the first fruits of those who are asleep.* *1 Cor 15:20*

So we, whoever we may be, follow our head the whole of this day on which we were formed and redeemed; we do not cease doing penance, we do not cease taking up our cross, but we persevere in this, as he persevered, until the Spirit tells us that we may rest from our labors. Let us not listen to anyone, my brethren—not flesh and blood, not any spirit—who would persuade us to come down from the cross. Let us remain on the cross, let us die on the cross; let us be taken down by the hands of others, not by our inconstancy. Righteous men took down our head; let the holy angels condescend to take us down, so that when the day of the cross has been courageously consummated[9] we may rest peacefully on the second day which comes after death, and that we may sleep happily in the tomb *while we wait for the blessed hope and the coming of the glory of the great God** who will at last *Ti 2:13* restore to life our bodies on the third day, conformed to the body of his glory.* Those dead four days stink, *Ph 3:21* as is written of Lazarus, *Lord, he already stinks, for he has been dead four days.** *Jn 11:39*

9. The ingenuity of the children of Adam fashioned the fourth day, one that did not come from the Lord. Therefore they became corrupt and were made abominable! Like beasts they rotted in their dung!* *Ps 13:1; Jl 1:17* The Triduum we have spoken of is God's arrangement, for labor, for rest, and for resurrection. These things are pleasing to human beings, but they choose to put their own day first, delaying repentance in order to indulge in pleasure. This is not the day that the Lord has made. They are four days dead, and by now they stink!

---

[8] *Novus homo.*
[9] *Consummata viriliter.*

The Holy One born of Mary does not accept this. He rose on the third day that he might not see corruption. *The Lion of the tribe of Judah has prevailed.** The Lamb was slain, but the Lion has prevailed. *The Lion will roar; who will not be afraid?** *The lion,* I say, *mightiest of beasts,* who *trembles at no one he meets**—this is the Lion of the tribe of Judah! Let those who have not acknowledged him tremble, those who said, *We have no king but Caesar!** Let those tremble who said, *We do not want this man to rule over us!* He returns, having received the kingdom,* and *he will bring those wretches to a wretched death.°* Do you want to know that he returns, having received the kingdom? *All authority in heaven and on earth has been given to me,** he says. And the Father says in the psalm, *Ask of me, and I will give you the nations as your inheritance, and the ends of the earth as your possession. You will rule with a rod of iron, and break them in pieces like a potter's vessel.** The Lion is mighty, not cruel. His indignation is severe, and the anger of the dove* is unbearable. But the Lion will roar for his own people, not against them. Let strangers tremble; the tribe of Judah will exult.

10. Let those rejoice who are clothed with praise;* all of their bones are saying, *Lord, who is like you? The Lion of the tribe of Judah, the root of David!** *David* means "greatly desired" or "strong in hand";[10] and David said, *All my desire is before you,** and, *I will keep my strength to you.°* The *Root of David,* Scripture says. David is not his root, but he is *the Root of David,* because he gives support and is not supported. Rightly, holy David, do you call your son your Lord,* because *you do not support the root, but the root supports you.** He is the root of your strength and your desire, the greatly desired root, the strong root.

Margin references: *Rv 5:12, 5; *Am 3:8; *Pr 30:30; *Jn 19:15; *Lk 19:14-15 °Mt 21:41; *Mt 28:18; *Ps 2:8-9; *Jer 25:38; *Ps 103:1; *Ps 34:10; Rv 5:5; *Ps 37:10 °Ps 58:10; *Ps 109:1; Mt 22:43-44; *Rm 11:8

[10] See Jerome, *Liber interpretationis Hebraicorum nominum; Hieronymus, Hebraicae quaestiones in libro Geneseos. Liber interpretationis hebraicorum nominum,* ed. P. de Lagarde, G. Morin, M. Adriaen, CCSL 72 (Turnhout: Brepols, 1959), 35, 11.

*The Lion of the tribe of Judah, the Root of David, has prevailed to open the book and to loosen its seven seals.** *Rv 5:5 These are the words of the book of Revelation. Let those who have not read them get to know them. Let those who know them ruminate on them. *I saw,* John says, *in the right hand of the one seated on the throne a book sealed with seven seals,** and no one could read it *Rv 5:1 or open it. *And I wept much,* he says, *because no one was found worthy to open the book. And one of the elders said to me, do not weep. See, the Lion of the tribe of Judah,* and so forth. *And I saw, and lo, in the midst of the throne a Lamb standing as if it had been slain.* And he went and took the book from the right hand of the one seated upon the throne,* and he opened the book; and there was *Rv 5:4-7 great joy and thanksgiving. John had heard the Lion, and he saw the Lamb. The Lamb was slain, the Lamb took the book; the Lamb opened it and the Lion appeared. Then the elders say, *Worthy is the Lamb that was slain to receive strength**—not to lose its mildness but *to* *Rv 5:12 *receive strength* so that it may both remain a lamb and be a lion.

I say more. It seems to me that he himself is the book that could not be opened! Who was found worthy to open that book? Even John the Baptist, than whom no one greater has arisen among those born of women, confesses himself unworthy. *I am not worthy to untie the thong of his sandals,* he says.* His majesty had *Mt 11:11; Lk 3:16 come to us wearing sandals, his divinity was clothed in flesh. The Wisdom of God had come, but in a closed and sealed book. What the thong of his sandal bound, the seals of the book closed.

11. But what are we to say about the seven [seals]?* *Rv 5:1 Are we perhaps to see the threefold soul—reason, memory, and will—and the four-part composition of the body—made from the four elements—in these seven, so that we may be sure that no part of true humanity was lacking to the Savior? Or is it that the

book is his humanity itself and the seven seals need to be sought?

I think that we find seven things that completely hid the presence of his majesty in the flesh, so that the book could not be opened, and the wisdom hidden there could not be recognized. They are these. First was his Mother's betrothal, which veiled his virgin birth and the purity of his conception so that the crafter of humans might be reckoned the son of a human craftsman. Then, his bodily weakness, whereby he wept and wailed, nursed and slept, and was subject to the other exigencies of the flesh, hid the power of his divinity. Next, he who had come to take away all weakness and sin received the sign of circumcision,* the remedy of sin, and the medicine against all disease.* Then his fleeing from Herod into Egypt where he would not be recognized as the Son of God or the King of heaven. What, next, of the threefold temptation by the enemy in the desert, on the pinnacle, and on the mountain top? *If you are the Son of God*, he said, *command these stones to become loaves of bread*, and again, *Cast yourself down*.* Christ did neither, that the book might remain sealed and the cunning one be deceived. The latter was misled to such a point that, having decided he was a simple human being, in his blind pride he burst out in such great madness that he no longer said, *If you are the son of God*, but, *All these I will give you, if you will fall down and worship me*.* The sixth is the seal of the cross, when the Lord of majesty hung between thieves and *was reckoned with the wicked*.* His burial also closed this book, and no other seal so bound up and so hid this great mystery of holiness.* When the Lord was buried, only despair seemed to be left, so much so that the disciples themselves said, *We used to hope*.* Who would not weep at that time with the book firmly closed and with no one to open it?

12. But weep no more, John, holy one; you too, Mary, do not weep. Let grief be far away, let the cloud

*Rm 4:11
*Mt 2:13

*Mt 4:3, 6

*Mt 4:9

*Lk 23:33; 22:37
*1 Tm 3:16

*Lk 24:21

of sadness disperse. *Rejoice in the Lord, you righteous, and exult with joy, all you upright in heart!** Worthy is the Lamb that was slain,* the Lion that rose from the dead, and finally, the book worthy to open itself! Rising from the dead, rising by his own power, and *after three days*, as he had foretold—as his enemies testified;* and rising in such majesty and glory he shows clearly that whatever seals and covers there were, which we pointed out above, were there because he chose them, not because they were necessary; they were not due to the circumstances but to condescension.

*Pss 32:1; 31:11
*Rv 5:12

*Mt 27:63

Why were you just now sealing the stone of the tomb, O Jew?* Because *that deceiver said while he was still alive, after three days I will rise again.** Truly he is a deceiver, but he is holy, not malicious. *You deceived me, Lord, and I was deceived*, says your prophet for you; *you were stronger, and you have prevailed.** He has deceived you, Jews, in his passion; for in his resurrection the conquering Lion of the tribe of Judah grew strong and prevailed. *If they had known, they would not have crucified the Lord of glory.** What are you going to do, then? He foretold it, and he has already returned to life.

*Mt 27:66
*Mt 27:63

*Jer 20:7

*1 Cor 2:8

Look carefully at the seal of the sepulcher—it has been opened. You are given the sign of the prophet Jonah, for he himself foretold this. Jonah came out of the whale's belly: Christ came out of the heart of the earth on the third day. But clearly something more than Jonah is here, one who manfully brought himself up from the very womb of death. Therefore the men of Nineveh will rise up against you at the judgment,* therefore *they themselves will be your judges,** because they obeyed the prophet, and you did not obey the Lord of prophets.

*Mt 12:39-41
*Mt 12:27

13. Where is that saying of yours, *Let him come down from the cross, and we will believe in him?** You wanted to break the seal of the cross, promising that you were going to enter upon believing. Look!—it is open, not

*Mt 27:42

broken, so enter! In any case, if you do not believe the
one rising from the dead you would not have believed
the one coming down from the cross. If the cross of

Gal 5:11

Christ is an offense to you*—*the message of the cross is

1 Cor 1:18, 23

an offense to the Jews, says the Apostle*—at least let the
novelty of his resurrection rouse you. We find glory in
the cross; to us who are being saved, it is the power of

Gal 6:14

God* and the fullness of all virtues, as we have shown.
May you at least have a part in the resurrection.

But perhaps that too, but even more so, is an offense
to you, and the aroma of life unto life for us is the

2 Cor 2:16

aroma of death unto death for you!* Why then do we
dwell upon it? The older brother cannot bear to listen
to the music and dancing; he is indignant when the
fattened calf is killed for us. He stands outside and will

Lk 15:25-28

not on any account agree to go in.* Let us go in, my
brothers, and *let us feast on the unleavened bread of sincer-*

1 Cor 5:8, 7

*ity and truth, for Christ our Pasch has been sacrificed.** Let
us embrace the virtues commended to us on the cross,
humility and patience, obedience and charity.

14. Let us consider with eager thought what is
commended to us in this great and solemn celebration—certainly a resurrection, a passing over, an entering into another state. Christ did not revert today,
my brothers, he rose! He did not return but passed
over; he entered into a different state, he did not come
back to the same one. The *Pasch* we celebrate is inter-

Ex 12:11

preted *passover,** not *return,* and Galilee, where he who
arose promises that we will see him, does not signify a
return but an entering into another state.[11]

I think that some people's imagination flies ahead,
and they embrace the meaning they want these things
to have. Yet I speak briefly so that a superfluity of

---

[11] Mt 28:7, 10; see Saint Jerome, *Liber interpr Libr. nom.,* ed. de
Lagarde, p. 58, 2.

words will not seem to burden your devotion on so great a feast. If Christ the Lord had been revived into our mortality and the burdens of this present life after the consummation of the cross, I would not say he had passed over, my brothers, but that he had passed back; not that he had entered a higher state, but that he had returned to his former state. But now, because he has passed into newness of life,* he invites us to pass over as well, he calls us to Galilee. Therefore *in that he died to sin, he died once for all*; in that he now lives, he lives not to the flesh, but to God.* *Rm 6:4

*Rm 6:10;
Gal 2:20

15. What are we to say, we who strip the Lord's sacred resurrection of the name *Pasch* so that it is to us a return rather than a passing over? We have been mourning during these days, given up to compunction and prayer, to gravity and abstinence, desiring to redeem and wash away the negligence of other seasons during these sacred forty days.* We have shared in the sufferings of Christ,* we have been planted together with him* once again by a baptism of tears, of repentance, and of confession. *If then we are dead to sin, how will we live in it any longer?** If we bemoan our negligences, why do we relapse into them? Will we now be found once more as meddlesome as we were before, as talkative as before, as lazy and negligent as before—vain, suspicious, slanderous, bad-tempered, and caught up in the other vices we have deplored with such distress during these days? *I have washed my feet; how will I soil them once more? I have put off my garment; how will I put it on?** This is not entering another state, my brothers; not thus is Christ seen; this is not the way by which God shows us his salvation.* One who looks back is not worthy of the kingdom of God.* *RB 49
*1 Pt 4:13
*Rm 6:5

*Rm 6:2

*Sg 5:3

*Ps 90:16
*Lk 9:62

16. Thus do those who love this world, the enemies of Christ's cross,* who are called Christians though they have received that name to no effect, long throughout this whole period of forty days for the present days of *Ph 3:18

the resurrection so that—it pains me to say it!—they may indulge in pleasure more freely! So a sad reality, brothers, clouds over the joy of this solemnity. We lament over the injury done to this festival, an injury we cannot ignore in principle, much less when carried out on the solemnity itself. How sad this is! The resurrection of the Savior is made a season for sinning, a time for relapsing! From this moment reveling and drunkenness return, debauchery and wantonness are indulged again,* and the reins of concupiscence are loosened, as though it was for this that Christ arose, and not rather for our justification.*

Rm 13:13

Rm 4:25

Is this how, unhappy ones, you honor the Christ you took up? You prepared a welcome for him who is to come, confessing your sins with groans, punishing your bodies, and giving alms, and now you betray to his enemies the one you embraced, forcing him to leave while you give free rein to your former depravities! Light has no partnership with darkness, nor Christ* with pride, with greed, with ambition, with hatred of the brothers, with excess, with fornication. Why do you owe him less now when he is present than when he was yet to come? Why does the season of the resurrection require less respect than that of the passion? But clearly you honor neither. If you had suffered with him,* you would reign with him; if you died with him, you would rise with him.

2 Cor 6:14-15

Rm 8:17

17. There is a certain humbling, but it is just out of custom and so is pretentious; no spiritual exaltation follows it. *Because of this*, the Apostle says, *many are weak and sickly and many have fallen asleep.** Because of this, death abounds in the various regions of humanity, particularly during these days. You, practicers of collusion, have been caught among calamities—not because you practice collusion, but because you persist in sin, augmenting your collusion.* Either you are completely impenitent, or your penitence is lukewarm; you flee

1 Cor 11:30

Is 1:5

neither from danger nor, after unhappily experiencing it, from the occasion of sin.

The enemy has ensnared you, as Scripture says, *in the tangled sinews of his testicles.** If you flee from the sacraments of Christ with the knowledge that this is so, you have nothing in common with Christ, nor have you life in you. Listen to him speaking: *Unless you eat the flesh of the Son of Man and drink his blood, you have no life in you.** If you receive it unworthily, you eat judgment against yourselves, not discerning the holy thing of the Lord.* *Recall it to mind, transgressors,*° seek the Lord with your whole heart, and hate evil, repenting not only in word and speech, but in spirit and in truth.

*Jb 40:17 [*Vulg* 40:12]

*Jn 6:53 (54)

*1 Cor 11:29
°Is 46:8

Seeing, then, that it does not sufficiently grieve a person that he has died, that he is disposed to remain in a dangerous situation or, not seeking a guide, to go astray, let there be a sign of true compunction, a flight from the opportunity for sin, a drawing back from its occasions. Otherwise we must truly fear that this day—it too being set for the falling and rising of many*—will stand as a rebuke to you, either clearly as aliens from Christ, having nothing to do with Christ, or as companions of Judas, into whom Satan entered after he received the morsel.*

*Lk 2:34

*Jn 13:27

18. But what have we to do, my brothers, with judging those who are outside?* We lament only because we have been in the same trap in which our fraternal love makes us grieve that they are miserably detained, and from which we rejoice that we have been released solely by the working of mercy. Would that, with the coming of the resurrection, we be found sanctified and wholly alien to this unhappy and unholy way of life; that no part of ourselves pass away or our spiritual exercise be lessened; but rather that we strive to pass over and to grow. Those who truly rise with Christ, who celebrate the Pasch and hasten to Galilee, are all who do not return to the consolations of the flesh

*1 Cor 5:12

after their tears of repentance, but who advance in confidence in the divine pity and enter into a new devotion and joy in the Holy Spirit—not so much afflicted by remorse at the remembrance of their former sins as delighted by the memory and inflamed by the desire for heavenly rewards.

You, then, beloved, *if you have risen with Christ, seek the things that are above, where Christ is, sitting at the right hand of God. Set your minds on things that are above, not on things that are on earth.** Then, as Christ rose from the dead by the glory of the Father, so you too may walk in newness of life.** Then you may rejoice to pass from secular pleasures and the consolations of the world, through the compunction and sadness that are of God, to holy devotion and spiritual exultation, by the gift of the one who passed from this world to the Father, and who deigns to draw us after himself, and to call us into Galilee, that he may show us himself, who is God over all, blessed forever.**

Col 3:1-2

Rm 6:4

Rm 9:5

Of the Holy Day of Easter, about the venomous saying of the Jews, *If he is the King of Israel, let him come down from the cross*, and of what we read in the book of Revelation, *The Root of David, from the tribe of Judah, has prevailed; he has opened the book and loosed its seven seals*

1. *T*HE LION OF THE TRIBE of Judah, the Root of David, has prevailed to open the book and to loosen its seven seals.* Where are those who said, *Let Christ, the King of Israel, come down from the cross, and we will believe in him?** Where are those, I say, who taunted him as they wagged their heads before the cross,* demanding that our Head be removed from it? Where are those who, when God our king before the ages worked salvation in the midst of the earth,* when he inspired the prophet who said that *the Lord has reigned from the tree*[1]—where, I say, are those who said then, *If he is the King of Israel, let him come down from the cross?** O venomous tongue, O deceitful tongue!* Truly *their tongue is a sharp sword*, truly they have sharpened their tongues like swords, and *the poison of asps is under their lips.**

    2. You urge him, O Jew, to come down from the cross. What then am I to do? I implore you, Lord, I

*Rv 5:5

*Mk 15:32

*Mt 27:44, 39

*Ps 73:12

*Mt 27:42
*Pss 139:4; 51:6

*Pss 56:5; 139:4

---

[1] Ps 95:10 and hymn *Vexilla Regis* for Passiontide.

*Pr 1:10

*Mt 10:22

implore you not to give way to them.* If only those who endure can be saved,* how much less can he be Savior [if he were not to endure]? What am I to say to my brothers, who are your limbs, if you come down from the cross? How will I encourage the fainthearted, how will I admonish the lazy and those who have almost gone back from the way of truth? How am I to say to people of this kind, *do not desert your post*, if they can reply that Christ deserted his? How many are even now tempted to come down from their cross, and some have even come down! Who will remain, if you come down and give to the fainthearted and to our impatience an opportunity that will find us totally ready? *The human imagination and thought are prone to*

*Gen 8:21

*Mt 16:24

*evil from youth.** How will you now say, *Those who want to follow me, let them take up their cross,** if you first leave your own?

*Mt 16:22

*2 K 16:15;
Ezr 9:4
*Ex 29:22;
Lv 3:9

*Far be it from you, Lord!** Be gracious to us. Don't let this happen! It is Satan who tries to persuade you thus; he is the enemy of salvation who is trying to hinder the work of salvation. What will this sacrifice profit—this evening sacrifice*—what will it profit if the tail is missing?* Perseverance alone is the crown of the virtues, and the enemy wishes to snatch it away from me. But how, my brothers, how will he endure on the cross when he sees on one side the Jews decrying him and on the other his disciples sighing? Must we not fear that he will come down to comfort his disciples and confute his enemies? The Jews say, *He saved others,*

*Mt 27:42

*Lk 24:21

*himself he cannot save.** His disciples say, *We were hoping that he would redeem Israel.** The Jews exult and insult; Peter despairs and denies. By his advice you would not have ascended the cross, as you know!

3. If you descend, what then? In the first place, do we not lose the four greatest virtues, which are fixed to the four arms of the cross? If you lay aside the cross before you lay down your life, where is that great love

than which no one has greater?* Where is what the
disciple whom you loved said, *Having loved his own, he
loved them to the end*?* If they too want you to come
down, I would say, with their leave, "Let them get behind you since they think wrongly,* and their counsel is not good, since it is to their advantage that you
go away.* Where is your full and perfect obedience if
you are not obedient to the point of death?* Where
is your patience, your humility, which you set before
us as a model, if you reveal your power by descending
from the cross because of the mockery of the Jews?
The well-known words, sweeter than honey and the
honeycomb, will have to be removed from the gospel:
*No one has greater love than this, to lay down one's life for
one's friends*; and this, *as the father has commanded me,
so I do*; and, [addressed] to the Father, *I have finished
the work that you gave me to do*; and this no less, *learn
from me, for I am meek and humble in heart*.* The Apostle
could not have said, *Christ loved us and gave himself up
for us*, or this, *Christ became obedient to the Father to the
point of death, even the death of the cross*.* You would not
say yourself, *I was filled with insults*, nor this from the
psalms, *I am a worm and not human, the reproach of others, and the outcast of the people*.* All this we lose, if you
come down. There will no longer be an incentive for
charity, nor a model of obedience; we will have no
example of patience and humility."

This is the mystery, brothers, this is the great sacrament of the Lord's cross, for in it we have those four
virtues. Let surpassing charity be at the head; let obedience be on the right side—it makes children of the
right hand; let patience be on the left side—which
we must show to those who oppose us; let humility be at the foot—it is the root and foundation of
all virtue. Here the Jew, or rather the devil through
the Jew's mouth, tried to persuade the Son of God
to come down. Truly, Lord, as you were wounded by

*Jn 15:13

*Jn 13:1

*Mk 8:33

*Jn 16:7
*Ph 2:8

**Jn 15:13; 14:31;
17:2; Mt 11:29*

*Eph 5:2; Ph 2:8

**Lam 3:30;
Ps 2:8*

nails in the body, so you were wounded by tongues in the heart; you accepted both for me, and for me you overlooked both.*

Ps 11:3

4. But see how the subject of temptation grows—as if temptation could harm him! Now he is one whom no enemy will impose upon, whom the son of iniquity will not have the power to harm.* Listen to what he says: *If he is the King of Israel, let him come down from the cross, and we will believe in him.** He who once spoke through the mouth of the serpent* was saying this through the mouth of the Jews. We know, brothers, that with desire Christ desired the salvation of his people;* because of them he makes this reproach full of devotion: *O all you who pass by the way, look and see if there is any sorrow like my sorrow,** especially to those who flee from salvation, for whom chiefly the Savior came, as he himself said: *I was sent only to the lost sheep of the house of Israel.** But now, when they say *let him come down and we will believe,* what remains except for him to come down for them to believe? O Lord, you know the hearts of all; you know that they are not seeking their own salvation but my damnation; they do not want to believe in God, but they are working that I may not be able to believe, since the Scripture says that *God's works are perfect.**

Ps 88:23

Mt 27:42
Gen 3:7

Lk 22:15

Lam 1:12

Mt 15:24

Dt 32:4

Yes, he is speaking, he is striving to persuade him to come down who dared with unholy daring to tempt him, placed on the pinnacle of the temple, to throw himself down.* If the Jews want to believe, have you not shown them greater works?* Was it not greater for them to see demons come out of haunted bodies at your command than for you to make the nails leap from the wood of the cross? What reply will you make to these people, Lord? *Look for me on the day of my resurrection.** Why do you hasten, why do you pass along the way?* *Wait for me,* he says, *on the day of my resurrection*—for the things written of me have their

Mt 4:5-6
Jn 5:20

Zep 3:8
Ps 79:13

time,* and you cannot disturb it. You were trying to bring about my passion before its time, and you have heard the words, *my hour is not yet come.* *

Lk 22:37

Jn 2:4

5. So now too, O Jew, if you are asking for a sign, *Look for me on the day of my resurrection.* This wicked and adulterous generation asks for a sign, and no sign will be given it except the sign of the prophet Jonah.* Do you ask for the sign of his coming down? I will not give you that, but the sign of his resurrection instead. There you were, saying, *Let him come down from the cross, and we will believe in him*, and here he is, having done greater things than this, much greater things. Is it not greater to leave a sealed tomb than to come down from the cross?

Mt 12:29

6. But perhaps you ask how I know that he came forth from a closed tomb. Yesterday you heard that as the holy women were coming to the tomb an earthquake occurred; an angel came down from heaven and rolled back the stone about which they were complaining and sat upon it, saying that he whom they sought was not there but had already risen.* Obviously then, the great stone that the Jews had put there and sealed had not yet been rolled back when the Savior came forth. Certainly this was a greater miracle than if he had come down from the cross. He did a much more marvelous thing when he rose from the dead.

*Mt 28:1-7;
Mk 16:1-7*

True, other resurrections had taken place earlier,* but they were preambles to this one, and they were surpassed by this one in two respects. First, they rose to die again, but Christ being raised now dies no more!* Hence Christ is the first fruits° of those who arise, because he was the first to rise after dying. Again, others, dying again, need to be restored to life again; Christ died once for all* and rose once for all.

Mt 27:52

Rm 6:9
°1 Cor 15:20, 23

Rm 6:10

7. The Lord's resurrection surpasses all the others in another way. Some had been restored to life by others, but none before Christ had been able to restore

themselves to life. Elisha, who restored the dead to life,* has long lain dead and has not yet risen. Christ alone has been able to restore himself to life, he who alone was free among the dead.* What will he be able to do, he who is living eternally and saying to the Father, *I have risen and I am still with you*,[2] he who alone with respect to all the dead was so powerful?

8. It was absolutely fitting for him to rise on the third day because of the text, *after two days he will revive us, and on the third day he will raise us up*.* Thus should it happen to us as to our head before us. The first day he was on the cross, the second in the tomb, and on the third he was glorified by the triumph of the resurrection. So we also, if we are his members* and if we choose to follow our head, on the first day—that is, while we are in this mortal flesh—we will persevere in the cross of our penitence, concerning which he himself said, *If any want to come after me, let them take up their cross and follow me*.* We will not come down, as Christ did not come down.

Righteous men took him down when he was already dead;* may the holy angels take us down! Thus with this day successfully finished, the second, which is after death, we will spend in the tomb, sleeping in peace* and resting from all labor. *Henceforth now, says the Spirit, they may rest from their labors*.*

On the third day we will rise again to be forever in glory and eternal life. Christ was unable to wait for a fourth day, because those who are dead for four days stink,* and of him it was written, *You will not let your holy one see corruption*.*

9. The children of Adam devised the fourth day; because of this they rotted like beasts in their dung.* God ordained three days: the first for labor, the second

*2 K 4:35

*Ps 87:6

*Hos 6:2

*Eph 4:15-16

*Mt 16:24

*Lk 23:50

*Ps 4:8
*Rv 14:3

*Jn 11:39
*Ps 15:10

*Jl 1:17

---

[2] Ps 138:18 as in the introit *Resurrexi* for Easter Sunday.

for rest, the third for dominion. The children of Adam devised a fourth, wanting now for a time to live in softness and good repute, and to put off repentance. Therefore they have become four days dead, and they already stink. The Lord does not know this fourth day, and so, rising on the third day, he does not see corruption. *The Lion of the tribe of Judah has prevailed.** The lamb has been slain,* but the lion has prevailed. *The lion will roar; who will not be afraid?* The lion*, I say, *mightiest of beasts*, who *trembles at no one he meets.** He is the Lion of the tribe of Judah. Let those who are from elsewhere tremble. Why should the tribe of Judah tremble? The Lion's anger does not roar against its own but against those from elsewhere. This lion is mighty, not cruel, yet still great is his indignation, and the anger of the dove is unbearable!* *Rv 5:5*

Rv 5:12

Am 3:8

Pr 30:30

Jer 25:38 Vulg

10. Blessed then are those of the *tribe of Judah.* They are clothed with praise,* so that all of their bones may say, *Lord, who is like you?** All their works, because they are works of God, praise him.* *The Lion of the tribe of Judah* is also *the Root of David.** David is not his root. David himself confesses, *O my strength, to you will I turn.** David means "strong in hand" and "desirable";[3] the Lord is the root of strength, the root of desire, the desirable root, the strong root. *Ps 103:1*

Ps 34:10

Ps 144:10

Rv 5:5

Ps 58:10

This Lion prevailed to open the book and to undo its seals. Those who are familiar with the narrative of the book of Revelation know how John saw the book closed and sealed and wanted to see what was written in it. He began to weep because no one was found worthy to open the book. One of the elders, however, said to him, *Do not weep. The Lion of the tribe of Judah, the Root of David, has prevailed to open the book and to loosen its seals.** A little later he heard them singing, *Rv 5:5*

---

[3] Saint Jerome, *Liber interpr. hesr. nominum*, ed. de Lagarde, 35, 11.

*Worthy is the lamb that was slain to open the book and to loosen its seals.** He is the Lamb, he is the Lion—indeed he is the Book. What wonder if no one was worthy to open this book? John himself—than whom no one greater has arisen among those born of women*— confesses himself unworthy. *I am not worthy*, he says, *to untie the thong of his sandals.** Divinity comes to us wearing sandals; the Wisdom of God* comes enclosed in a book; what the thong of his sandal binds is also symbolized by the seals of the book.

*Rv 5:9

*Mt 11:11

*Lk 3:16
*1 Cor 1:24

*Rv 5:1-2

*Mt 2:13

*Lk 2:26

*Mt 4:9
*Lk 23:33

*1 Tm 3:16

11. But what are these seven seals? There are seven things, I think, that chiefly concealed the presence of majesty in the flesh, and in some way prevented the book from being opened and the Wisdom of God from being recognized. Among these are the be- trothal of his mother, by which the virgin birth and his holy conception were concealed so that he might be thought to be the carpenter's son; also his physical weakness, his wailing, and suffering hunger, and nurs- ing, and the other kinds of physical distress he bore, greatly obscured the Lord of majesty. Circumcision, too—the brand mark of robbers, the medicine of the sick, and the remedy for sinners—was no less instru- mental in closing and sealing this book. But it was the flight into Egypt away from Herod the king* that provided the greatest concealment to the Son of God and King of heaven.

And who would have recognized the Christ of the Lord* in his temptation by the devil, when the tempter was bold enough to suggest that he should fall down and worship him?* Need I speak of the cross, where he hung between two thieves* as though he was one of them? His burial too most certainly closed this great mystery of holiness,* because when the Lord was bur- ied, it seemed that only despair remained.

12. Rightly did John weep because no one was found to loosen the seals and open the book to reveal

the Wisdom of God enclosed within.* But worthy is *Rv 5:3-4
the Lamb that was slain,* the Lion who rose from *Rv 5:12
the dead, and the Book worthy to open itself, which
we cannot doubt was done at the resurrection—by
which, among all the rest, it is clearly shown that all
we mentioned before was a matter of choice, not of
necessity; a matter of condescension, not of contract.

13. See, you Jews, you who strove to break apart
the seal of the cross, see, now it has been opened, not
broken apart.

14. He did not choose to break it apart because in it
he wished to commit and commend to us those virtues mentioned above. See, we have obtained something great from the cross: do you also receive it from
the resurrection, *and do not be faithless, but believing.** *Jn 20:27
Or rather, because the obstinate Jew spurned him, let
the true Jew, one circumcised in the spirit, not in the
letter, a Jew inwardly, not outwardly,* receive riches *Rm 2:28-29
and glory in the cross, in the resurrection, and in the
ascension. As it is written, *Riches and glory are in his left
hand, long life is in his right hand.** *On the cross are wealth* *Pr 3:16
and glory because the remission of sins is in the resurrection—*he died*, as the Apostle says, *for our transgressions*[4]—as is also our justification, that is, the bestowal
of merits—for *he rose for our justification.** Similarly *Rm 4:25
in the ascension are hope and the expectation of rewards—he ascended for our glorification. *If I go away*,
he says, *I will come again and will take you to myself.** *And* *Jn 14:3
now God the Father *has lifted up my head*;* we can- *Ps 27:6;
Ac 2:33
not doubt that he will lift up his limbs as well, if they
choose to follow their head and go through the same
opening, which is the passion; otherwise they must be
separated from the head and perish. For the head to go

---

[4] Rm 4:25 as in the responsory *Expurgate* for the Friday after
Easter.

through one opening and the limbs through another is quite impossible.

Let them have no doubt that they cleave to him; let them hope with confidence, let them wait free from care. *I will*, he says, *that where I am, there also they may be with me.** If he wills this, who will stand in his way? Is there not *life in his will?** *If God is for us, who is against us?** Therefore in affirmation he says, *Where I am, there will my servant also be.**

I am only his servant, his beloved, setting the Paschal Lamb before you. He of his goodness allows me so to serve, that I may be found among the faithful stewards,* and that my ministry may be for my salvation and yours.

*Jn 17:24

*Ps 29:6 Vulg

*Rm 8:31

*Jn 12:26

*1 Cor 4:2

On the Holy Day of Easter, about the Gospel Reading: *Mary Magdalene, and so on.**

**Mt 16:1*

1. WE HAVE RECEIVED from the Apostle that Christ dwells in our hearts through faith;* hence it seems that we **Eph 3:17* can reasonably suppose that as long as faith lives in us so does Christ. But if our faith has died, then Christ is in some measure dead in us. Moreover, works testify to the life of faith, as it is written, *the works that the Father has given me, these testify on my behalf.** The **Jn 5:36* one who declares that faith by itself without works is dead* does not seem to disagree with this. As we **Jm 2:17, 20* discern the life of this body from its movement, so we discern the life of faith from good works.* **Jm 2:18*

The life of the body is the soul, by which it moves and feels; the life of faith is love because it works through love, as you read in the Apostle, *faith that works through love.** So when love grows cold faith dies,° just as the **Gal 5:6* body does when the soul departs. Therefore if you see *°Mt 24:12* people active in good works* and cheerful in the fervor **Eph 2:10* of their way of life, have no doubt that faith lives in them, for you have undoubted proofs of that life.

But there are some, I hate to admit, who start with the Spirit but afterward end with the flesh. We know that the spirit of life no longer abides in them because it is written, *my spirit shall not abide in humanity forever,* *Gen 6:3* *for they are flesh.** If the spirit does not abide, we can have no doubt whatsoever that love is lost, *the love that has been poured out in our hearts through the Holy Spirit* *Rm 5:5* *that has been given to us.**

2. Furthermore, the life of faith, as we have already *Gal 5:6* said, consists of love; faith manifests itself through love.* From this we may gather that when the spirit *Jn 6:63* departs faith dies, because *it is the spirit that gives life.** Then if to live according to the sensibility of the flesh is death, we cannot doubt that those in whose lives we rejoiced as long as they were putting to death the deeds of the flesh by the Spirit are mourned as though dead when they live according to the flesh. Hence you read in the same Apostle, *If you live according to the flesh, you will die; but if by the Spirit you have put to death the* *Rm 8:13* *deeds of the flesh, you will live.**

Unhappy whoever is a *dog returned to its vomit, a sow* *2 Pt 2:22* *that was washed only to wallow again in the mire.** I am not speaking so much of those who return to Egypt in the body but of those who return in heart, following the blandishments of this present world, and lack the life of faith, which is love. *If any love the world, the love* *1 Jn 2:15* *of the father is not in them.** Who is deader than those *Pr 5:20; 6:27* who cherish fire in their bosom* and sin in their conscience, who neither feel, nor tremble, nor shake it off?

3. See, Christ is in the tomb, and faith is dead in the soul. What shall we do? What did the holy women do, who out of all his friends were held by greater affection? *They bought spices, so that they might go and* *Mk 16:1* *anoint Jesus.** Was this to restore him to life? We know, brothers, that it is not for us to restore to life; our duty is to anoint. Why? So that those in this state do not *Jn 11:39* stink,* that others may not catch the odor of death,° *2 Cor 2:16* and that they do not flow away and utterly dissolve. So the three women bought their spices—mind, tongue,

and hands. Concerning these, I think, Peter received a threefold command to feed the Lord's flock.* Feed them, he said, with the mind, with the mouth, and with action: feed them with interior prayer, with verbal exhortation, and by example. *Jn 21:15-17

4. Let the mind therefore seek its spices—above all affectionate compassion, then zeal for uprightness, and among these let it not forget the spirit of discretion. As often as you see a brother sinning, affectionate compassion should immediately appear as something belonging to human nature and which you give birth to in yourself. *You who are spiritual,* says the Apostle, *restore such a one in a spirit of gentleness, considering yourself, lest you also be tempted.** *Gal 6:1

And when the Lord went out carrying the cross by himself and they wept over him—not all the tribes of the earth, but a few women—he turned to them and said, *Daughters of Jerusalem, do not weep for me, but weep for yourselves and for your children.** Notice the order carefully: first, *for yourselves;* then *for your children.* Take note of yourself, that you may know how to be compassionate toward others, and that you may reprove in a *spirit of gentleness.* Take note of yourself, *lest you also be tempted.* *Lk 23:27-28

But because an example is more persuasive and effective and makes a greater impression on the mind, I send you to the holy old man who, hearing that one of his brethren had sinned, wept bitterly and said, *It is he today, and I tomorrow.*[1] Do you suppose that one who wept for himself had no compassion for his brother? This feeling of compassion benefits many, because a generous spirit is ashamed to sadden someone he sees is already sufficiently troubled.

5. But what are we to do when some are stiff-necked and have a hard forehead* so that the more we have *Ex 32:9;
Ez 3:7

---

[1] *Vitae patrum.* PL 74:380, 10; compare PL 73:1039, 3.

compassion on them, the more they abuse our compassion and patience? We were compassionate toward a brother. Should we not also be compassionate toward righteousness itself when we see it so shamelessly thrust aside and so thoughtlessly provoked? I know that if we have any love we cannot bear this scorn toward God with equanimity. This is the zeal for righteousness. It sets us on fire against wrongdoers so as to lead us by a sense of duty[2] toward that righteousness of God that we see scorned. Truly, the feeling of compassion[3] must claim better things for itself. Otherwise, with a violent wind we shatter the ships of Tarshish, break the bruised reed, and quench the smoking flax.* *Ps 47:8; Is 42:3

6. When both a feeling of compassion and zeal for righteousness are present, the spirit of discretion must be there too; otherwise, when it is necessary to bring one into play it happens that the other gets acted out instead and everything ends in confusion because of indiscretion. Let our minds, then, possess the third, the spirit of discretion, so that, suitably distinguishing circumstances, they may know when to emulate others and also how to pardon. Let them be Samaritans, watching and judging when to use the oil of mercy and when the wine of ardor.* *Lk 10:33-34 Do not think this my own opinion. Listen to the prophet praying for these same things and in the same order: *Teach me goodness and discipline and knowledge*, he says.* *Ps 118:66

7. But where are we to get these things? The soil of our heart does not make virtues like these sprout up for us, but rather produces thorns and thistles!* *Gen 3:18 So, we have to buy them. But from whom must we buy? From the one who said, *Come, buy wine and milk without money and without price.** *Is 55:1

---

[2] *Pietas.*
[3] *Compassionis affectus.*

You know very well that milk signifies sweetness and wine austerity. But what does it mean to buy without money and without price? This is not the kind of purchase lovers of this age make, but no other is possible with the maker of the world. The prophet said to the Lord, *You are my God, you have no need of my goods.** What price will humans give him for his grace° since he needs nothing, and all things are his? Grace is free and freely given. Even when it is bought, it is bought for nothing, because what is given for it is held for our betterment. *Ps 15:2 Vulg* °Mt 16:26

8. We must buy the three spices for the mind with the money of self-will; by losing it we lose nothing, we even gain more, for we change it for something better so that what was private might be common.[4] The common will is love. So we buy *without price*, receiving what we did not have while keeping more securely the things we had. How will someone ever have compassion on a brother if in his self-will he does not know how to have compassion on anyone but himself? Or how will the one who loves himself ever love righteousness or hate iniquity? Such a one can put on a good show before human eyes, and even deceive himself, so that when moved by self-referential love he thinks it is the feeling of compassion, or by hatred he thinks it is zeal for righteousness.

But clearly it is easy to know how alien to self-will are the things proper to love; the two are directly opposed. Love is kind, love does not rejoice at iniquity.* Now by the spirit of discretion we know that nothing destroys love as much as self-will, subverting human hearts and closing the eyes of reason. So we must buy three spices for the mind at the cost of self-will—the feeling of compassion, zeal for righteousness, and the *1 Cor 13:4, 6*

---

[4] *Ut communis fiat quae propria fuit.*

spirit of discretion, with the money, as was said, of self-will.

9. There are also three spices for the tongue—sobriety when reproving, generosity when encouraging, and efficacy when persuading. Do you want to have these spices? Buy them from the Lord your God. Buy them, I say, as you bought the previous ones, *without price*. You receive something, you lose nothing. Buy from the Lord moderate reproof because it is an extremely good thing, the best gift,* and few possess it. For, as blessed James says, *No one can tame the tongue.** You see many who, inspired by a sincere intention and good-will, make light in speech of serious matters they have heard. *Once a word flies you cannot bring it back,*[5] and because it seems more biting, it irritates and aggravates what it ought to cure. When impudence is added to negligence, impatience too increases, so that *those who were filthy, let them be filthy still.** They descend to words of malice to make excuses for sin* and, like madmen, not only fend off the doctor but try to bite the doctor's hand as well!

Not many people have a gift for words, so faced with a lack of words they feel their tongue stick to the roof of their mouth,* something that can cause no little irritation to their hearers. Others, however, have a considerable flow of words at their command, but what they say is neither wise nor heeded; because they lack grace, what they say has little efficacy.

So you see how necessary it is to buy, from the one who is the source of all goodness and knowledge, so-briety when reproving, generosity when encouraging, and efficacy when persuading.

10. Therefore buy these things with the coinage of confession, that you may confess your own sins be-

Jm 1:17
Jm 3:8

Rv 22:11
Ps 140:4 Vulg

Lam 4:4;
Ez 3:26

---

[5] Horace, *Ep* 1.18.71.

fore you go to clear away those of others. Restoring a soul to life is a great and wonderful sacrament: see that you do not come to it dirty! If perhaps you cannot be innocent—or rather, because you cannot be—wash your hands among the innocent before you go around the Lord's tomb—all things are washed in confession. This washing shall be reckoned to you as a kind of innocence so that you may stand among the innocent. No one comes to service at the altar in ordinary clothes; rather, whoever comes to it is clothed in white. You, then, when you are hastening to the Lord's tomb, wash yourself, make yourself bright, put on the garments of glory so that you may be told, *You have put on confession and beauty.** Where there is confession, there, in the Lord's sight, is beauty.* **Ps 103:1*
*Ps 95:6

These things have been said so that you may purchase with the coinage of confession sober reproof, generous encouragement, and efficacious persuasion.

11. We read, and we learn by daily experience, that the preaching of those whose lives are contemptible is despised.[6] Let the hand then prepare its spices, so that the Wise One may not mock us like that lazy person who found it a burden to raise his hand to his mouth,* **Pr 26:15*
and the one whom you accuse can say, *You who teach others, you do not teach yourself.** *You bind heavy and insupportable burdens and lay them on people's shoulders, and are unwilling to move them with a finger.** I say to you: the word that is living and active* is the example of one's deeds. It easily persuades and demonstrates that what we advise is doable. For this reason the hand, too, must have its spices—continence with respect to the flesh, mercy with respect to a brother, and patience with respect to godliness. That is why the Apostle says, *Let us live sober, righteous, and godly lives.** **Rm 2:21*
*Mt 23:4
*Heb 4:12

*Ti 2:12

---

[6] Gregory the Great, *Hom. in Ev.*, 12.1.

These three things are extremely necessary to our way of life, for we owe them first to ourselves, second to our neighbor, and third to God. *One who fornicates sins against his own body*,* depriving it of great respect, and adding to it disgrace by fear and shame, taking a member of Christ and making it a member of a prostitute.* But I say that you should abstain not only from that, which is so abominable, but from every pleasure of the flesh.

Before all else, then, seek this perfect continence that you owe to yourself; no one is nearer to you than yourself! Then, add the mercy that you owe to your neighbors, because you are to be saved along with them; and lastly the patience that you owe to God, because you are to be saved by him. *All who want to live a godly life in Christ suffer persecution*,* and *it is through many tribulations that we must enter the kingdom of God*.* See then that you do not perish through impatience, but bear all for him who bore greater things for you long ago, and with whom patience will not be fruitless. As the prophet says, *The patience of the poor will not perish for ever*.*

12. These spices of the hand are bought with the coinage of submission. This is what directs our steps and gains the grace of a holy way of life. If a hostile law is found in our members through disobedience,* who does not know that continence is the gift of obedience? Obedience knows how to govern mercy, it teaches patience and bestows it. Approach, then, with these spices one in whom faith is dead.* Truly if we consider what a great thing it is to restore someone in this state to life—how difficult it is to reach a heart closed by stony obstinacy and shamelessness—I think that we too must say, *Who will roll away the stone for us from the entrance to the sepulcher?**

But while we tremble and fear to approach, resisting so great a miracle, it sometimes happens that with its

*1 Cor 6:18

*1 Cor 6:15

*2 Tm 3:12
*Ac 14:22 (21)

*Ps 9:19

*Rm 7:23

*Jm 2:26

*Mk 16:3

usual loving-kindness the divine ear hears the preparation of our heart,* and with a mighty voice raises up   *Ps 9:38
again what was dead.*   *Ps 67:34

Then, so that his face may be seen clearly trans-
formed, behold, the Angel of the Lord, a certain mer-
riment in his expression, appears to us as it were in
the door of the tomb, and something like lightning as
a sign of resurrection. He offers us access to his heart;
even more, he calls us, and rolls away and takes his seat
upon that very stone of obstinacy—even the linen
cloths that covered [his face] are raised up by faith—so
that he might reveal himself! And while he opens up
everything that had before been played out in his heart,
and confesses how he had buried himself within, for-
saking his very temerity and negligence: *Come,* he says,
*and see the place where the Lord had been laid.**   *Mt 28:6

Concerning Naaman's Leprosy

1. IN THE MEDICAL treatment of the body, purgings are first employed, then nourishment; thus the body is first emptied of noxious humors and then strengthened with health-giving foods.

This is what the Lord Christ, the doctor of souls, did. His entire purpose, as he showed in the incarnation, was to be the medicine of salvation. Before his passion he gave us seven purgings; after his resurrection he gave us an equal number of wholesome and pleasant foods. Our Elisha ordered Naaman the leper to wash seven times in the Jordan,* which is interpreted "descent."[1] In the descent of our Lord Jesus Christ—that is, in the lowly way of life he exhibited before his passion—we are cleansed and purged; in his resurrection and in the life he exhibited during the forty days,* we are fashioned afresh and fed with food that brings delight.

The leprosy of pride overtook us in seven ways: one in ownership, one in showy clothing, one in bodily pleasure, two in our mouths, and another two in our hearts. First is leprosy of the house, which makes us want to be rich in this world. We are cleansed from this if we wash in the Jordan—that is, in Christ's de-

*2 K 5:10

*Ac 1:3

---

[1] Jerome, CCSL 72:7, 64.

scent. We find that, though he was rich, for our sake he
became poor.* He descended from the indescribable   *2 Cor 8:9*
riches of heaven. Coming into the world,* he chose to   *Jn 1:9*
have none of those riches at all, but he came in such
poverty that when he was born he was immediately
laid in a manger because there was no room in the inn.*   *Lk 2:7*
Everyone knows that the Son of Man had nowhere to
lay his head.* Will one who has plunged himself deep   *Lk 9:58*
into this river seek to gain the riches of this world? It
would be a great mistake, exceedingly great, for a lowly
worm, for whom the God of majesty and Lord of Hosts
chose to become poor, to want to be rich!

2. Next, take the leprosy of clothing to be the whole
empty show of this world. Nevertheless you will be
cleansed from this by washing in the Jordan, where
you find the Christ of the Lord wrapped in poor rags,
having become the *reproach of men and the outcast of the
people*.* We are cleansed from the leprosy of the body   *Ps 21:7*
in the Jordan if we consider well the passion of the
Lord and are ashamed to pursue bodily pleasure.

The leprosy in the mouth is, as I have said, twofold. When some misfortune occurs, we complain,
and an impatient word flows out like the bloody flux
of leprosy. We are cleansed from this if we attend to
him who *was led to the slaughter like a sheep, and did not
open his mouth*,* who, *when abused did not return abuse;*   *Ac 8:32; Is 53:7*
when he suffered, he did not threaten.* When things go   *1 Pt 2:23*
well, in opposition to him who said, *it is not those who
commend themselves who are approved*,* we *do* commend   *2 Cor 10:18*
ourselves, not in much patience, though, but in ar-
rogance, and so we are defiled by the second leprosy
of the mouth, boastfulness in speech. To be cleansed
from this let us wash in the Jordan and imitate the one
who did not seek his own glory.* This is why he bade   *Jn 8:50*
the demons who were calling out that he was the son
of God to be silent* and forbade the blind whose eyes   *Lk 4:34-35*
were opened to speak.*   *Mt 9:30*

3. In the heart, too, is a twofold leprosy: self-will and self-counsel. Each form of leprosy is profoundly wicked, and each is the more harmful for being the more interior.

I call self-will the will that is not common to God and humans, but is ours alone. We do what we want, not for the glory of God or to profit our brethren, but for ourselves; not intending to please God or benefit our brethren, but to satisfy our own whims. Love, which God is,* is exactly the opposite of this.

*1 Jn 4:8

Self-will engenders hostility toward him and a most cruel war. What does God hate or punish but self-will? Let self-will cease, and hell will be no more. What does that hellfire rage against but self-will? Even now, when we suffer cold or hunger or anything else of the kind, what is hurt except self-will? But if we bear these things willingly, the will becomes common will, even though a certain infirmity and, as it were, an itching of self-will still remain in us. Until it is utterly consumed we go on suffering.

The will, properly so-called, is that by which we assent, and by which our human liberty inclines. This means that the desires and longings that hold us without our consent are not the will, but are a corruption of the will. As to the frenzied war that self-will wages against the Lord of majesty, let those who serve self-will hear and be afraid. First it withdraws itself and, declaring itself autonomous, hides from him whom by rights it should serve as its Creator. But do you think it is satisfied with this affront? No, it brings to bear all its power, and lays hold of and lays waste all the things that are God's. What limit does human greed[2] set for itself? Anyone who acquires a modest sum of money in interest will try to gain the whole world in the same way, won't he, if the chance presents itself and the will

---

[2] *Cupiditas.*

is up to it? Believe me, the whole world would not be enough for one who is bound up in self-will.

But would that it might be content with these things, and would not rage—it's horrible to say it—against the very Creator! Self-will cuts off God himself, because it is wrapped up in itself. It would have God altogether unable to punish its sins, or unwilling to, or to be unaware of them. It wants, in short, that God not *be* God; it wants him impotent, or unjust, or unwise. The most savage malice, totally detestable, is the desire to destroy the power, the justice, and the wisdom of God. This is the savage beast, the wickedest wild creature,* the ravening wolf,* and the savage lioness. This is the foulest leprosy of the soul, because of which a person must wash in the Jordan and imitate him who did not come to do his own will;* wherefore the Lord says during his passion, *Not my will but yours be done.** *Gen 37:20
*Gen 49:27

*Jn 6:38
*Lk 22:42

4. But the leprosy of taking counsel with yourself alone is more pernicious than that because it is more hidden, and the more frequent the practice, the more sensible the person thinks he is! This is the vice of those who have zeal for God, but not according to knowledge.* They so obstinately follow their error that they are unwilling to agree with any advice.[3] They are destroyers of unity, enemies of peace; they are destitute of love, swollen with vanity; they please themselves, have a superlative opinion of themselves, and are ignorant of God's righteousness while wanting to establish their own.* What greater pride is there than for one person to prefer his own judgment[4] to the whole community, as though he alone possessed the Spirit of God?* *Rm 10:2

*Rm 10:3

*1 Cor 7:40

Not to agree is the crime of idolatry; it is like the sin of divination.* Have nothing to do with those who *1 Sm 15:23

---

[3] *Consiliis acquiescere*; see Gen 27:8.
[4] *Iudicium.*

make out that they are better religious than others, who are not like other people!* See how they have become diviners and idolaters—not in their own opinion, though, but according to the One who said it! Indeed, the Word of Truth makes the same statement when he says, *If someone will not listen to the church, let such a one be to you as a heathen and a publican.**

But where can this leprosy be cleansed except in the Jordan? Wash there, you who have this disease, whoever you may be, and see what the Angel of Great Counsel[5] does, how he esteems his counsel less than the counsel, or rather the will, of a single woman—I am speaking of the blessed Virgin—and of a poor workman, Joseph. He was found among the teachers, listening to them and asking them questions, and he was somewhat chided by his mother: *Child, why have you treated us like this?* And he said, *Why were you searching for me? Did you not know that I must be about my father's business? But they did not understand what he said.** And what did the Word do? He did not retreat into himself. *He went down* so that he might be subject to them.*

Are any not ashamed now to persist in their own plan[6] when Wisdom himself abandoned his own? He so changed his plan that from this time all the way to his thirtieth year he put aside completely what he had then undertaken. You find no teaching or works on his part from this twelfth year until he is thirty.

5. But perhaps we should ask him how he laid aside his will and his plan. O Lord, your will, of which you said, *Let it not be done**—if it was not good how was it yours? If it was good, why was it laid aside? So too your plan: if it was not good, how was it yours? And if it was good, how was it to be laid aside?

*Lk 18:11

*Mt 18:17

*Lk 2:46-51

*Lk 2:51

*Lk 22:42

---

[5] Is 9:6 as in the introit *Puer* for Christmas; counsel (*consilium*).
[6] *Consilium suum.*

They were both good, and they were both his. Nonetheless, they were to be laid aside so that better things might result. What is only one's own must never be prejudicial to what is held in common. The will was Christ's, and it was good, by which he said, *If it is possible, let this cup pass from me.** But that will of which he said, *Thy will be done,** was better, because it was possessed in common, not the Father's alone but Christ's too—for *he was offered because he willed it**— and also ours. Unless a grain of wheat falls into the earth and dies, it remains alone; when dead it bears much fruit.* This was the Father's will,° that he should have children to adopt; it was Christ's, *so that he might be the firstborn among many brothers and sisters;** it was ours, because it acted for us, that we might be redeemed.

We are speaking also of the plan.[7] The plan was Christ's, and it was good, when he said, *I must be about my father's business.** But because they did not understand, he changed the plan to cleanse us from the leprosy of taking counsel with ourselves alone. He gave us an example* that we should act in the same way. He knew from the first* what he would do, but he wanted to show us a model of his humility and to prepare a divine Jordan in himself to wash away this worst form of leprosy.

Listen, then, both equally, you who are befouled with the leprosy of self-will and you with the leprosy of taking counsel with yourselves alone. Hear what the Spirit says to the churches,* condemning both forms of leprosy in a single short verse: *The wisdom from above is first pure,* in contrast to the impurity of self-will, *then peaceable,** in contrast to the obstinate rebellion of taking counsel with yourself alone.

6. When the sick person is cleansed of these seven [forms of leprosy], it is as though he looks for seven

*Mt 26:39
*Mt 6:10
*Is 53:7 Vulg
*Jn 12:24-25
°Jn 6:39
*Rm 8:29
*Lk 2:49
*Jn 13:15
*Jn 6:65
*Rv 2:7
*Jm 3:17

---

[7] *Consilium.*

*Is 11:2-3 Vulg

plates of food, which are the seven gifts of the Holy Spirit,* after seven movements of his bowels. Moreover, as we find seven cleansings in the Lord's life before the passion, so too in the seven appearances that we read took place after the resurrection we can find the seven gifts of the Holy Spirit.

Take first the spirit of fear: an angel came down from heaven as the holy women were coming to the tomb, and the earth shook, so that they were stricken with fear and had to be comforted by the angel.*

*Mt 28:1-5
*Lk 24:34

In the spirit of godliness he appeared to Simon.* It was truly great kindness and worthy of the Lord Jesus to want to appear privately, ahead of the others, to the one who more than all the others was conscience-stricken over the denial.* Thus, where transgression increased, grace would increase too.*

*Mt 26:34
*Rm 5:20

In the spirit of knowledge he explained the Scriptures to the two travelers to Emmaus, beginning from Moses and the Prophets.*

*Lk 24:13, 27

In the spirit of might he entered through closed doors, and he showed his hands and his side* as the holes in a shield used to be shown as signs of courage.

*Jn 20:19-20

In the spirit of counsel he counseled those who were laboring in vain at fishing to let down their nets on the right side.*

*Jn 21:6

In the spirit of understanding he opened their minds to understand the Scriptures.*

*Lk 24:45

In the spirit of wisdom he appeared to them on the fortieth day and, *as they were watching, he was lifted up*, and they saw the Son of Man ascending to where he was before.* Until that day he was saving those who believed as though through the foolishness of preaching,* but after he ascended to the Father° in their sight, he began to be proclaimed with wisdom.

*Ac 1:3, 9;
Jn 6:63
*1 Cor 1:21
°Jn 20:17

On the Days of the Resurrection: How Christ Has Not Yet Been Born for Some

1. ALL WE READ of the Savior is medicine for our souls. Let us therefore take care that it may never be said of us, *we would have cured Baby-lon, but she is not healed.** Let all consider how effectual such health-giving medicines are in themselves. For some Christ has not yet been born, for some he has not yet suffered, for some he has not up to now risen. For others he has not yet ascended; for still others he has not yet sent the Holy Spirit.

Jer 51:9

How is his humility active in us, he *who, though he was in the form of God, did not regard equality with God as some-thing to be grasped, but emptied himself, taking the form of a servant?** How, I ask, is God's humility active in a proud person? What traces of his humility are present in those who are still dazzled by the desire for earthly riches and honors? Is not your conscience stirred now, my broth-ers, when you can say *a child has been born for us?**

Ph 2:6-7

Is 9:6

For some Christ has not yet suffered; they avoid hardships, and still fear death, as though he had not conquered hardships by enduring them, and death by dying.[1]

---

[1] See the preface for Easter.

2. For some he has not yet risen. They experience death all day long in anxiety over their works and the pain of penitence; they have not yet received spiritual consolation. But *if those days had not been shortened** who could bear them?

*Mt 24:22

For others, Christ has risen but has not yet ascended; instead, with them he still remains on earth in holy consolation; they spend the whole day in devotion, they weep at their prayers, they sigh during their meditations; everything is festive and joyful for them, and the days pass in a continual song of Alleluia. But the milk must be withdrawn from them, and they must learn to live on solid food.* It is to their advantage that Christ go away* and that this passing devotion be withdrawn.

*Heb 5:12

*Jn 16:7

But when will they understand this? They complain that they are deserted by the Lord and bereft of grace. But let them wait a little, let them stay in the city until they are clothed with stronger power from on high and receive the greater gifts of the Holy Spirit. When the Apostles were moved to a higher place, and entered the more excellent way of love,* they were no longer anxious how they might weep a little, but how by a great victory they might triumph over our common adversary and trample Satan under their feet.*

*1 Cor 12:31

*Mt 7:6

SERMON ONE

Of the Reading of the Letter of Saint John

1. *WHATEVER IS BORN OF GOD over-comes the world.** Inasmuch as the only-begotten Son of God *did not think equality with God something to be grasped* but deigned to become Son of Man and *to be found in human condition,** not without reason does our meager human estate now presume a heavenly birth.

*1 Jn 5:4

*Jn 3:18;
Ph 2:6-7

It is worthy of God that he should become the father of those whom Christ has made his brothers. So it is that blessed John, who time and again has assiduously commended to us this adoption as children of God,* writes at the very beginning of his gospel, *to as many as received him he gave power to become children of God.** This is echoed by the words we heard read today from his letter when he says, *Whatever is born of God overcomes the world.*

*Rm 8:23

*Jn 1:12

As many as are of Christ the world hates along with Christ, but it is overcome equally by them along with Christ. *Do not be astonished*, he says, *if the world hates you: know that it hated me before it hated you.** And again, *Take courage*, he says, *because I have overcome the world.** Thus is made manifest the truth of the saying of the Apostle, *Those whom he foreknew*—he means God the

*1 Jn 3:13;
Jn 15:18
*Jn 16:33

Father—*he also predestined to be conformed to the image of his Son.* See how the conforming takes place—they are adopted after him, *that he may be the firstborn among many brothers and sisters.** The world hated them after him; the world is overcome by them after him.

*Rm 8:29

2. It is well said that *whatever is born of God overcomes the world,* so that a victory over temptation may be proof of heavenly birth. As he who is a son by nature triumphed over the world with its ruler,* so may we too, as many of us as are children by adoption,* be found victors. Victors indeed, but in him who strengthens us, in whom also we can do all things,* because *this is the victory* that overcomes the world, our faith.* If we are adopted as children of God by faith, the world lying in wickedness hates and persecutes the faith in us but is also overcome by faith, as is written: *the saints through faith overcame kingdoms.** Why should victory not be attributed to faith, whose life it is? *The righteous live by faith.**

*Jn 12:31
*Rm 8:15

*Ph 4:13

*1 Jn 5:4

*Heb 11:33
*Rm 1:17;
Gal 3:11

Whenever you resist temptation, whenever you overcome wickedness,* do not credit your own strength; do not glory in yourself, but rather in the Lord.* When will the strong man armed* give way to your weakness? Hear what warning the shepherd of the sheep, appointed by the Lord,* gives: *Your adversary the devil,* he says, *like a roaring lion, prowls around looking for someone to devour. Resist him, steadfast in faith.** You see how the testimonies of truth coincide: Paul says that the saints overcame kingdoms by faith; Peter says that in faith he must resist the world's rules; and John, *this is the victory that overcomes the world, our faith.*

*1 Jn 2:13
*1 Cor 1:31
*Lk 11:21

*Jn 2:15

*1 Pt 5:8-9

3. He goes on: *Who is it that overcomes the world but the one who believes that Jesus is the son of God?** It is certain, my brothers, that everyone who does not believe in the Son of God for this reason is not only overcome but also judged.* *Without faith it is impossible to please God.*°

*1 Jn 5:5

*Jn 3:18
°Heb 11:6

Maybe someone can say that we see many who believe Jesus is the Son of God but are nevertheless entangled in the passions of the world. Why then does it say, *who is it that overcomes the world but the one who believes that Jesus is the Son of God*, if the world itself now believes this? Do not *even the demons believe and shudder?**   *Jm 2:19*

But I say, do you think that a person, whoever it might be, who is neither afraid of his threats nor attracted by his promises, who neither obeys his commands, nor follows his counsels, considers Jesus to be the Son of God?* Does not that person deny it in fact even while claiming to know God?* Besides, faith without works is dead in itself.* It cannot seem strange if those who are not even alive do not overcome.   *Gen 27:8*   *1 Jn 2:4*   *Jm 2:17, 20*

4. Do you ask what a living and victorious faith is? Without a doubt it is that through which Christ dwells in our hearts,* for Christ is our strength and our life. *When Christ, who is your life, appears*, says the Apostle, *then you also will appear with him in glory.** What is the source of glory if not victory? And why will we appear with him if not because we also overcome in him? If power to become children of God* is given only to those who accept Christ, then we must take his words, *whatever is born of God overcomes the world*, as referring only to them.   *Eph 3:17*   *Col 3:4*   *1 Jn 1:12*

That is why, in order more obviously to commend the faith through which, as was said, Christ dwells in our hearts, the same one who asked, *Who is it that overcomes the world but the one who believes that Jesus is the Son of God*, immediately adds concerning his coming, *This is the one who came by water and blood, Jesus Christ.** And showing us a more excellent way, he says, *and the Spirit is the one who bears witness that Jesus is the Son of God.** What he interposes, with a significant repetition, *not by water only, but by water and blood,** we must take, I think, as distinguishing him from Moses. Moses came by water, from which he also received his name so that he was called *Moses.**   *1 Jn 5:6*   *1 Jn 5:6*   *1 Jn 5:6*   *Ex 2:10*

5. Let those familiar with the narrative of the Old Testament recall how in Egypt, when all the baby boys of Israelite stock were being killed, Pharaoh's daughter *Ex 1:16; 2:3-5* took Moses after he was placed in the waters.* See if Christ is not clearly prefigured in this event.

Mt 2:16 Like Pharaoh, Herod was troubled by suspicion* and turned to the same acts of cruelty, but in the same way he too was fooled. In both cases a large number of boys were massacred in place of one suspected person; in both cases the one who was sought escaped. As Pharaoh's daughter received Moses to keep him from harm, so did Egypt—which is not unreasonably identified with Pharaoh's daughter—receive Christ.

Mt 12:42 But clearly something more than Moses is here,* since he comes not by water only, but by water and *Rv 17:15* blood. Many waters are many peoples.* The one who assembled the people but did not redeem them came by water only. The true liberation from slavery in Egypt was accomplished not by Moses but by the *Rv 7:14; 22:14* blood of the Lamb;* it prefigured us who are to be *1 Pt 1:18* liberated from our empty commerce with this world* by the blood of the spotless Lamb, Jesus Christ. This is *Is 33:22 Vulg* the true Lawgiver,* with whom is plenteous redemp-*Ps 129:7* tion.* He died not for the nation only, but to gather *Jn 11:51-52* into one the dispersed children of God.*

Jn 19:35 Remember that this is John who saw and testified—*and we know that his testimony is true*—that blood and water came out of the Lord's side as he slept on the *Jn 19:34* cross,* so that the new church might be brought forth and redeemed by the new Adam from his side as he slept.

6. So today he comes to us by water and blood, that the water and blood may be testimony to his coming as well to the faith that overcomes. Not only this, though, but there is a testimony still greater than this, *Jn 15:26* which the Spirit of truth provides.* The testimony of these three is true and certain, and happy is the soul

worthy to receive it: *There are three that testify on earth,
the Spirit, the water, and the blood.**

Take the water as baptism, the blood as martyrdom, and the Spirit as love. *It is the Spirit that gives
life,** and the life of faith is love. If you ask what links
the Spirit and love, let Paul reply: *because God's love has
been poured out in our hearts through the Holy Spirit that
has been given to us.** And so the Spirit must be added
to the water and the blood since, as the same apostle
testifies, without love whatever you have profits you
nothing.**

*Jn 6:63

*Rm 5:5

*1 Cor 13:3

7. Now we have said that baptism is represented by
the water and martyrdom by the blood. Remember
that baptism and martyrdom both happen once for
all, and yet both are experienced every day. There is a
kind of martyrdom and a certain shedding of blood in
the daily suffering of the body; there is also a baptism
in compunction of heart and constant tears.

Thus the weak and fearful, who are not up to laying
down their lives for Christ once and for all, must at
least shed their blood in a milder but daily martyrdom.
So, too, the sacrament of baptism, since it may not be
repeated, must be complemented by frequent washing
on the part of those who offend often in many things.
For this reason the prophet says, *Every night I will wash
my bed; I will water my couch with my tears.**

*Ps 6:7

Do you want to know *who it is who overcomes the
world?** Give careful attention to what must be overcome in it. Blessed John tells us this when he says,
*Beloved, do not love the world or the things in the world. All
that is in the world is the desire of the flesh, the desire of the
eyes, and worldly ambition.** These are the three squadrons that the Chaldeans made.** But I remember that
holy Jacob also made three squadrons when, returning from Mesopotamia, he feared to face Esau.** You
too need a threefold defense against the three kinds
of temptation, so that the desire of the flesh may be

*1 Jn 5:5

*1 Jn 2:15-16;
Vulg, "the pride
of life"
*Jb 1:17

*Gen 32:7; Vulg,
"two squadrons"

overcome by its mortification which, if you remember, we said must be understood by the testimony of the blood. The exertion of compunction and constant tears may conquer the desire of the eyes. The virtue of love, which alone makes the soul chaste and alone purifies the intention, may cut off vain ambition.

It is a sure testimony to triumph over the world if you punish the body and bring it into subjection* lest in its destructive freedom it becomes subject to pleasure; if you give your eyes over to weeping rather than to wantonness and curiosity; and finally, if you do not give your mind to vanity but burn with spiritual love.

8. Truly there is one Spirit that testifies equally on earth and in heaven* that even if bodily affliction shall cease, even if the fountain of tears* dries up, *love never ends.** There is some foretaste in the present, but the completion and the fullness are still to come. But although the Spirit remains after the blood—water and blood will not possess the kingdom of God*—yet for the present the Spirit is scarcely, or not at all, found without them because *these three*, John says, *are one.**

Thus if any of these three is absent you cannot assume that the others are present. Yet these witnesses, when joined together, are totally credible,* nor can one to whom these things were present on earth lack testimony in heaven. Such a one acknowledges the Son of God before humans, not by word or speech but in action and truth,* and the Son will also acknowledge that one before the angels of God.*

Can the Father refuse testimony to one to whom he sees the Son testifying? Surely he will acknowledge what he himself sees in secret.* And the Spirit will not fail to agree with the Father and the Son, since he is the Spirit of the Father and the Son. How then can one lack testimony in heaven who has been found worthy of it on earth? *There are three that testify in heaven: the Father, the Son, and the Holy Spirit.*

*1 Cor 9:27
*1 Jn 5:7-8
*Jer 9:1
*1 Cor 13:8
*1 Cor 15:50
*1 Jn 5:7
*Ps 92:5
*1 Jn 3:18
*Lk 12:8
*Mt 6:4

And, lest you should imagine any disagreement, *these three are one.** Those the Father will receive in heaven as children and heirs, whom the Son will receive as brothers and sisters and fellow-heirs, and whom, as they are united to God, the Holy Spirit will make one with himself,* will possess a great testimony. The Spirit himself is the indestructible bond of the Trinity, through whom, as the Father and Son are one,* so we also may be one in them, through the mercy of him who deigned to pray this for his disciples, Jesus Christ our Lord.

*1 Jn 5:7

*1 Cor 6:17

*Jn 10:30

Of the Words of the Same Reading:
There are three that testify in heaven

1. The reading proclaimed for us today was from the Letter of blessed John. In it we learn that threefold is the witness given in heaven, and threefold on earth.* This suggests to me that the former is the sign of stability, the latter of restoration; the one refers to angels, the other to humans; one divides the blessed from the wretched, the other the righteous from the ungodly. The vision of the Trinity bears witness to the angels who, in the first trespass when Lucifer became proud, stood in the truth.* To human beings, whom divine mercy saves, the Spirit, the water, and the blood bear witness.

*1 Jn 5:7-8

*Jn 8:44; Eph 6:14

Why does the Father not bear witness to those who honor him as a father? Instead he says: Wicked one, *if I am a father, where is my honor?** You must do without the witness of the Father whose glory you try to usurp for yourself when you desire to equal him rather than to honor him. *I will sit*, he says, *on the mountain of the covenant; I will be like the most high.** Really? Created just now, will you sit with the Father of spirits? Surely he has not yet told you, *sit at my right hand!**

*Mal 1:6

*Is 14:13-14

*Ps 109:1

184

If you don't know, shameless one, he is the Only-Begotten, to whom equality with the Father and sitting with him are conferred by an eternal begetting. You, thinking equality with God something to be grasped,* begrudge the Son his glory, *glory as of the only-begotten of the Father,** so that you do not deserve witness from him. Indeed can a person abhorred by the Father and the Son be justified by the Spirit of both? Such a one is held in abomination as proud and restless by the lover of peace who rests upon the peaceful and humble;* he who is dedicated to unity strives against you in his zeal for peace and unity.

Ph 2:6
Jn 1:14

Is 11:2-4

2. Should it surprise us, my brothers, if we are afraid that an individual[1] wild beast may begin to feed on this little vineyard of the Lord?* How many shoots of the heavenly vine has that individualism[2] trodden down? You can easily enough notice the pride in him, but not the individualism. So I ask, whereas the whole angelic creation was standing, the vice of individualism wasn't lacking the one that presumed to try to sit, was it?

Ps 79:14; Is 5:7

But perhaps you ask how I know about this standing of the angels? I have two sure witnesses, each of whom testifies to what he saw. *I saw the Lord sitting*, says Isaiah, *and the seraphim were standing;** and Daniel says, *A thousand thousands served him, and ten thousand times ten thousand stood attending him.** Do you want a third, so that every word may be established by the mouth of three witnesses?* I refer you to the Apostle who was caught up to the third heaven* and when he returned said, *Are they not all ministering spirits?**

Is 6:1-2

Dn 7:10

Mt 18:16
2 Cor 12:2
Heb 1:14

Thus where they all stand, they all minister. Will you sit then, you enemy of peace? Clearly you grieve the Spirit,* who makes people of one mind to dwell in a

Eph 4:30

---

[1] *Singularis.*
[2] *Singularitas.*

*Ps 67:7 Vulg

*Eph 4:3
house;* you offend against love, you rend unity, and you break the bond of peace.* Rightly does the Spirit attest to the love, unity, and peace of the angels, who have abandoned neither their rank nor their abiding place; by them your envy, individualism, and restlessness are condemned. And this is the evidence given in heaven.

3. That given on earth is different. It is for distinguishing between exiles and those who belong on earth—that is, between citizens of heaven and those of Babylon. I mean, when does God leave his elect without evidence? What consolation would there be for them, wavering as they are anxiously between hope and fear, if they were thought undeserving to have any evidence at all to their own election? *The Lord knows*

*2 Tm 2:19

*Jn 6:65; 13:18
those who are his, and he alone knows whom he has chosen from the beginning.*

Who knows whether a person is worthy of love or hatred? If certainty is altogether denied us—and it certainly is!—then the signs of this election, if we should happen to find any, will be that much more delightful, won't they? What rest would our spirit have so long as it held no evidence of its predestination? *The saying is*

*1 Tm 1:15
sure and worthy of full acceptance, by which the evidences of salvation are given. By this word consolation truly is provided the elect, and excuses are withdrawn from the condemned. If the signs of life are known, those who disregard them are plainly convicted of taking their souls in vain and proven to have despised the pleasant land.

4. *There are three*, he says, *that give evidence on earth,*

*1 Jn 5:8

*Rm 5:12

*Hg 2:8

*Rm 8:26
the Spirit, the water, and the blood. You know, brothers, that we all sinned in the first man, and in him also we all fell.* We fell into a prison full of mud and of stones; there we lay captive, filthy and broken, until the desired of the nations* came to redeem, wash, and help us. He gave his own blood for our redemption, he poured forth water from his side to wash us, and he sent his Spirit from on high to help our weakness.*

Take care to know whether or not these things are at work in you so that you do not become guilty of the blood of the Lord* by emptying it of its preciousness, and so the water that ought to cleanse does not instead collect in dirty puddles as a judgment of everlasting damnation, and lest the Spirit, too, whom you resist,* *does not acquit those who slander with their lips.*° Be careful, then, because if these things bear no fruit in you, they will work against you.

*1 Cor 11:27

*Ac 7:51
°Ws 1:6

5. Who has the evidence that the blood of Christ was not shed in vain except one who refrains from sin? Those who sin are slaves of sin,* so that if they can refrain from sin and cast away the yoke of miserable slavery, they will be a most certain evidence of the redemption that the blood of Christ accomplishes.

*Jn 8:34

True, refraining from sin is not enough for a sinner unless repentance is present too. Those who are weary with their moaning, who flood their bed with tears every night,* have evidence from the water. Just as the blood redeems so that sin will not rule in our mortal body,* so the water washes us from those sins we committed before.

*Ps 6:6

*Rm 6:12

But what will happen to us if, broken and beaten by the long use of chains and cruel imprisonment, we become disheartened on the way of life? Let us call upon the Spirit, the Life-Giver and Supporter, confident that the Father who is in heaven will give the good Spirit to those who ask.* Clearly a new way of life[3] is evidence that a new Spirit has arrived!

*Lk 11:13;
Mt 7:11

Now, to sum up, you have evidence from the blood, the water, and the Spirit, if you refrain from sin, bear fruit worthy of repentance,* and do the works of life.

*Lk 3:8

---

[3] *Nova conversatio.*